SHAD FISHING

0 11557 03067 9

SHAD FISHING

Techniques, Tactics, and Tackle

By
C. Boyd Pfeiffer

STACKPOLE
BOOKS

Published by
STACKPOLE BOOKS
5067 Ritter Road
Mechanicsburg, PA 17055
www.stackpolebooks.com

Printed in the United States

10 9 8 7 6 5 4 3 2 1

First edition

Cover design by Wendy A. Reynolds
Cover photographs by C. Boyd Pfeiffer

Library of Congress Cataloging-in-Publication Data

Pfeiffer, C. Boyd
Shad fishing / C. Boyd Pfeiffer.—1st ed.
p. cm.
Includes bibliographical references (p.).
ISBN 0-8117-3067-0 (pbk.)
1. Shad fishing. I. Title.

SH691.S38 P46 2002
799.1'745—dc21 2001034408

To Brenda, who has brought
both beauty and purpose
to my life.

Contents

Acknowledgments

When I was about eleven or twelve, my parents moved from a row house in Baltimore to a single home near the edge of the city. Next door lived an elderly gentleman. Fred Klemcke, a bachelor, was in the import-export business after leaving Germany during the rise of Hitler and after four years of bitter conflict as a young German cavalry officer during World War I. Soon after my parents moved into the new home, we all learned that Fred Klemcke liked to take kids fishing. I learned later that, yes, my parents had him checked out before releasing me to his tutelage.

It was lucky for them, with my avid interest in fishing. It was also lucky for me, since no one in my family had any knowledge of or interest in fishing of any type. In a very real sense, Fred Klemcke introduced me to and gave me the life that I now enjoy and have enjoyed for so many years—fishing, seriously, passionately, and writing about it.

After some excursions for bass in local waters, trips for trout in western Maryland streams, and rowing a boat for pickerel in brackish water, he took me shad fishing one spring on the Susquehanna River and Deer Creek, one of its tributaries. I was about thirteen at the time, and though I don't remember my success (or lack thereof), I guess it was less than outstanding. But I met fishermen such as Simeon Yaruta and Gurney Godfrey, as well as tackle shop owner Burt Dillon, met their fishing friends, heard the tales of Tom Loving's shad flies, fished the early Quilby darts for shad, and learned to love this sport as I did all fresh- and saltwater fishing.

That early fishing for shad with those older mentors, and the experiences that resulted, began to pave the way for my earlier edition of *Shad Fishing* (Crown Publishers, 1975). To them, the early mentors almost all gone now, my thanks for their help to a boy that led him to this life.

Since then, a lot of shad trips later, enduring the ban on shad fishing in Maryland on my local waters, fishing with longtime friends, tying and trying shad flies and darts, casting for shad in West Coast rivers, fishing other states, and experimenting with new techniques showed me the need for an updated book on shad—thus this volume.

Along the way, I have continued to fish for shad—and a lot of other species—with good friends and fine fishermen such as Chuck Edghill, Norm Bartlett, Ed Russell, Lefty Kreh (who taught me how to fly cast and corrected the earlier "lessons" of well-meaning Fred Klemcke), Joe Zimmer, Irv Swope, Jim Heim, Bill May, Tony Tochterman, Jack Goellner, and so many others. They have all helped me more than they will ever know, by teaching me and experimenting with me on shad and a host of other species, becoming the subjects of photos and text for articles and books, and most important of all, remaining true friends and fishing companions. To them, my thanks for their companionship on shad rivers and other waters, and for their help and assistance in other ventures and publications.

Many fly tiers have helped by providing me with samples of their flies and sharing their theories on shad fishing and shad flies. Other fly tiers shared with me their patterns for my original book. Legendary fly tier Poul Jorgensen deserves special credit for the flies that he tied that were used for photos in the original *Shad Fishing*, and which were also used—along with samples from other fly tiers—for this volume. Those who in addition cooperated with this new version include Jim Victorine, Floyd Franke, Thom Rivell, John Stercho, Craig Bentley, Carl Blackledge, Dr. Michael Jeavons, Dean Havron, Jack Denny, Joe Bruce, Phil Chapman, Mark Lewchik, Dave Bailey, Brian Wiprud, and others. Brian Wiprud deserves special thanks. From the start, he has been enthusiastic about this work and shared with me his thoughts on such things as shad feeding, shad foods, bioluminescence, and fly and dart size. As a fellow writer, his cooperation is especially appreciated.

Authors such as John Shewey and Terry Hellekson allowed me to use flies from their books in my works, and I appreciate that.

Many representatives of state agencies corresponded with me and sent me far more material, some including flies and fly patterns, than I could possibly use in this book. They include Steve Gephard, supervising fisheries biologist for the state of Connecticut; Albin Sonski, hatchery supervisor for the Kensington Fish Hatchery of Connecticut; Bert Deener, regional fisheries supervisor for the south-central area of Georgia; Ron Klauda, Rudy Lukacovic, and Dale Weinrich of the Maryland Department of Natural Resources; Richard McBride of the Florida Fish and Wildlife Conservation Commission; Kent Nelson of the North Carolina Wildlife Commission; Steven D. Leach of the South Carolina Department of

Natural Resources; Joseph Hightower of the North Carolina Cooperative Fish and Wildlife Unit; James W. Watts of the Oregon Department of Fish and Wildlife; Mike Hendricks of the Pennsylvania Fish and Boat Commission; Alan Weaver of the Virginia Department of Game and Inland Fisheries; Caleb Slater, anadromous fish project leader for the Massachusetts Division of Fisheries and Wildlife; Philip Edwards, fisheries biologist for the state of Rhode Island; Pat Festa of New York State; Hugh Carberry, biologist with the Department of Environmental Protection for the state of New Jersey; and so many others.

Much thanks also goes to Bill Goldsborough of the Chesapeake Bay Foundation, who allowed me to use slides taken of 100-year-old photos of commercial shad fishing and to reproduce them for this book, with credit for each accompanying the photo.

The boning shad photos would have been impossible without the help of Gibby's Seafood in Timonium, Maryland, and the cooperation of Brian Moore, manager, and Adrian Bonaventura who boned the shad for the photos included. Much thanks to them both.

Chuck Edghill, mentioned above as a good friend and longtime fishing companion, deserves special mention and special thanks. For several of my more recent books, Chuck has volunteered to read the manuscript, offering corrections of spelling, typos, and grammar and suggesting any changes that he thought would improve the book. He did so again with this book, and to him my special thanks for his talent and thoughtfulness in this thankless task. As an excellent editor, grammarian, and writer, Chuck corrected typos and spelling errors, and made the suggestions that make this a better book than it would be otherwise. Any errors or faults that remain are mine and my responsibility, but the book is better because of his hand.

Finally, my thanks to Judith Schnell, editorial director of Stackpole, for her interest in this, another book with Stackpole, and to Stackpole editor Jon Rounds for his interest, patience, and understanding as the book changed back and forth several times and my deadline was stretched to the limit.

C. Boyd Pfeiffer

Introduction

There are more reasons than ever to fish for shad. Shad fishing along both the Atlantic and Pacific coasts continues to gain popularity. Light tackle spinning gear is better than ever. Fly fishing for shad is increasing in popularity as the closely related saltwater fly fishing continues to have a meteoric rise in interest. And last but not least, shad populations are relatively stable in most areas, or slightly improving, as many old dams are removed. These efforts coincide with state stocking and restoration plans, as well as the practice of catch-and-release fishing by ever-increasing numbers of anglers.

Shad are not large by some angling criteria—averaging less than 2 pounds for the hickory shad and 4 pounds for the American shad—but they more than make up for any lack of size by their jolting strikes, long runs, hard fight, high jumps, and preference for flies and small artificial lures. They are fun on light tackle without exhausting either the fisherman or the fish.

Compared with most fish, shad are relatively easy to catch. In fact, much of shad fishing is almost like the mantra of the real estate salesperson: "location, location, location." Get in the right spot in the river or stream for the shad dart or fly to swing properly, and you have solved much of the problem of shad fishing.

Shad are fun with any tackle, but especially so with light spinning gear and fly tackle. Each year, more and more fishermen are discovering shad and ways to take them on everything from fly rods fished with floating lines in small streams, to deep-sinking lines in the strong currents of the principal rivers, to spinning from the shore, to still fishing with spinning tackle in major rivers, to using a downrigger to get your spoons on the bottom for the big American shad. But basically, it's not hard to fish for the gamy shad, since they hit eagerly, fight hard, jump readily, and can be counted on each spring to repeat this same performance.

They are also a great family fish, since they are plentiful during the spring runs and ideal for introducing youngsters to spinning or fly fishing in running water and on something larger that puts more stretch in the string than the local pond bluegills. For fishermen with a yen for gourmet meals, both shad species are tasty, although the American shad is better and, being larger, provides more meals. Check to make sure that the taking of either species is legal in your area before keeping fish.

The one problem with both hickory and American shad is the numerous bones, although some shad recipes solve this through long cooking, which reduces the bones to mush. The roe from both species is delicious and highly regarded as gourmet fare.

Though the shad runs in the streams and rivers last only through the spring, angler interest has been growing annually. And there is increasing information on fall hickory shad fishing that promises to produce a second season of sport on the Atlantic coast. During the popular spring runs, shad are a welcome respite from the rigors of winter and often offer the first serious fishing of the angler's year—a few weeks before the earliest trout fishing and well before the first good bass fishing. Fall concentrations of hickory shad may offer still another species for your rod late in the season.

In a sense, it's good that shad are as plentiful as they are and that the runs don't last all year. If they did, we probably would not pay any attention to them or would fish them to the exclusion of almost everything else. My fishing partner Chuck Edghill has been saying for years—decades, really—that he is "glad when they come, since they are a lot of fun, but also glad when they leave, so I can get on with serious fishing." I feel a little the same way. It's great to have a fish this plentiful and cooperative early in the spring to break the fishing ice, certainly figuratively and sometimes literally. It's a time when the fish can be just fun and taken a little casually. Shad put the fun back into the sport of fishing, which is often taken too seriously.

CHAPTER 1

Shad Fishing, Past and Present

SHAD AND THE INDIANS

Shad fishing was commercially important long before the general Colonial population had the time, inclination, or money to pursue any type of sportfishing. In fact, shad were well known to the Indians long before the white man made his way to this country, and before sport angling developed and fishermen discovered the shad's sporting qualities.

The History of the Mission of the United Brethren among the Indians in North America, written in German in 1794 by George Henry, described shad and a method of fishing for them, but only as food for the Indians.

> When the shad-fish *(Clupea alosa)* [today *Alosa sapidissima*] come up the rivers, the Indians run a dam of stones across the stream, where its depth will admit of it, not in a straight line, but in two parts, verging towards each other in an angle. An opening is left in the middle for the water to run off. At this opening, they place a large box, the bottom of which is full of holes. They then make a rope of the twigs of the wild vine, reaching across the stream, upon which boughs of about six feet in length are fastened at a distance of about two fathoms from each other. A party is detached about a mile above the dam with this rope and its appendages, who begin to move gently down the current, some guiding one, some the opposite end, whilst others keep the branches from sinking by supporting the rope in the middle with wooden forks. Thus, they proceed, frightening the fishes into the opening left in the middle of the dam, where a number of Indians are placed on each side, who standing upon the two legs of the angles, drive the fishes with poles and a hideous noise, through the openings into the above mentioned box or chest. Here they

> lie, the water running off through the holes in the bottom, and other Indians stationed on each side of the chest take them out, kill them and fill their canoes. By this contrivance they sometimes catch about a thousand shad and other fish in half a day.

This is what we would today call a fish weir, the remnants of which can sometimes still be seen on some Atlantic coastal rivers.

GEORGE WASHINGTON, SHAD FISHERMAN

George Washington is credited with netting shad, and an early run of shad is credited with saving the fledgling and floundering Continental Army under Washington during a time when food, morale, and supplies were low. He fished for shad, albeit with a net and as a gentleman farmer, long before his clash with the British and debut with history. In his diary entry on April 11, 1760, the father of our country noted, "About 11:00 set the people to hauling the seine and in the night catched and dressed barrels of herring and 60 white fish." Since shad and herring run at the same time and in the same rivers, these "white fish" had to be shad. Many river landowners and planters of the period, like Washington, engaged in this form of commercial or subsistence shad fishing.

History suggests that the Continental Army captured and seined shad during the early spring battles of 1778 in the Valley Forge area. The story goes that the army captured shad ascending the Schuylkill River, and this saved the army to fight again another day, perhaps saving the nation. Shad were instrumental in feeding the army, but this particular account seems to have no basis in historical fact or records, according to a recent article in *Shad Journal* (vol. 4, no. 2, 1999). The article lists the frantic efforts to find salted, smoked, or pickled shad and herring for the soldiers, and says that efforts were made from Connecticut to Maryland and Virginia, principally for shad from the Potomac and Delaware Rivers. They often lacked barrels in which to keep the shad and wagons by which to transport the barrels. There are also indications that the British might have run a seine or netting across the Schuylkill for the express purpose of preventing early runs of shad from reaching the Continental Army, where they might have aided in feeding the troops. Regardless, shad were important to the Revolution, even if captured elsewhere and transported, and even if the last-minute "saved-by-the-shad" story is not true.

EARLY SHAD SPORTFISHING

Some of the early sportfishing clubs used seines for shad, obviously with a greater interest in eating the shad or its roe than in the thrill of the catch. Early on, the catch was more important than the catching, and

Pulling out of seines full of shad in the Susquehanna Flats area at the head of the Chesapeake Bay. Photo taken at the late 1800s or early 1900s. ***(courtesy, Bill Goldsborough, Chesapeake Bay Foundation from photos at the Cecil County Historical Society.)***

early slave and indentured servant agreements generally prohibited feeding pickled shad to slaves and servants more than twice a week. By 1766 the fishing was so intense for shad in the Raritan River of New Jersey that special regulations were enacted to control the methods used, and by 1799 haul seining was the only legal method allowed.

Early sportfishing with rod and reel was done with the fly rod. Revolving spool-casting tackle was developed in the early 1800s but was not able to cast the light lures required for shad. It could be—and was—used for trolling and still fishing, but records indicate little if any use in shad fishing. Spinning was not developed until the late 1800s and even then did not become popular in this country until after World War II. Early sport fly fishing in this country was for trout, although some coastal fly fishing did begin in the mid-1800s. John Brown, writing in his 1849 *American Angler's Guide,* noted that herring were taken on the fly and that a "fish similar to the herring and called by the same name is taken in the bay of New York off Fort Lafayette. They jump readily at a white, red or fancy colored fly." These may well have been shad. He also noted that they were very shy fish and quite suitable for fly fishing, remarking that they "take the fly and require long rods and fine tackle, similar to that used for trout."

Commercial fishermen with concentrated and full nets of shad from market seining in the late 1800s or early 1900s. ***(courtesy, Bill Goldsborough, Chesapeake Bay Foundation from photos at the Cecil County Historical Society.)***

Frank Forrester, who used the pen name of Henry William Herbert, was an Englishman who came to this country in 1831 under a hint of scandal (for reasons still unknown). He became a well-known fishing and hunting writer, and noted that coastal fishing for striped bass, shad, and herring with a fly rod was excellent sport. Fly fishing must have been well established by then, since he also noted in his writings that shad flies specifically tied to catch shad were available at a tackle shop called Conroy's, on Fulton Street in New York.

Thaddeus Norris, in his 1864 *American Angler's Book,* predicted that shad would never be classed as a game fish. Today thousands of fly fishermen and spinning sport anglers know differently.

One well-known and otherwise accurate writer who was wrong about shad and shad fishing was Genio Scott. In his 1888 book, *Fishing in American Waters,* Scott said that the shad "is exclusively caught with nets." Considering that this was in a sportfishing book, it seems strange that Scott did not check with other sources, such as tackle shops, shad fishermen of the time, or previous writings on fly-fishing for shad. A look at Forrester's writings would have educated him about fly-fishing for shad and herring and the shad flies available early on from Conroy's in New York.

Charles Hallock, author of the 1873 book *The Fishing Tourist* and the 1877 *Sportsman's Gazetteer and General Guide,* noted that shad could be taken on flies, along with bait and lures, in the Delaware, Housatonic, and Connecticut Rivers in New England and in the St. Johns in Florida. Wet flies were then standard, and "casts" of several flies, usually three, were a common practice in fly-fishing for all fish. For shad, Hallock noted that the flies must be small, although he did not list sizes. He also suggested a "white miller for leader, with red ibis, snipe and any drab fly with lighter body, arranged as you please." The idea of drab flies contrasts with the idea of the bright-colored fluorescent shades and some flash used in current patterns, but dark—even black—flies will work. Generally shad anglers just don't try them, but instead stick to the bright fluorescent-colored patterns.

Although there are exceptions (see chapters 6 and 8), anglers also don't usually fish for shad with bait, another of Hallock's suggestions. Hallock described one angler who fished and chummed successfully, catching seven shad, including four roe shad, one of 5½ pounds, using a chum mixture of Irish moss, gluten from wheat flour, oyster juice, fibrine from bullock's blood, and powered "sulphate of barytes" prepared into a glutinous mass, mixed, and somehow miraculously stuck onto a size 6 Kirby hook.

The first possible mention of taking shad on a dry fly was reported by John McPhee in his article "A Selective Advantage," in the September 11, 2000, issue of the *New Yorker,* on shad fishing in the Northeast. Thomas Chalmers, fishing a dry fly below Holyoke Dam on the Connecticut River, took up to one hundred American shad using drys that were, even then, almost the exception in fishing. The story of Chalmers newfound dry-fly shad-fishing success was reported in the March 13, 1874, edition of *The Turf, Field & Farm,* placing him in the rich company and time period of John Brown, Frank Forrester, Charles Hallock, and other early writers on the sport of shad fishing. Dry-fly fishing was unusual then, with most fly fishing for trout. It is telling that it was sixteen years later that Theodore Gordon, considered the father of dry-fly fishing in America, first wrote to Frederic Halford about dry-fly trout fishing in England, which was being popularized and written about by Halford.

Perhaps the first mention of possible dry-fly shad fishing in a book is found in *The Fishes of the East Atlantic Coast,* written by Louis O. Van Doren and Samuel C. Clarke and published in 1884. They noted that shad is a surface feeder, a fact later picked up by writers after the 1970s, and made a few references to taking shad late in the season on dry flies. Van Doren and Clarke also noted that at the time, interest in fly-fishing for shad had died out, primarily because the larger and stronger striped bass could also be taken in the same waters on a fly. As to flies, they suggest "a white miller, a red fly with red wings, a scarlet fly with mottled-brown wings. The hooks used are numbers one, two and three, Limerick."

Shad fishing did not seem to get its own special recognition as a sport until the 1920s and 1930s. On the East Coast, Tom Loving, a Baltimore-area angler, designed a bucktail fly for shad that consisted of a black-and-white ribbed wool body, white bucktail wing, and large painted head with white eyes and black pupils. Occasionally he tied them with a yellow bucktail wing, and sometimes with a little red fur for color. They were tied on double salmon hooks. He tied small flies for the American shad and used larger flies for the hickory—the exact opposite of prevailing size theory today. And even with that, most of his flies were of a larger size than anglers would use today.

On the West Coast, shad fishing seemed to have a surge of popularity around 1950 and the very early 1960s, about twenty to thirty years later than on the East Coast.

STATISTICS

Statistics and records on shad and shad fishing were not kept until 1837, when a Samuel Howell noted of shad, "Their average weight may be about seven pounds but individuals are occasionally caught which weigh as high as 12 and even 13 pounds." Those figures were for American shad, since few states, then or now, have kept records on the smaller hickory shad. Those weights may have peaked in the 1800s, since the commercial peak catch of 50 million pounds occurred in 1897. Today fly-rod records are little more than half of those weights, with the International Game Fish Association (IGFA) maintaining records for catches of American shad with both general tackle and fly tackle.

The current world record is 11 pounds, 4 ounces, caught in the Connecticut River, Massachusetts, by Bob Thibodo on May 19, 1986, using 12-pound class line. The current fly-rod world record is 7 pounds, 4 ounces, caught in the Feather River, California, by Rod Neubert on June 30, 1983, using a 2-pound class tippet. As recorded by the International Game Fish Association all tackle records for species from other countries are smaller, as follows:

allis shad: 1 pound, 12 ounces, from the North Sea, The Netherlands
Mediterranean shad: 1 pound, 10 ounces, from the Ombrone River, Grosette, Italy
twaite shad: 1 pound, 8 ounces, from the North Sea, The Netherlands

Our hickory shad is not included in IGFA record keeping, although I have suggested this and it may be added in the near future.

Shad records as of 2001 are as follows:

GENERAL TACKLE FRESHWATER RECORDS

Line class	Weight
2-pound	7 pounds, 13 ounces
4-pound	8 pounds, 14 ounces
6-pound	5 pounds, 0 ounces
8-pound	11 pounds, 1 ounce
12-pound	11 pounds, 4 ounces

FLY-ROD FRESHWATER RECORDS

Tippet	Weight
2-pound	7 pounds, 4 ounces
4-pound	5 pounds, 15 ounces
6-pound	5 pounds, 12 ounces
8-pound	6 pounds, 7 ounces
12-pound	6 pounds, 12 ounces
16-pound	5 pounds, 0 ounces
20-pound	5 pounds, 10 ounces

SHAD DECLINE AND RESTORATION

Pollution, the erection of dams for hydroelectric power, farming, and development were all factors in the decline of shad and other freshwater and anadromous species, such as herring and striped bass. Pollution killed the fish outright or destroyed their eggs. Dams of various types prevented natural migration and spawning runs. Poor farming practices and construction silted shad habitat and buried eggs. All of this had a negative effect on many rivers and river-running species.

Additionally, the increasing human coastal population continually exploited shad. Delaware shad catches in 1837, the first year such statistics are available, noted that 1.5 million pounds of shad were taken from shore seines and drift nets. Coastwise, commercial fishing built to a peak fifty years later. In 1897, 50 million pounds of shad were taken and this was followed by continual declines. The peak catch in the 1940s was about 15 million pounds, later stabilizing at about 8 million pounds annually. Pollution was so bad in the Delaware River that by 1950, only twenty-two shad were caught above Trenton, New Jersey. Fortunately, that was reversed, and today the upper Delaware features some fine shad fishing.

Shad restortation is occurring in other areas as well, and the outcome looks guardedly bright. In 1972, a low point for shad in the Chesapeake Bay area, only 172 shad were captured at Conowingo Dam—the first dam up from the bay on the Susquehanna River. By 1999 the number had increased to 79,370 shad, which were captured here and then moved with a fish lift to upstream waters.

Changes in regulations also bode well for the future of shad. In Florida, commercial fishing for shad has been virtually eliminated. It is hoped that this will lead to an increased abundance of shad in the St. Johns River, once the site of the largest sport fishery for shad among the Atlantic states.

Federal regulations are also contributing to the future of recreational shad fishing. The Atlantic States Marine Fisheries Commission has enacted regulations to eliminate ocean-intercept commercial shad fishing by 2004 or 2005. This type of fishing involves intercepting shad at the mouth of a bay or river system, thereby preventing them from getting to their upstream spawning grounds and producing the next generation of shad. While this intercept fishing has targeted American shad, hickory shad have often been an unintended catch of this commercial effort, and thus their populations have been damaged by it as well.

Fish commissions and DNR agencies are also conducting extensive studies on shad. One example is in Maryland, where the Department of Nature Resources has for several years been conducting angler catch surveys for the Susquehanna River, distributing logbooks that ask for fishing success, date, location, hours fished, and method of fishing.

Results for 1999 showed that bank anglers using spinning tackle with artificial lures or fly rods with flies caught 2,220 fish and released 100 percent of the fish, as required by law. Of these catches, hickory shad accounted for 60 percent, American shad 21 percent, white perch 12 percent, river herring 4 percent, striped bass 2 percent, and other fish less than 1 percent.

A similar Maryland shad study in Deer Creek, a tributary of the Susquehanna River, showed 4,980 hickory shad caught in 1998, with a catch rate of over 8 shad per hour. For 1999 the catch was 5,110 hickory shad caught between March 18 and May 21, with a catch rate of 6 fish per hour.

Other efforts are paying off for shad and for shad fishermen and will continue to do so. Since 1986 the Chesapeake Bay area alone, the cooperating states, U.S. Fish and Wildlife Services, and Native American tribal goverments reared over 250 million shad and released them into bay tributaries. In addition, more than one thousand miles of dammed tributaries in the bay, including five hundred miles of the Susquehanna River watershed, have been reopened with dam removal or construction of fish lifts or fishways. In Virginia, 240 miles of rivers and streams have been opened by fish passages or dam removal, another 120 miles have been opened but currently remain inaccessible, and another 117 miles are planned to be opened.

FISH LADDERS AND FISHWAYS

Historically, shad were know to have ascended the Cape Fear River in North Carolina to Smiley Falls near Lillington, about 180 miles from the ocean. Today dams are located at mile 67, mile 101, and mile 124. These prevent shad runs, although fish ladders erected in 1962 by the Army Corps of Engineers and the North Carolina Fish and Wildlife Service helped in part to alleviate this blockage.

On some rivers, fishways and fish ladders have helped shad ascend farther upriver, but not all have been successful. Unfortunately, there is no way to know in advance what type of ladder or fishway will work best with a given species or on a certain spot of a given river. What is known is that ladders or fishways that will work for herring will not necessarily work for shad, unless the entrance for the fishway is made large enough to attract these larger species.

Even though widespread construction of fish ladders is relatively new, occurring only in the past fifty years, the concept is old—an 1874 New Jersey law stipulated that any dams have fishways built over or around them, at the dam owner's expense. Today, whenever possible, fishways are being erected, while low dams that are no longer used are being torn down to allow for freer migrations and spawning runs of these and other fish.

Mike Hendricks of the Pennsylvania Fish and Boat Commission, who has worked with shad since 1985, reports that in Pennsylvania thirty-three projects have been completed to date to help restore shad to Pennsylvania rivers, primarily the Susquehanna. These included two fish lifts (not including that at the Conowingo Dam, which is in Maryland); two vertical slot fishways; two Denil fishways, which have steplike vertical boards that impede flow and create small resting pools; and twenty-seven dam removals.

Major design changes in fish ladders are helping shad find new upriver spawning grounds. Dam removal is also expanding the range of the shad to some long-lost spawning areas and sections of rivers. This fish ladder in Maryland makes a 180-degree bend, creating a gradual slope to help shad and herring ascend past the dam.

And the good news is that this trend is continuing in all coastal states. In Connecticut, Steve Gephard, supervising fisheries biologist, reports that there are now four fish passages on the Connecticut River: a fish lift (elevator) at Dam 1 at Holyoke, Massachusetts; West Coast–style fish ladders at Dam 2 at Turners Falls, Massachusetts, and Vernon, Vermont; and a vertical slot fish ladder at Dam 4 at Bellows Falls, Vermont, at the end of the natural range of shad, where a waterfall historically blocked them.

Other advances in creating fishways, fish lifts, and fish ladders have resulted in bringing shad back to areas denied to them just several decades ago. Twenty-five years ago, there was no shad fishing to speak of in New Hampshire or in the Merrimack River in Massachusetts. However, shad surveys show shad returns on the Merrimack of twenty-two thousand for 1997, twenty-seven thousand for 1998, fifty-six thousand for 1999, and seventy-two thousand for 2000, the result of fish lifts at Essex Dam at Lawrence, Massachusetts; the Pawtucket Dam at Lowell, Massachusetts; and a fish ladder at Amoskeag Dam at Manchester, New Hampshire, which now allows the shad to run as far at the dam at Hooksett, New Hampshire, a distance of about ninety miles from the ocean. Stockings from other shad rivers, from the mid-1970s on through the present, have helped in this shad restoration.

On the Susquehanna River, the Conowingo Dam, built in 1928, was the first block to shad runs, which originally went the full length of the river into New York. But that is changing. The first lift at the dam in 1999 allowed the passage of 79,400 American shad, 30 hickory shad, 139,200 blueback herring, and 1,800 alewife herring.

SHAD CULTURE, STOCKING, AND TRANSPLANTING

Fish culture—the raising of fish for stocking purposes—began in the 1860s and 1870s. Shad, along with salmon, were a frequent aim of these programs. By 1870 nineteen of the then thirty-seven states had hatchery programs, with fish commissions established in six New England states, New York, New Jersey, Pennsylvania, California, and Alabama. The fish commissions of Maine, Massachusetts, Connecticut, Vermont, and New York hatched almost 200 million shad eggs between 1866 and 1871.

Even with the U.S. Fish Commission in place, the states did most of the work. Connecticut and Massachusetts alone stocked 92 million shad in 1872, compared with 8 million shad fry released into the Connecticut River by the feds.

Today fish commissions and environmental agencies are involved both in dam removal, to expand upriver access to shad and herring, and in stocking and transplanting shad to restore them to their original range where they have been decimated by dams, pollution, and overfishing. Pennsylvania and Maine are two states that are currently raising and stocking shad fry into rivers. In Maine, both adults and eggs are collected from the Connecticut River and placed in a hatchery, where the adults are allowed to spawn. The resulting fry are then stocked into the Kennebec and the Sebasticook, a tributary of the Kennebec. The shad are marked before release to further evaluate returns and future possibilities.

Pennsylvania, in cooperation with the U.S. Fish and Wildlife Service, has been stocking the Susquehanna River with juvenile shad obtained from adult shad from the Hudson, Delaware, and Connecticut Rivers. If baby shad are stocked early enough, they will imprint or home in on the river where they are stocked. They will return to their new home river as adults in four to six years, just as wild shad do.

Other efforts involve capturing prespawn shad at shad lifts located at dams and stocking them in new waters. They then spawn in these new river systems, and the fry or young imprint on the new river and will return there to spawn in the future. Connecticut is doing this, capturing shad from the Connecticut River and stocking them in the upper portions of other rivers targeted for shad restortation.

Though originally native only to the Atlantic coast, American shad have been introduced to the Pacific coast, where they are doing well—and have been since the late 1800s. The first stocking was in 1871, after a California fisheries commission formed on April 2, 1870, decided to make arrangements with Seth Green, "the noted pisciculturist of Rochester, N.Y.," to introduce young shad to the Sacramento River. Green left New York by train on June 20, 1871, with 15,000 shad fry and arrived in California one week later with 10,000 of them still alive. Most were carried in tanks or milk cans. These were released into the Sacramento River at Tehama on June 27. A second attempt to stock more shad met with disaster when the train was derailed leaving Omaha, killing the engineer and destroying the aquarium car filled with shad. More shad, in a later shipment, were released at the same spot in the Sacramento on July 2, 1873. Continued stocking through 1880 or 1881 released a total of 600,000 to 800,000 shad (reports vary) into California waters by the U.S. Fish Commission. Today they can be found as far south as San Diego and as far north as Kodiak Island, Alaska. Principal shad sportfishing on the West Coast ranges from northern California through northern Washington.

SHAD-FISHING RESURGENCE

Shad fishing has never died out, but it has had up-and-down swings in popularity, based on tackle available for it, the shift from netting to sportfishing, and the unfortunate lack of availability of shad as a result of dams and pollution. But there is a current resurgence in the sport.

It is impossible to name the exact timetable for the resurgence of shad fishing in particular areas, states, or rivers. Probably there are many early pioneers who led to its popularity in small geographic areas. But in spite of the smaller size of the fish today compared with the catches of 150 or more years ago, as well as pollution, dams, and commercial exploitation, fishing for both hickory and American shad is a well-established sport during the early balmy days of spring that mark the beginning of the spawning runs of this fabulous light-tackle fly-rod fish, and the super sport to follow.

FALL FISHING FOR HICKORY SHAD

An entirely new fishery for hickory shad has recently developed on the East Coast. Fall populations of hickory shad have been found in scattered areas along the Atlantic coast, where fly fishermen and light-tackle spinning anglers take them from August through October, depending upon latitude. Capt. Norm Bartlett, a light-tackle guide on the Chesapeake Bay, has caught them while jigging around the Chesapeake Bay Bridge in mid-August, and Capt. Ritchie Gaines has caught them in the nearby Kent Narrows, which separates Kent Island from the rest of Maryland's Eastern Shore. Mike Hendricks of the Pennsylvania Fish and Boat Commission reports catching adult hickory shad in Indian River Inlet, Delaware, from August through November using small bucktails and plastic-tailed jigs. Outdoor writer Joe Reynolds has caught them in the winter at the Ocean City, Maryland, inlet.

The states bordering Long Island Sound and west (New York, Connecticut, Rhode Island) perhaps first developed and popularized this still little-known fishery. One of the best spots for this estuary fishery has been in Niantic Bay and the Niantic-Waterford area. Other good spots are the mouths of coastal river systems around Old Lyme, Connecticut, and Thames, Rhode Island. This fishery was discovered during summer and fall fly-fishing for stripers, with the shad often the prey for the larger stripers in the same area. Ultimately a fishery for shad developed.

Most of this fishery is by spin fishermen casting from shore with darts, tandem darts, or a dart with additional weight, allowing the dart to sink in the 10- to 15-foot-deep water, then retrieving. The best fishing is on a moving tide, and when the hickory shad are found, catches of over one hundred fish in a few hours are possible and have been recorded. Fly-fishing from shore or boat is also possible, with sinking lines, sinking flies, or both required to get deep, especially with the moving tide. Strong tides require more weight for both spinning and fly fishermen, to counter the current action, which will belly the line and plane the fly or dart up.

It's quite possible that similar fishing exists throughout hickory shad range but has yet to be explored in all areas. And it's quite possible that hickory shad could be found—but perhaps are being overlooked—in all Atlantic coast locations in which American shad are found. The lack of past fishing for them, or the possibility that anglers thought their hickory shad catches were just smaller or buck American shad, might have led to a mistaken belief that they were nonexistent in certain areas.

Some New England anglers raise the point that this summer and fall estuary hickory shad fishery did not exist in the past. If so, these experienced longtime fishermen insist, they would have caught them while fishing for other species or while blind-fishing during these periods. I believe one possible explanation is that though the original range of hickory shad is said to have extended up to the Bay of Fundy, it is now no farther north than the New England coastal areas south of Maine. Since the American and hickory shad have traditionally spent summers and the fall in the Bay of Fundy, and since hickory shad are no longer found there, is it possible that they have switched their summer-fall foraging area to the New England coastal waters because of a lack of food in the Bay of Fundy, an inability to compete with the larger American shad for any available food, or other reasons? One argument against this explanation is the fact that hickory shad are being caught in the summer and fall in other, more southern estuary areas. Right now no one seems to know the answer, but it's an intriguing question.

CHAPTER 2

Biology and Life History

The shad of the hard strikes, high leaps, and fun fishing is one of two popular species in the United States: the American (also called white or common) shad and the hickory shad. These are just two of the thirty-plus species worldwide, many of which provide sportfishing for anglers in other parts of the globe. We in the United States also have the Alabama shad in the Gulf of Mexico, along with the skipjack herring, a close relative. Gizzard shad, threadfin shad, blueback herring, alewife, and other related species are too small for game fish but are often used for bait for other species.

Among those fish belonging to the family Clupeidae in this country are the shads, herring, menhaden, pilchards, and sardines—almost thirty species off the Atlantic and Pacific coasts or found in fresh water.

Other shad are also sought in other parts of the world. The English have the twaite shad *(Allosa fallax)*, and the French have the allis shad, both of which are also found elsewhere on the European coast. The allis shad *(Alosa alosa)* can reach a length of 24 inches and a weight of 6 pounds, making it a fine sport fish. Shad are also found in Eastern Europe, the Mideast, Africa, Southeast Asia, and China. Many of these are underutilized as game fish but in danger from the sadly common worldwide problems of pollution, dams, commercial overfishing, and human overpopulation. In Europe, shad were held in gustatorial esteem by the ancient Greeks, and the various European shad, along with hummingbird tongues and baby mice, graced the table of many Roman emperors.

Other fish that are not true shad have the shad name. In Bermuda, six different fish are known as Bermuda shad, some as small as 6 inches in length, and rarely exceeding 15 inches. Off Africa, the bluefish is sometimes called a shad or occasionally an elf. In New Hampshire, the freshwater whitefish is sometimes called shad, even though it is not at all

An American shad.

related. And several of the smaller and brackish water species of the *Alosa* family are not game fish but often end up as bait.

The American shad in this country also goes by a number of other names, including alose, white shad, common shad, Potomac River shad, Susquehanna River shad, Connecticut River shad, Delaware River shad, North River shad, Atlantic shad, and so forth, depending on their spawning run. Some fanciful names, such as poor man's salmon, poor man's steelhead (West Coast), poor man's tarpon, white lightning, silver shad, and Susquehanna salmon have also been given to them. They are also called the "mother of herring," since they are similar to herring, although larger. In the Canadian Maritime Provinces, where shad are caught even though not heavily fished for, American shad are sometimes called *Alose savoureuse,* or just alose.

IDENTIFYING NORTH AMERICAN SHAD SPECIES

Both American and hickory shad are easily identified and distinguished from other species of the same family. The American shad *(Alosa sapidissima)* is a compressed, flat (side-to-side) fish with a tapered shape gener-

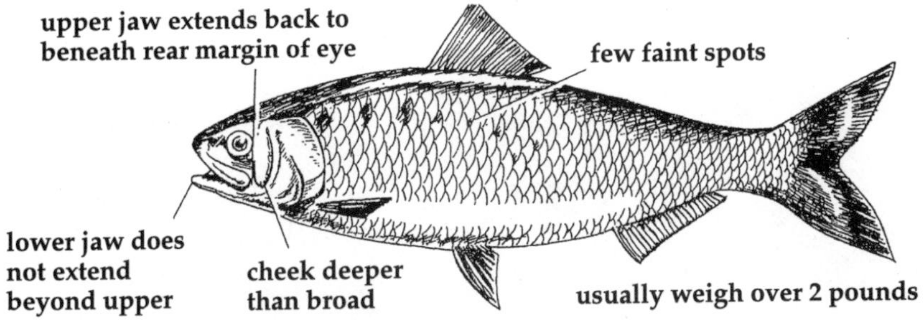

AMERICAN SHAD *Alosa sapidissima*

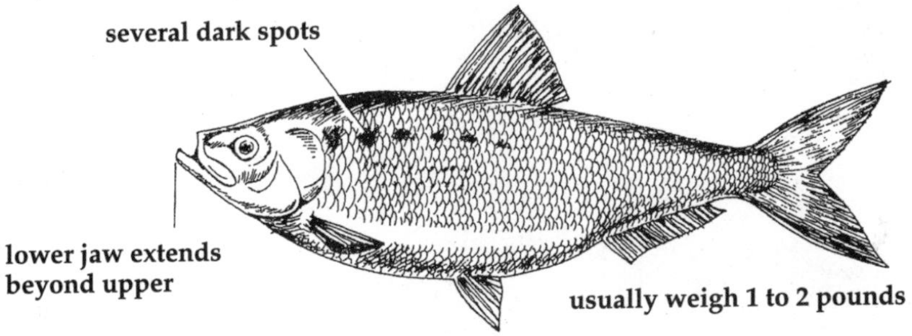

HICKORY SHAD *Alosa mediocris*

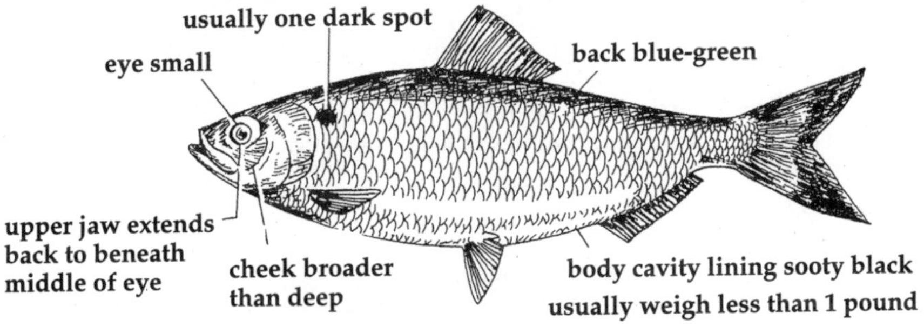

GLUT HERRING *Alosa aestivalis*

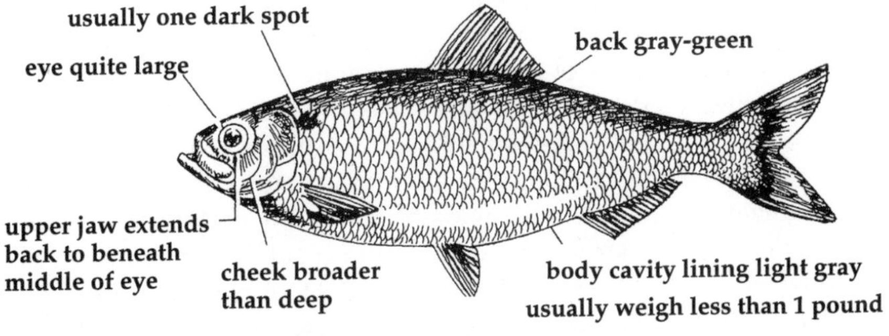

ALEWIFE *Alosa pseudoharengus*

Species identification between American shad, hickory shad, and the various herrings is easy with a few distinguishing characteristics such as general shape, jaw structure, and shoulder spots.

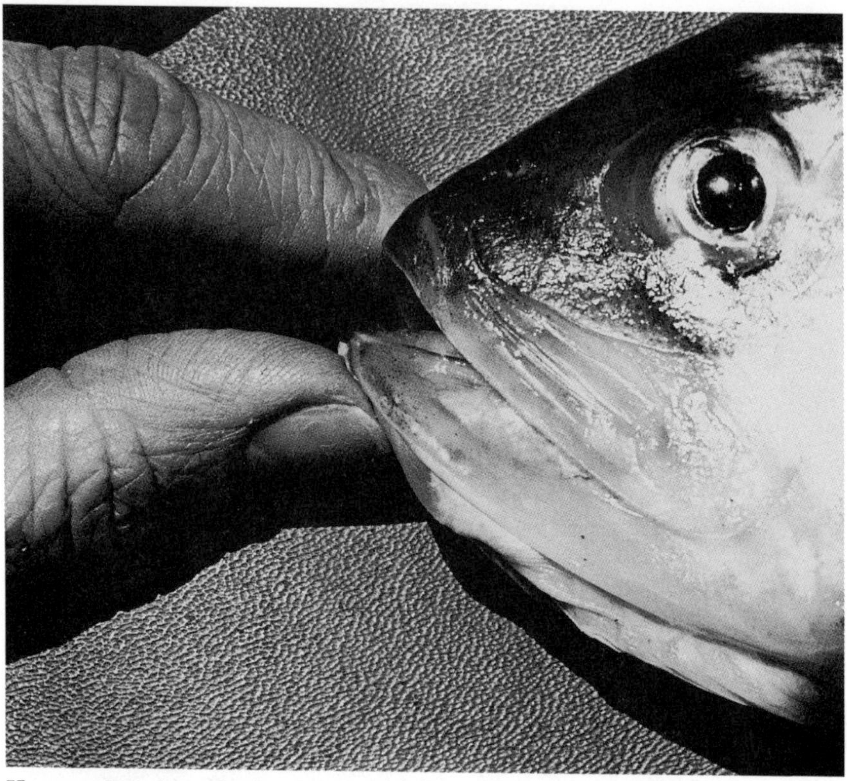

Here, an American shad is shown with the jaws meeting—an easy identifying characteristic.

ally described by biologists as fusiform. Its dorsal fin is single and soft rayed, as is the anal fin. The tail is deeply forked. The lower jaw does not extend beyond the upper jaw, but meets the upper jaw closely. The upper jaw extends back, or posterior, of the rear margin of the eye, and its shoulder is marked with a few dark spots, diminishing in color and often size toward the tail. The back of the fish is moderately dark green or bluish, fading into silvery sides and belly. The scales come off easily when the fish is handled and the belly ridge is marked by the serrated edge of the scales from both sides that touch there. Weight for the returning American shad is generally over 2 pounds, averaging from 3 to 5 pounds in most areas. In all cases, the males are smaller in size and weight than the females.

The hickory shad *(Alosa mediocris)* is similar to American shad in that they have soft ray fins, a deeply forked tail, loose scales, a serrated belly ridge, similar coloration, and one or more dark spots behind the gill cover. They differ in that they are smaller and have a more pronounced curve to the belly and a protruding lower jaw. This protruding lower jaw is perhaps the most prominent identifying feature, since it differs markedly from the matching upper and lower jaws of the American shad. Hickory shad usually weigh less than 2 pounds.

The Alabama shad *(Alosa alabamae)* is indigenous only to the Gulf coast, primarily along the Florida Panhandle. It is similar to the American shad and hickory shad but has a more pointed head, more projecting lower jaw than the hickory shad, and is smaller than both, usually averaging only about 15 inches in length. Perhaps because of its small size in an area that is blessed with other fine coastal and river fishing, sport angling for the Alabama shad is infrequent, and any catches are usually incidental to fishing for other species.

The glut herring is similar to the hickory shad but smaller, usually less than 1 pound, and has a single dark spot on the shoulder, a small eye, and a sooty black body cavity lining. The alewife is also smaller, usually less than 1 pound in weight, but has a large eye, one dark shoulder spot, and a light gray body cavity. Neither of these are game fish.

The closely related family of anchovies includes a dozen and a half species, some of which might be confused with shad by the angler. These include the blueback herring, skipjack herring, alewife, Atlantic herring, Pacific herring, gizzard shad, threadfin shad, round herring, flatiron herring, dwarf herring, and several other herring species. Most of these are small, and even the larger members might only be mistaken as being a very small hickory or American shad. The herring and alewife—like the American and hickory shad—live in the ocean and do ascend freshwater rivers and streams in the spring. They are occasionally caught by shad fishermen, with herring at least taking darts and flies. They may be misidentified as very small or buck (male) hickory shad.

RANGES

The ranges of the American shad and the hickory shad differ. The American shad now swims far beyond its original native waters of the Atlantic coast. It was originally native from the St. Johns River in Florida to the St. John River in Canada. Since the first transplants in 1871 from the Hudson to the Sacramento River in California, the Pacific range now extends from San Diego in Southern California to Kodiak Island, Alaska.

Hickory shad are confined to the Atlantic, since these smaller fish apparently were not thought of as having commercial importance and thus were never transplanted to the Pacific. Their range originally extended from the Bay of Fundy to Florida, but today they are seldom found north of New England. Their popularity is currently increasing, with the principle interest in them found in Massachusetts, Connecticut, Rhode Island, Maryland, Virginia, and North Carolina.

LIFE HISTORIES

Although sportfishermen see shad only during the spring spawning runs up rivers, their life history is important both to understand those spring runs and also in helping to maintain those annual runs for sportfishing.

Like salmon, shad are anadromous fish, which means that they live in salt water (the ocean) but must ascend freshwater rivers and streams to spawn and lay their eggs. Historically, there were many theories as to the movements of shad throughout the year. The most recent research indicates that the two keys to their movements, particularly during spawning, are water temperature and the amount of sunlight, or phototropic periods. Most of the research deals with the more commercially popular American shad.

American Shad

William C. Leggett, writing in the March 1973 issue of *Scientific American,* noted that his studies led him to believe that the movements of shad along the coast through most of the year—in the rivers during the spawning season and again along the coast in postspawning movements—are all controlled by the American shad's preference for certain water temperatures.

Movements

It is known that American shad do not stay year-round off the coastline of their natal river, nor do they mysteriously disappear, as was once supposed. Instead, annual migrations can be described in a long ellipse. In this ellipse of movement, they spawn in the spring in their natal stream (early in the South and later in the North), and then head north along the coast to the Bay of Fundy. Some indications are that they stay there during the summer, from June through September. Later, they reverse their travels farther off the coastline. Although migrations are still little understood, some shad arrive off the St. Johns River by November to December. Others, depending on their river of origin some three to four years prior, continue up the coastline and then peel off into their spawning river when they reach it during their northward travels. Ample evidence of this and the fact that seemingly all shad spend the summer and fall in the Bay of Fundy can be found from research done in which ten thousand shad were tagged in the Bay of Fundy, with later recaptures from every river system along the Atlantic coast, from the Canadian Maritimes to Florida.

Importance of water temperature

Tagging studies and correlation of previous studies by Leggett and others indicate that the shad in all these movements are following specific temperature strata or isotherms found in the ocean current. These coastal migrations were found to be closely associated with water temperatures ranging from about 55 to 64 degrees F.

Further studies by Leggett, over eleven years, as to the freshwater movements of American shad in the Connecticut River indicate that few shad enter the river when the temperature is below 39 degrees F and that the number of shad entering the river increases as the temperature rises to 55 degrees F, with commercial catches declining at temperatures above that.

These figures indicate the temperatures at which the shad enter the river, not necessarily the temperatures at which the sport angler will find them upstream. Temperature studies at the fish lift on the Holyoke Hydroelectric Dam on the Connecticut River at Holyoke, Massachusetts, a popular place for shad fishing, indicate that the peak movement of shad there has been at temperatures from 62 to 71 degrees F. This can be explained by the fact that this dam is 86 miles above the river mouth, thus receiving the main body of shad some four weeks later than those entering the mouth. By that time, the water temperatures have warmed considerably.

Similar findings at Bonneville Dam on the Columbia River in Washington indicate that most of the peak movements of shad there between 1938 and 1969 were at temperatures from 62 to 66 degrees F. For twenty-six of those thirty-two years, the temperature range during which 90 percent of the shad appeared varied no more than these 4 degrees.

One interesting fact concerning the movements of shad along their coastal migration is that whereas in most rivers, shad wait for the water to rise to the proper temperature, in the St. Johns in Florida, they wait for it to fall to the proper temperature. Thus the shad runs and optimal angling there are during the winter months, when it is the coldest. Equally interesting is that when the Atlantic warms during the summer and early fall months, the only waters on the whole coastline having the preferred temperatures of the shad are the Gulf of Maine and the Bay of Fundy.

The same preference for water temperatures controls the migrations of shad once they begin the initial stages of their spawning runs, leaving the true coastline and venturing upstream from the mouth of major coastal rivers.

Spawning run movements

Once committed to their spawning run, the shad enter the wedge of river water extending into the ocean but do not make an immediate direct run into the river. Instead, they face the current and swim into it, reversing their direction as the direction of the tide changes. Thus they yo-yo, or zigzag, back and forth for some time as the tides change and as temperatures warm to their liking. The only reason they make any progress into the river during this zigzag course is that they swim forcefully and strongly against the current while running upstream (toward the river), yet barely hold their position while swimming against the current when facing out to sea on an incoming tide. This type of activity can continue into the river itself when salt water is mixed with fresh water at the river mouth.

Once in the river, they abandon these movements and stick to the deep channels. Here they swim directly upstream, going into the tributaries, smaller streams, and creeks, and following the river up toward its headwaters until they reach the areas where they were spawned a few years before.

In some cases, natural falls such as the Great Falls on the Potomac River and Bellows Falls on the Connecticut River (originally) prevented the further upstream movement of shad. In other cases, dams and heavy pollution have prevented the shad from reaching their original spawning areas.

Research also suggests that shad somehow return to the specific area on the specific river where they were hatched years before. A study done on the Hudson River indicates this, although the spawning areas there are quite extensive shoal areas, and further work in this area is needed to pinpoint the degree of specific site returns.

Spawning activity

Once the shad reach their spawning grounds, the female, or roe fish, deposits the eggs, ranging from about 100,000 to 600,000 per fish. (Researchers vary in their results of such studies, some having found from 30,000 to 300,000, others from 155,000 to 410,000.) The quantity of eggs produced depends upon such factors as the age and size of the fish and the river of origin. Generally, fish from south of the Chesapeake Bay deposit more eggs than those north of the Chesapeake, presumably as natural compensation for the larger number of repeat spawners that are found in the more northern rivers.

Fertilization

Fertilization by the buck, or male shad, occurs over a hard bottom of sand, gravel, or both, usually adjacent to river channels and at varying depths, depending on the river and the spawning location. Spawning has been found at depths from 3 to 30 feet (1 to 10 meters) and is often in areas shallower than 9 feet (3 meters).

The act of egg depositing and fertilization occurs with the fish paired, swimming together on or near the surface, in a fast, splashing, back-out-of-water movement. Usually fish are about three to five years old when first spawning, with the buck often a year younger than the roe shad.

Eggs and fry

The eggs when deposited by the female are a clear pink-amber to pink or yellowish. When fertilized, they absorb water, increase slightly in diameter, and gradually sink. They are carried along with the current, which usually varies from about 1 to 3 feet per second and keeps the eggs floating or suspended. The eggs hatch in three to eight days, depending on the water temperature. Higher temperatures produce shorter hatching times.

Less than a half inch long when hatched, the baby shad grow rapidly. The yolk sac is absorbed, and transformation into a slender shad shape gradually occurs over a period of four to five weeks, after which the shad are about an inch long. They stay in fresh water through the autumn, feeding on tiny insects and crustaceans while at the same time being fed upon by larger predator fish and aquatic animals.

Movements of young shad

In the fall, when the young shad are about 3 to 5 inches long, they leave fresh water by swimming downstream. They head into the ocean to begin the ellptical, temperature-following, coastal cycle with adult shad. Indications are that shad continue this coastal cycle until about three to five years old, at which time they make their first spawning run to deposit the eggs of another year class of shad, repeating the life cycle and ensuring future shad-fishing fun.

Growth rates

Growth rates differ between the sexes (females grow larger) and with the latitude of the natal river of the fish. In southern Atlantic coast rivers, most of the spawning fish are four to five years old, while farther north, spawning fish vary in age from about four to seven years.

Surprisingly, in view of their origin from the Atlantic, shad on the Pacific coast apparently have better growing conditions. There they average about one pound heavier than the Atlantic coast shad.

Maximum age and size

The maximum age for American shad appears to be about seven years, and the maximum size (rarely) up to 12 to 14 pounds. Most of these figures are from the late 1800s, however, and the maximum today is about 9 to 10 pounds. The average size for the buck shad is about 2 to 3 pounds and for the female about 3 to 4 pounds.

Feeding during spawning runs

Twenty-five years ago it was thought that shad do not eat while making spawning runs, as reported in my earlier edition of *Shad Fishing*. That whole discussion of anadromous fish eating or not seems to depend upon the species. Today we know that Pacific salmon do not eat, or eat only reflexively on spawning runs. Once they enter a spawning river, they do not digest food well. Atlantic salmon do seem to eat but, unlike the Pacific salmon, live after spawning and often return to spawn again. Shad seem to fit into this latter category and do feed at least some when in spawning rivers.

Biologists still question this, with some arguing that shad do not feed or feed only a little when on a spawning run in fresh water. This argument is primarily based on some feeding research done twenty years ago, in which shad were found with little food in their stomachs; some were found with food, however, although these were discounted in the final study. Some studies by Dr. Jill Leonard on the Connecticut River had inconclusive results, with indications that shad can feed, although they were less likely to have food in their gastrointestinal systems the farther upstream they were taken. Another study on the York River, Virginia, by John F. Walter III of the Department of Fisheries Science, Virginia Institute of Marine Science, also concluded that feeding activity dropped as the shad went farther upriver. He did find some incidental feeding on the spawning grounds, and some of the shad sampled had stomachs as full as if they were feeding in the ocean. Shad do feed differently on different rivers. For example, it was found that shad feed less on the York River than on other Virginia rivers of the same study. We know at least that they "feed" or react reflexively, since otherwise they would not take shad flies, darts, spoons, and other lures that they hit. They would keep their mouths shut, and there would be no sport shad fishery!

Repeat spawning

The more southerly the river, the greater the likelihood that more shad will die after spawning. Studies indicate that in Florida's St. Johns River, the shad spawn once and then die. The higher egg production of shad in the St. Johns adjusts for this annual loss of spawning fish and keeps the shad population stable. The shad from the New England area return to spawn several times before dying.

Hickory Shad

Less is known about hickory shad than about American shad. In many ways, other than size and a slightly earlier run in most rivers, their his-

A hickory shad catch taken with fly tackle on a small stream.

tory and life cycle are the same as or very similar to that of the American shad.

The runs of the two shad do overlap, with the hickory found in the rivers first, and overlapping with the American shad run, but ending before the American shad runs end. Hickory shad were originally found as far north as the Bay of Fundy but, perhaps because of overfishing, pollution, or other factors, now seem to be most prevalent south of the New York–Massachusetts–Connecticut area, and particularly prevalent from the Chesapeake Bay waters south. Spawning has been confirmed in the Connecticut River. Their distribution and movements in the ocean seem to be largely unknown, although they may closely parallel those of American shad.

Foods of Both Species

Foods for both American and hickory shad is basically based on ocean forage, since that's where they spend most of their lives. Food habits are important for fishermen to be aware of, since they might shed some light

Hickory shad, although smaller than the American shad, are especially prized by fly fishermen because of their jumping antics.

as to why shad strike what they do and what might be the best color, size, and shape of lure or fly to use in a particular situation.

American shad seem to eat mostly small crustaceans and such found in the open ocean, including copepods, mysid shrimp, and amphipods. Most of these are small—much smaller than the lures and flies we use. They are often colored and even glow, or bioluminesce, which might be why shad seem to be attracted to brightly painted lures and fluorescent-material flies. It might also suggest that making some lures painted with phosphorescent paint or tied with phosphorescent materials might produce even better results. These glow-in-the-dark lures and flies might work best under low-light conditions, such as at dawn or dusk.

The copepods that are much of the shad's food resemble the miniature sand fleas that we find along the beach, although copepods are tiny—generally less than about 1 millimeter in length (1⁄25 inch). Mysid shrimp resemble larger shrimp but are only about 10 to 15 millimeters long (3⁄8 to 5⁄8 inch), still much shorter than the average fly, shad dart, or spoon used.

Hickory shad eat the same organisms as American shad but will also eat small fish more readily. Other food items include small squid, fish eggs, and small crabs. Thus it would seem that hickory shad might be more receptive to a larger lure than would be readily taken by an American shad. This was reflected in some of the early flies used for the two species. Tom Loving, an early (1920s) shad fisherman on the Susquehanna River, tied shad flies with alternating black and white bands of yarn for the body and white bucktail for the wing. He mostly tied them on double-point salmon hooks, using larger flies for the hickory shad and smaller, sometimes tied on single hooks, for the larger American shad.

CHAPTER 3

Fly-Fishing Tackle

Fly-fishing for shad does not require any new or special fly-fishing equipment or tackle. The tackle you already have for trout, panfish, bass, or light saltwater fly fishing will do fine for shad. Shad are not sophisticated or highly spooky fish, as are trout and salmon. Fishing for them is primarily fun, not a difficult challenge or mental exercise as to the precisely correct fly and right drift to get the fish to take.

For hickory shad, you can use light trout tackle such as 4- or 5-weight systems. Realize, however, that the rod has to match the line and the fly being used. You won't be able to cast weighted or larger flies with these light outfits. Even the lightest size 8 flies will be at the upper limits of weight and mass for these light outfits. A 6-weight outfit is a better choice. In the smaller streams frequented by hickory shad, floating lines are usually fine, although sinking-tip lines are also popular.

For American shad, a 6-, 7-, or 8-weight system is best, with the heavier outfits usually a little better. This is particularly true for long-distance casting with shooting tapers on larger rivers. You may need sinking lines to get down deep to the shad in some areas, but there are ways of coping with that also, to be discussed shortly.

RODS

Graphite rods are best, but if you have an older fiberglass fly rod, or one of fiberglass-graphite composite, it will work fine also. Rod actions vary with each manufacturer, as do prices. If outfitting for shad or adding tackle to your assortment, you don't have to go overboard on price. Many mid-priced and even low-priced rods are ideal. It does pay to try rods, since some manufacturers build rods with a fast action; others make rods with a slower parabolic action. There is no right or wrong—only what suits you and your casting style.

Avoid rods with a whippy or light tip. These tend to be harder to cast and tend to throw shock waves into the line or collapse with long casts. Whippy rods are not good, particularly when throwing heavier lines, or some specialty lines such as fast-sinking lines, lead-core shooting tapers, or sinking-tip lines.

Rod Length

Rod length is also a personal preference, with rods from 7½ to about 9½ feet typical for shad fishing. Since long casts may be required in some situations, the longer rods are best. They give you more line control and power to push out a long line. This is particularly true if wading for shad or fishing from a float tube, pontoon boat, or kayak, where you will be closer to the water. Here a longer rod is a must for easy casting and to keep the line off the water during the casts. I prefer 9-foot rods for all my shad fishing, whether by boat or miniboat, wading, or shore fishing.

Fly rods for shad fishing include those from about 4 through 9 weights, depending on whether they are used for the smaller hickory shad or for casting sinking lines in larger rivers for the American shad. The detachable extension butts on the third and fourth rods from the top are ideal for fighting big shad when casting on large rivers.

Multipiece Rods

Two-piece rods are standard, although more and more anglers are going to the three- or four-piece travel rods, which pack easily and are less susceptible to baggage breakage.

Guides

Pick rods with large, adequate guides—snake, single-foot snake, or single-foot ceramic guides of silicon carbide, Hardloy, aluminum oxide, or similar materials. Stripper guides—either two or three of them—should be large also. More and more rod companies are going with large strippers, particularly the butt guide, which should be 12 millimeters or larger. Larger guides help in clearing a line on a cast to get maximum distance. Make sure that there are enough guides. The total number of guides, not counting the tip-top, should equal the length of the rod in feet or fractions. Thus the number of guides for 8-, 8½, 9-, and 9½-foot rods, respectively, would be 8, 9, 9, and 10 guides. More guides are better than fewer.

Grips

While some very inexpensive fly rods have foam grips, cork is best. It has a firmness lacking in foam and thus allows punching out a cast more authoritatively than with the soft foam—often necessary for the long casts of shad fishing. Also, with large rods (6-weight and up) such as are normally used for shad fishing, grip shape is important. I firmly believe that the full Wells or half Wells grip is best. Unfortunately, some manufacturers are placing the half Wells grips on rods in reverse—more like the so-called "fishtail" grip—since they look more streamlined and aesthetic that way. Insist on a rod with the grip mounted correctly. The swelling of the grip at the front end of the half Wells or full Wells helps position your thumb to punch out the long casts often necessary for shad.

Reel Seats

Up-locking reel seats are best, since they allow you to hide the forward hood in the rear of the cork grip, and also make for a very slight extension of the butt end. This helps position the reel away from your body when bracing the rod and prevents clothes from tangling in the reel spool. If you use an extension butt, make sure that it is short. About 1 to 2 inches is right; longer than that only causes problems.

REELS

Fly reels come in direct-drive, antireverse, and multiplying models, along with a few subcategories.

Direct-Drive Reels

The direct-drive is just what it says—one turn of the handle (which is attached to the spool) makes one turn of the reel spool. When a fish runs, the handle turns as the spool releases line. These reels, in simple, barebones styles, are ideal for most shad fishing.

Antireverse Reels

Antireverse reels have the handle attached to a separate plate that allows turning the spool as with a direct-drive. A one-way bearing or ratchet prevents the handle from moving as the spool turns backward when a fish takes line. This presumably makes the reel a little safer with the blistering runs of some fish, since the handle can't become a knuckle buster. Although some manufacturers do make small, suitably sized antireverse reels for shad, most are too large. Also, the concept is not really needed for fish the size of American or hickory shad. The basic problem with antireverse reels for smaller fish and tippets is that you often have to set the drag light for the tippet size used. This means that you can end up cranking against the drag (cranking and fighting the drag without retrieving line) or really fighting the fish. These reels, designed so that the spool will rotate without the handle turning, likewise allow turning the handle without the spool rotating. The light tippets and light handle/drag resistance can make it impossible to determine whether you are retrieving line or merely fighting the drag and not gaining line.

Multiplying Reels

Only a few multipliers are made, basically by Martin and J. W. Young, although more manufacturers will probably return to this old idea in the near future. Multiplying reels are just what they sound like, with extra gearing between the handle and reel spool that allows for more than one turn of the spool with each turn of the handle. Most are about a 1.5:1 or 2:1 ratio. The big advantage of these when river fishing for shad is that they allow a faster retrieve of excess line or to reel in line to prevent drag in the water.

Large-Arbor Reels

Large-arbor fly reels became popular in the mid-1990s and are still sometimes misunderstood. In principle, they are larger-diameter direct-drive (usually, though not always) reels that in theory allow retrieving more line with each turn of the reel handle. The key to this is not the diameter of the arbor, but the external diameter of the spool. A reel with a 3-inch-diameter spool will retrieve about 10 inches of line with each turn of the handle; a reel with a 4-inch-diameter spool will retrieve about 13 inches of line per handle turn. If you switch to a larger-diameter reel for the same shad fishing and line and rod size, the principle works. If not, you are just exchanging your standard reel for a reduced-capacity reel with a large arbor.

Necessary Fly Reel Features

Any shad fly reel should include the following features:

- Rim control to allow palming the reel on a long run as an adjunct to the drag.
- Enough line capacity to take the full fly line plus enough backing. "Enough backing" might be no more than 50 yards of Dacron, although on a large, fast-running river with American shad, a fish could presumably run farther. For these situations, 100 to 150 yards of backing is better.
- A good drag. Shad aren't tarpon or big stripers, so drag is less important than it would be with those or other large species. Click drags are nothing more than one or two pawl ratchets that click against a gear on the spool to slow the reel revolutions, prevent line overruns, and present some resistance to a fish taking line. Reels can have one or two of these click drags, and they can usually be turned on or off. With two, you have a choice of one or two clickers working as drags. Don't completely eliminate the click drag, since this allows no control of line overruns.
- Cork disk drags are excellent for shad fishing, even though these reels often have a slight click drag in addition, as a signal of a shad running or of line retrieved. A cork drag has a cork disk on the inside of the frame or back of the spool. Drag adjustment controls the pressure on the cork drag, and thus the resistance to the line pulled from the reel. Other drag systems, including the spindle type and the caliper-style system that works on a rotating disk, are also ideal and equivalent to cork disk drags.

LINES

Fly lines provide the weight to make the cast, thus the thick diameter of the line. And just as spinning and casting outfits require different weight lures for optimal performance (each rod will work best with one lure weight), so fly lines come in different "sizes," or weights, for optimal casting with fly rods of different lengths, stiffnesses, and actions.

These different line weights are designated by a series of numbers that indicate the weight of the first 30 feet of fly line for lines up through 6-weight, and the first 40 feet in sizes 7 and larger.

Line Sizes and Weights

The line sizes and weights determined as standard by the industry are presently as follows, based on the first 30 feet of line as established by the industry. Heavier lines are available, but most shad fishing will be with 6- through 9-weight lines. The new weights listed are for the first 40 feet of line, at this writing being strongly considered by the fly-tackle industry and likely to become the standard.

LINE SIZE	WEIGHT	NEW WEIGHTS (grains/grams)
1	60 grains	
2	80 grains	
3	100 grains	
4	120 grains	
5	140 grains	
6	160 grains	
7	185 grains	234/15.14
8	210 grains	286/18.56
9	240 grains	327/21.17
10	280 grains	384/24.87
11	330 grains	387/25.06
12	380 grains	443/28.71

Grain-weight fly lines

Some fly lines are sold by grain weight rather than the designated number sizes as listed above. Notably, these are lines by Teeny, along with some by Scientific Anglers, Cortland, and Rio. Thus it is important to realize the weights of these lines in conjunction with the rod to be used with them. While the line manufacturers usually list suggested rod weights for their grain-weight lines, some give a wide range that, in truth, can really overload a rod by several line sizes. Be careful about this, or make appropriate changes in your casting style—slow down and throw a wider loop—to adjust for these extreme weight lines when used with some rods.

Line Tapers

All lines, regardless of weight, come in several different taper styles, including level, double-taper, and weight-forward. Weight-forward tapers have the advantage of front tapers, similar to that of many double-tapers, assuring a light, delicate presentation of the fly. This is more important in trout fishing than for shad. The front belly of a weight-forward also makes casting long distances easier, something most important in shad fishing. Weight-forward tapers come in many styles, with different belly lengths, and even with different characteristics for fishing in warm climates (stiffer lines) or cold weather or water (very flexible lines). If you have the choice, use a cold-weather-style weight-forward taper or shooting taper for shad fishing.

Specialized shooting lines

Shooting tapers, also known as Shooting Heads, are specialized lines developed and used for shad more on the roaring rivers of the West Coast than elsewhere, although they are becoming increasingly popular for shad in the East, particularly in the sinking versions and for long-distance casting. These specialized fly lines are about 30 to 40 feet long.

While they do allow greater casting distances, the casting method is slightly different from that of standard fly lines and requires some practice. Since they are far shorter than the standard 90- to 105-foot length of fly lines, they must be used with a running line between the shooting taper and the backing. Double-taper lines can be cut in half to make two or more 30- to 40-foot-long shooting tapers.

Running line for shooting tapers

Running, or shooting, lines are used with shooting tapers and are about 100 feet long. This running line becomes, in effect, part of the fly line. In casting, the shooting taper is worked out of the rod tip and false-cast before being released and "shooting" a long line. With the 100 feet of running line and 30 to 40 feet of shooting taper, this makes for a usable, workable line of 130 to 140 feet before reaching the backing. Specific running lines are similar to a thin fly line or braided material. They are made by Scientific Anglers, Cortland, Rio, Elite, and Gudebrod. Another possibility is flat or oval mono, such as Cobra, made by Cortland. You can also use a small-diameter level line for a running line. Most of these are plenty strong. Cortland makes a 4-weight level line with a 20-pound-test core, while their 5- through 9-weight lines have a 30-pound-test core. Scientific Anglers also has level lines with core strengths similar to that of Cortland and strong enough for shad fishing, usually with a 20- to 30-pound-test core.

Sinking Lines and Sink Rates

At one time, fly lines were made only in floating versions, although those early floating lines did not float that well. Today floating lines really float, but lines of various sink rates are also available. Fly lines were once characterized simply as floating, slow-sinking, medium-sinking, or fast-sinking, but there's now a newly proposed (not yet enacted at this writing) numbering system to rate lines with a specific sink rate as follows. The number represents the approximate sink rate in inches per second, plus or minus ½ inch.

SINK RATE NUMBER	SINK RATE (inches per second)
1	½"–1½"
2	1½"–2½"
3	2½"–3½"
4	3½"–4½"
5	4½"–5½"
6	5½"–6½"
7	6½"–7½"
8	7½"–8½"
9	8½"–9½"
10	9½"–10½"

While full-sinking lines are made, sinking-tip lines are also available. These are ideal for shad fishing. They are floating lines with a sinking-tip end that can vary as to sink rate and length. The sinking-tip end of these lines varies from 5 to 30 feet. In addition, multiple-tip lines are now made that consist of a standard floating line with tip ends that are interchangeable through interconnecting loops. These tip ends include a floating section and two or three sections of various sink rates, allowing fishing at different levels of the water column or coping with varying river currents. Each of these types of lines has a place in shad fishing.

Full-sinking lines

For fishing large, fast-flowing rivers, where you must get down to get to the shad, use a full-sinking line, often with a fast sink rate. This will allow maximum depth through the full length of the cast and retrieve to get down to the fish. With full-sinking lines, retrieve almost all of the line, then make an aerial roll cast to get the line in the air and ready for a back-cast and the next forward cast to get the fly out to the shad again.

Sinking-tip lines

For smaller rivers and streams, sinking-tip lines are often fine, since they do allow getting down in all but very fast waters. Much of the line floats, making them easier to fish, since the floating line allows planing the sinking tip to the surface when ready for a new cast, and making a cast similar to that used for a floating line.

Lead-core lines

Lead-core lines also allow fishing deep with a fly. In addition, heavily weighted lines are available from all the major companies. These are often made by adding tungsten powder to the fly-line coating. They are often incorporated into shooting tapers. Sometimes heavier grain weights than are recommended for a rod are fished, but this requires a slowed casting process and care to avoid tangles. It is also possible to make your own fast-sinking lines or shooting tapers from regular lead-core line available from the standard line companies, or from lines such as the Cortland LC-13 line, so named for the lead core and the 13 grains-per-foot weight. This also allows you to custom-make a line of a specific weight by measuring out the right length: 130 grains for a 4-weight would be 10 feet; 260 grains for a 9-weight would measure 20 feet.

Mini lead heads are ideal for fishing deep for shad. These are short lengths of lead-core line commercially available from companies such as Cortland and Gudebrod. Most are about 2 to 5 feet long, with loop

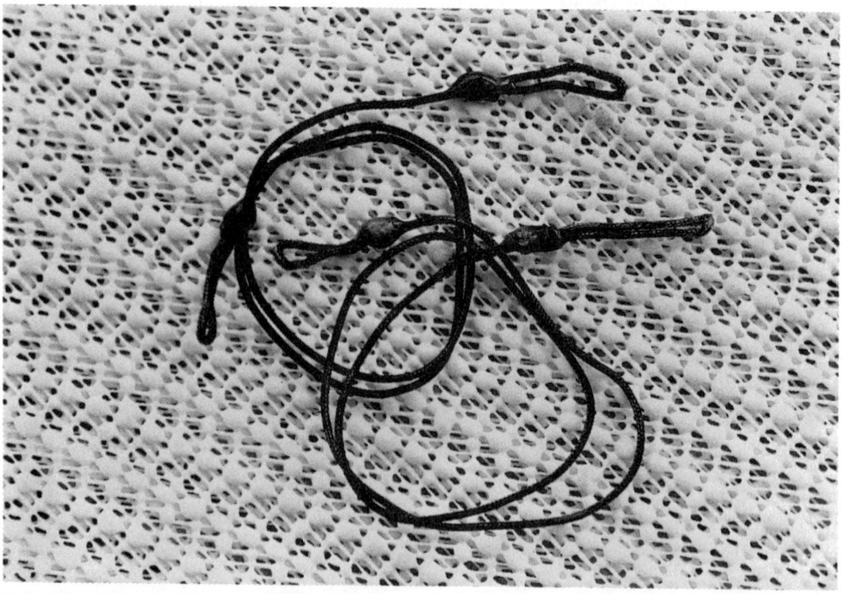

Mini lead head tips like these can be bought (Cortland, Gudebrod) or made at home using lead-core or lead-substitute lines in short sections, with loops whipped on each end. Place these sinking ends between the end of the line and the short leader to help the line and fly sink in fast currents.

connections on each end. You can make your own with lead-core line, folding over the end of the line, then wrapping and whip finishing it with fly-tying thread as suggested for fly lines. I make these in 2-foot lengths, using 27-pound-test lead-core line. The 2-foot lengths with loops on each end allow me to fish one or more lengths to keep a sinking fly down or to temporarily convert a floating line to a sinking-tip style.

Lead-core lines range from about 15- to 60-pound-test. Use the lightest you can safely fish, since the strength of the line is in the braided sleeve, not the lead core, and lighter-pound-test line will sink faster than heavier-pound-test that is thicker but contains no more lead. (Most companies use two sizes of lead core, such as Cortland, which uses 0.012-inch lead core in its 14-pound-test line and 0.020-inch in all its other lines, 18- to 60-pound-test.) If the area you are fishing has legal prohibitions against using lead in your fishing tackle, non-lead lines are also available.

Backing

Since fly lines usually measure between 90 and 105 feet in length (longer for Spey lines or the shooting-taper/running line combination), you need some backing if a shad catches the current and makes a long run. I like 20-pound Dacron for this. Fill the reel with the Dacron line, leaving enough room for the fly line or running line/shooting-taper combo. It is bothersome, but the best way to do this is to add the fly line to the reel, then tie on the backing and fill the reel. Reel this onto a second reel or winder, then onto another spare reel or winder, and then back onto the fly reel. Make sure that the weight-forward line is on correctly, and check all knots or loop-to-loop connections.

LEADERS

Monofilament leaders can be tied to the line via a nail knot or connected through loops. Loops are best, since they allow maximum versatility of adjusting the line and leader for changing shad-fishing conditions. The best mono leaders are about 7½ feet to 9 feet long for floating lines when the fish are shallow in small streams or late in the season. Commercial leaders are fine for shad fishing. Pick those that have a tippet section of about 4- to 8-pound-test for hickory shad, 6- to 10-pound-test for American shad.

Making Leaders

You can also make your own leaders, starting with a 30- to 40-pound butt section, tapering down through a series of smaller-diameter mono, and ending with the tippet. An easy formula is to make the butt section about

40 percent of the total length, the tapering portion about 40 percent, and the tippet about 20 percent. Thus for a 10-foot leader, there will be 4 feet of level butt section, 4 feet of taper, and 2 feet of tippet. Use shorter leaders for sinking or sinking-tip lines, since a short leader helps keep the fly down with the fish. Best length for these conditions is about 2 to 4 feet.

Shad are not particularly leader shy. If possible, pick a leader color based on the water you fish. Often early-season stream and river conditions make waters slightly turbid and milky; here, mist, brown, or camouflage leader colors are best. You don't need fluorocarbon leaders for shad.

CONNECTIONS AND KNOTS

You only need a few knots for fly fishing. My favorite method for all backing-line-leader connections is to use interconnecting loops. Use a nail knot or interconnecting loops for attaching the line to the leader. Use an Albright knot or interconnecting loops to add the backing to the line. Use loops in both ends of the fly line for quick connections. For the loop in the backing, use a splicing needle or tie a Bimini twist. For a loop in the butt end of the leader, tie a perfection loop knot, surgeon's loop, or figure-

Here, connecting loops are shown where a line and a mini lead head section are joined. This is a simple method of adding these sections to line to help it sink.

eight loop. Use blood knots to tie together tapered leader sections, and an improved clinch or Palomar to tie the fly to the tippet. For details on knots, see one of the knot booklets available through Stren, Berkley, or Ande, or one of the knot books listed in the Bibliography.

Basic Knots

While the arbor knot, the blood knot for tying leader sections, and the improved clinch or Palomar knot to tie the fly to the tippet are "musts," the best connection of backing to line and line to leader is with loops. For the leader part of the line-to-leader connection, use a perfection loop knot, figure-eight loop knot, or surgeon's loop knot. Follow the directions with your braided Dacron line to make a spliced loop, or tie a Bimini twist for maximum knot strength in your backing. Make sure that any backing loop is large enough that you can run the reel through it to change lines if needed.

Making Whipped Loops

On the front and back end of the fly line, make a whipped loop. To do this, fold over 1½ or 2 inches of the end of the line, then hold this in your left hand and begin to wrap around the folded part with fly-tying thread. Make sure that you leave about 1 inch of loop open. This is easiest to do with a fly-tying bobbin, by wrapping over the end of the thread, then swinging the bobbin around the loop while holding it with both hands. Cover the end of the fly line with the wraps, and finish by making it level and smooth.

Tie off the wraps by holding the finished loop in the left hand (loop protruding to the right), then make a whip finish, as in fly tying, over the wraps. This is the same as the whipped end of a rope that we all learned in Boy Scouts, or get a fly-tying friend to show you the process. Once the whip finish is complete, clip the thread. Seal and protect the whipping with a thin coating of flexible sealer or glue such as Pliobond or Scientific Anglers UltraFlex.

CHAPTER 4

Flies, Patterns, and Tying Techniques

Ever since shad were first caught on hook and line, flies have held an important place in the history of the sport. Locally popular shad patterns have a long history, but little emphasis has been given to them, unlike the highly developed interest in flies for trout, bass, salmon, steelhead, and more recently, saltwater species. Unlike trout, shad do not require highly developed patterns or different flies for different conditions and seasons. Even so, today there are a lot of colorful, as well as some not-so-colorful, patterns for shad.

Prior to 1884, successful patterns for shad included a White Miller (an all-white fly), a red fly with red wings, and a scarlet fly with mottled brown wings. Hooks used then were mostly Limerick, sizes 1, 2, and 3. One of the early fly-fishing offerings was not really a fly at all, but nothing more than a red glass bead strung onto the silkworm gut leader (mono was not available until the early 1940s) ahead of a bare hook. A variation of this was to use two or three beads of contrasting colors, often red and yellow, sometimes with a bright gold-plated hook. You can do the same thing easily, and with less possibility of abrasion and damage to the mono leader, by using bright, fluorescent-colored plastic beads in 4-, 6-, 8-, and 10-millimeter sizes. Fishing with two to four small, colored beads on the leader just above a bare gold hook is a common method on the Columbia River (along the Washington-Oregon borders), according to angler Dave "Scaly" Bailey of Sequim, Washington.

Today shad flies number in the hundreds, often locally popular and known and used only on one small stream, a part of a major river, one river system, or in one geographic area. Shad flies do not have to be widely publicized nor do they have to be tied in any particular color or style, to be successful. Indeed, successful flies are often only locally known, with a completely different fly pattern equally well known and equally effective in another nearby area or stretch of river.

EAST AND WEST COAST SHAD FLIES

Shad flies of the East and West Coast vary widely. East Coast patterns are generally slimmer, bright but not flashy, and use a lot of fluorescent colors in the body and wing of the fly. West Coast patterns are often more like the western steelhead flies. They are bulkier and often have a few more materials or parts to the flies, such as tails, ribbing, collars, and tags. Sometimes a little more flash material is included in the wing or hackle. They also seem to use more cactus or ice chenille, and thus have more bulk than the slimmer eastern patterns.

This similarity to steelhead flies is not surprising, since steelhead are a native species and are more widely fished for and sought after than shad. Also, steelhead and shad are found in some of the same rivers at the same time, so a crossover or compromise in fly design is not unlikely when an angler is trying to cover all the bases and might not be sure of what will hit his or her offering on any particular drift.

FLY SIZES

Most of the flies for both the East and West Coast are tied on smaller and shorter length hooks than those of the past. While flies of the past were sometimes tied on flies as large as 1/0, most flies for American shad today are tied on sizes 2 to 8. Flies for hickory shad are usually tied on smaller hooks, such as sizes 4 to 10. Most shad flies are tied on regular or 1X to 3X long hooks, similar to nymph hooks used for trout fishing. Since the flies need to get deep, stout hooks with heavy shanks are best. Flies can also be weighted, or weight can be added to the leader with wraparound lead or split shot, or with a mini lead head added in the middle of the leader or between the leader and fly line, as described in the chapter on tackle.

FLY PATTERNS, COLORS, AND FLASH

While fly patterns vary by region, similar color combinations have proven effective on rivers throughout the Atlantic and Pacific coasts where shad are found. In buying shad flies or materials for tying your own, you won't need subtle shades or complex ties. Stick to bright white, yellow, red, light green, purple, orange, pink, medium green, light blue, lavender, and similar colors, in mix-and-match combinations of the fly body and wing.

Although shad flies are typically colorful, in my opinion, as well as that of most experts, they should not include too much flash material, such as Mylar, Flashabou, Krystal Flash, or similar products. Some years ago, before writing my first book on shad (*Shad Fishing*, Crown Publishers, 1975), I experimented with flies for shad and tied some with the then-new Mylar. Mylar is a very shiny, metallic-looking plastic material. It comes in silver and other bright metallic colors, almost like the stiff metallic tinsel used in fly tying. In addition to sheets and braided tubing, it is also available in thin, stranded ribbon form that can be used as a wing or as an adjunct to wing material. Originally I tied some flies with wings cut from the flat Mylar, but then quickly switched to the stranded material for wings and bodies or the braided Mylar for bodies. For bodies, the stranded material can be wrapped around the hook shank, just as you would wrap a shank with metallic tinsel or spiral through a chenille or yarn body as a ribbing. The braided material can be slipped onto the hook like a cigar wrapper onto a cigar, and then tied off at both ends.

I tried flies tied wholly of Mylar, with conventional (colored) bodies and Mylar wings, with Mylar bodies and calf-tail wings, and various other combinations. I also tried a few strands of the bright material mixed in with or tied alongside the regular wing material.

In almost all cases, the Mylar flies proved to be too bright for the shad and scared them. With polarizing glasses, I could see the shad swim away from the fly as it swung in the current. This will sometimes happen with conventional bright, fluorescent-colored flies, but you will also usually see the shad return to the fly and one eventually hit it once it swings into the right location in the drift. That didn't happen with the bright Mylar flies. Fishing a short line, I could watch the shad swim upstream, see the fly, and shy off to the side. The flies with a few strands of Mylar mixed into the wing seemed to work equally as well, but no better than, the established bright, fluorescent flies.

There does seem to be a place for the shiny Mylar flies, however. This is when fishing at night or during very low-light conditions, such as when fishing at dawn or dusk under hazy or heavily overcast skies, or even during the day if it's extremely overcast or if rain threatens. The Mylar flies may also be appropriate in turbid water, although this is more difficult to determine, as water turbidity makes it more difficult to see a shad reaction to the fly.

Black Flies

As an experiment a few years ago, I tried some black flies. While bright, fluorescent flies have proven themselves and seemed to be popular all along both coasts for both American and hickory shad fishing, some anglers have also reported catching shad on nymphs and similar dark or dull patterns. Taking this one step further, I tied up some simple black flies that consisted of nothing more than a black metal bead in back of the hook eye and a body of plain black chenille. In the few test runs, I caught about as many shad as did other anglers using more traditional bright-colored flies. It pays to experiment.

Phosphorescent Flies

An almost unexplored possibility in shad fishing exists with phosphorescent, or glow-in-the-dark, flies. Brian Wiprud, a New York–based writer and shad fisherman, in his research of the literature, learned that both hickory and American shad feed on mysid shrimp (krill), copepods, and other small ocean invertebrates, many of which bioluminesce, or glow in the dark. If this bioluminescence is a triggering factor for feeding by shad, then a glow-in-the-dark fly might be a distinct advantage in certain fishing situations, such as when fishing at night, during the low light of dawn or dusk, under overcast skies during the day, or during bright, sunny days.

DRY FLIES

At the headwaters of some streams and rivers, anglers have reported catching shad on dry flies. This can be done, but dry flies work best in shallow streams and tributaries and at the headwaters of main rivers, as well as at the end of the season when shad have spawned and are feeding, or are feeding more than they are earlier in the run. Almost any dry fly can be used, although Bivisibles seem to be best, both because of their ability to float high with the extra hackle tied in the fly, and also their increased visibility. Try light brown, tan, cream, and other colors that will simulate the natural mayflies, caddis, and stoneflies found on those waters in mid to late spring. Trout flies and patterns in sizes 4 through 8 are ideal for this, although smaller sizes also work well.

Michael Jeavons of Toronto, Ontario, Canada, wote to me in 1995 of his fly fishing in the West Branch of the Delaware River:

> "Since the last trip I made to the Catskills in shad season was nearly ten years ago, the following technique may by now be well known, but when I was last there, no one seemed to talk of it. The pool I fished most often for shad also held a population of brown trout, and it was these I took to be rising to mayfly spinners in the riffles very late in the evening. However, when I cast over them with a 5-weight outfit and polywing spinner I was startled to connect with a shad. For the rest of that trip, I would start

fishing in the early evening in the heavy water with the sinking-tip and the Jerk [a dartlike fly] and as it grew dark . . . that signaled a change to the dry fly. The 'locals' would leave the river as it began to get dark and before the rise started, so I had the pool to myself. I found the polywing spinner [a dry fly] quite easy to see in the gloom, especially as the shad seemed to prefer a size 12 to 10. The main problem was finding my way back to the car to head for a late supper at the Roscoe Diner. Shad are a lot of fun on a 6- or 7-weight rod, but on a 5-weight they are something else!"

Shad angler Jack Denny of Belleville, New Jersey, also fishes dry flies late in the season on the Delaware, drifting them to take rising and surface-cruising shad.

SIMPLE SHAD FLIES

The Simple One

Since shad flies can be simple, I developed an extremely simple design years ago that I called The Simple One. I originally tied it with a Mylar, tinsel, or chenille body and a calf-tail or impala wing. Since then, I've modified it by making it even simpler, with no body and only a wing tied

Simple shad flies can be made with bright chenille bodies, ribbing, and a simple wing. This shad fly has had the tail tied in place and the body wrapped up the hook shank, with the ribbing ready to be added next.

Finishing shad flies is easy using the whip.

on the hook. As a basic design, it's a great saltwater pattern, for which it was originally designed, but it can be tied in any size for any fish. The secret of this fly—if there is one—is that the wing, in both the original and modified versions, is tied so that it completely encircles the hook shank, veiling, or hiding, the hook shank and making the wing more of a cone around the hook than an angled wing on top of the fly.

To tie the simple one, tie down the thread, clip the excess thread, then position a bundle of wing material (usually calf tail) over the hook shank in back of the hook eye. Make two loose loops of thread around this wing, pull tight, and at the same time, use your thumb to push down on the base of the wing to spread and flare the wing around the hook shank, then make several more tight turns to secure it. Trim the butt ends, complete the head, and then tie off with a whip finish. Seal with head cement, and you're finished. As with most shad flies, use bright colors, such as calf tail dyed fluorescent colors.

Other Simple Patterns

Another pattern that I like is one that was developed years ago by my fishing buddies Joe Zimmer and Irv Swope. This is a fly that closely imitates the basic colors of the standard spin fisherman's shad dart, although any combination of bright colors can be used. Shad darts are tapered lead

To protect the completed wrapped head, it is best to add a drop of head cement or clear fingernail polish.

body lures, with the original basic color combinations a yellow calf tail and painted lead body, white with a red head. Originally these were commercially available as the Quilby Minnow, manufactured by the Pequea Company of Strasburg, Pennsylvania. The original design incorporated a turkey quill body into which low-melt metal (often called Wood's metal) was poured. (Molten lead at over 600 degrees F would burn the turkey quill.) The tail was tied on and the red head painted, with the quill left unpainted and the metal showing through the translucent quill body. They also made a lightweight fly-rod version of the Quilby.

Later it was discovered that the shad would just as readily hit a painted body, so the time-consuming task of making them with turkey quills was replaced by simple lead-head jig molding methods.

The Zimmer/Swope fly employs a bright chenille body, optional silver ribbing, and an impala (calf-tail) wing. There is no tail or throat. Most shad fishermen tie or buy these in a wide range of color combinations, including white, red, yellow, orange, pink, green, purple, and similar colors, all in fluorescent dyes for maximum brightness. Most are tied with contrasting wing and body colors.

WEIGHTED FLIES

Shad flies are best when they are fished deep. While it is possible to get shad flies down with a sinking line, sinking-tip line, mini lead heads at the leader, or split shot, it's also easy to weight any existing pattern. Also, shad are not as concerned as other fish about action of a fly or a fluttering, undulating movement in the water. They are mostly concerned about the fly being colorful (usually) and in the right place in the current (location, location, location). Thus the weight that tends to stifle movement and action in a fly is of less concern with shad flies. There are several ways to tie weighted shad flies, including the following:

- Using lead wire. Lead wire, or wire of a non-lead substitute, is available in a number of sizes, from about 0.015 to 0.035 inch in diameter. When tied in identical ways, the thicker wire will add more weight. There are several ways to use lead wire. One is to wrap the hook shank with the lead, either in a tight wrap or in a looser spiral. Generally the tight wrap is best, since it makes it easier

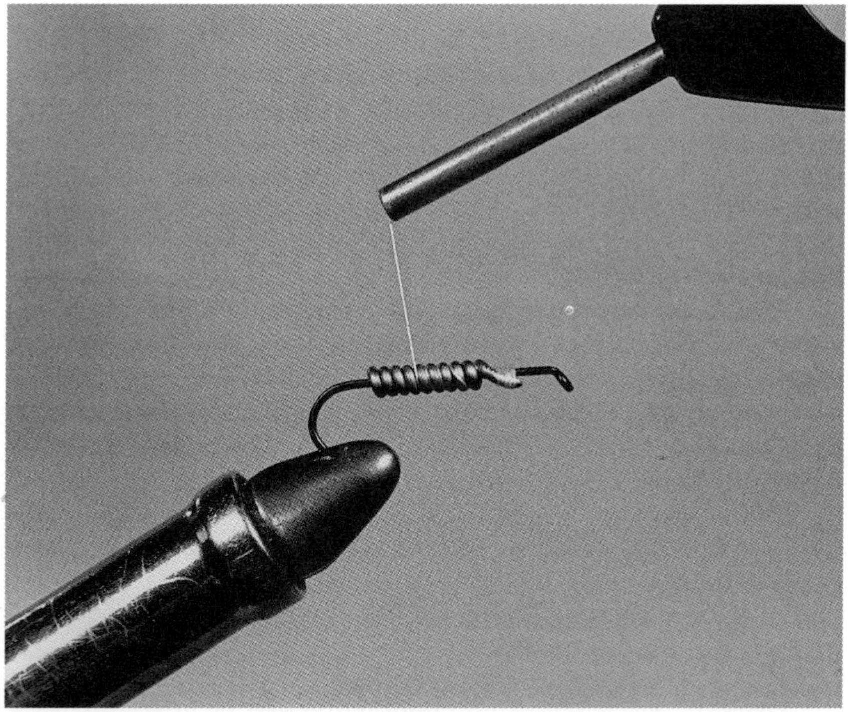

Tying shad flies is easy, since most involve only a few materials and simple methods. Here, lead wire is added to a hook and wrapped over before tying the rest of the shad fly to help the fly sink in fast currents.

to get a smooth body when overwrapped with chenille, yarn, floss, or similar body materials. The tight wrap is a must if covering with a wrap of tinsel. Wrap with floss over the lead wire for the smoothest tinsel wrap. With a tight wrap, tie it down with thread at each end, and make a taper of the thread for a smooth transition of the body material up over the now-thicker lead body. Then coat the lead wire with head cement or a similar sealer to prevent the lead from discoloring the body material and making the fly useless.

- Another method of using lead wire is to cut two, three, or four strands (two are typical) of lead the length of the hook shank, less the bend and the hook eye. Then tie in the thread, hold the lead wire parallel to the hook shank, and wrap with tight turns of thread to completely cover the lead. Position the two strands on either side of the hook shank, three strands with one on each side and one on top, or four strands equally around the hook shank. Then secure them in place with wraps of thread.

  You can also tie lead wire just at the head or tail of the fly to make for an up-and-down action in the water. Unfortunately, you can't see where the lead is located or how much is tied on the fly once it's finished.
- Dumbbell and hourglass eyes can also add weight to shad flies. The Clouser Minnow, one of the best deep-water flies, is tied this way, and if tied in bright colors and on the right size hooks, Clousers will take shad. Dumbbell eyes also give a fly a peculiar up-and-down, yo-yo action in the water. This may or may not attract shad, but the weight does allow the fly to get down. You can weight a fly as little or as much as you like with dumbbell eyes, as they are available in a number of sizes, including mini to large—about 1/100 to 1/16 ounce. To keep from having to use the steelhead anglers' "chuck-and-duck" method of casting heavily weighted flies, stick to the mini and small sizes of dumbbell eyes. To tie any fly with these, tie in the thread, position the dumbbell eye in back of the hook eye, and figure-eight the thread around it to position and tightly wrap the eye in place. Then continue to tie the rest of the fly. These eyes are available in lead, as well as plated finishes of nickel, copper, gold, and black, along with some Spirit River hot fluorescent colors, such as chartreuse and orange.
- Bead chain eyes add a little weight, but certainly not as much as that of the lead or lead-substitute eyes. These are made from bead chain that is cut with wire cutters into pairs, the pair of eyes tied in place through the connecting strand just as are hourglass and

dumbbell eyes. They are available in silver (really nickel) and gold (brass), and in several sizes. Terry Hellekson, in the chapter on shad flies in his book *Fish Flies,* suggests bead and hook size matching as follows:

CHAIN SIZE	HOOK SIZE
Small (0.0940)	8 and smaller
Medium (0.1250)	6
Large (0.1562)	4
Extra large (0.1875)	2 and larger

- Beads and cones are available in metal, glass, and plastic. Metal cones, available in nickel, gold, black, copper, and bright-colored finishes, provide the maximum weight for fishing deep. While the plain metallic finishes are fine, I also like the new "hot" color cones that are available from Spirit River. These give you a bright-colored head, just like those of the spinning anglers' shad darts, and the rest of the fly can be finished as you prefer with normal fly-tying materials.

  To use these, first bend down the barb of the hook to slide the bead or cone in place over the hook point and around the bend. In general, you want to use the smallest bead or cone that you can fit onto the hook. Also, hook choice is important, since a round or perfect bend will make it easier to slide the bead or cone in place than on hooks with a sharp bend, such as Limerick styles.

  Slide the bead or cone to the hook eye, tie down the thread in back of it, and proceed to tie the fly, ending with wraps of thread and a whip finish just in back of the cone or bead. Hot color beads from Spirit River come in 1⁄8, 5⁄32, and 3⁄16 inch in chartreuse, roe red, hot orange, and pink. The cones are available in chartreuse, orange, and red in 5⁄32, 3⁄16, and 1⁄4 inch.
- Use jig hooks to tie your shad flies. Jig hooks are being used more and more in fly fishing, since they allow adding weight (cone heads or dumbbell eyes) to the hook at the bend and keep the hook riding point up to lessen snags. You can buy hooks and add your own weight to the sharp bend in the hook shank, or buy the hooks with painted or unpainted lead heads already molded onto them.

  You can get molded-head jig hooks as light as 1⁄100 and 1⁄80 ounce, but most of these are on hooks that are too small for shad fishing. Most catalogs will list painted and unpainted jig heads in 1⁄64 ounce on a size 8 hook and 1⁄32 ounce on a size 6 hook. These are about right for shad fishing, and the weights are within the range of those of the dumbbell eyes used for flies, which weigh from about 1⁄100 to 1⁄16 ounce. The best for tying are those with just the round head molded onto the hook, with the head lacking any collar or barbed shank or sleeve, such as that used for fishing bait or soft plastics. This leaves the entire length of the bare hook shank on which to tie the body and tail. (It's not fly tying, but you can also use the sliced or barbed shank heavier-weight jig hooks, or those with a button-end collar, for attaching and fishing with the bright-colored tiny tube lures, Sassy Shad type of body, and tiny grubs.)

The main advantage of jig hooks is when fishing snag-filled shad rivers. Since the shad darts of spin fishermen are specialized jigs that are fished point up, this makes sense for fly fishermen too. Just make sure that in tying your flies, you stick to small jig heads that will not be difficult to cast with the fly rod.

Marking Weighted Flies

You can see the effect and guess the approximate weight of flies tied with dumbbell eyes, beads, or cones. If tying different ways with lead, develop some sort of system to keep from mixing your unweighted flies with the weighted patterns. One way is to use different fly boxes for weighted and unweighted patterns. Label with the fly boxes with a felt-tip marker if they are otherwise identical.

Another method is to use different thread colors for tying weighted and unweighted flies. You can use two colors for just weighted or unweighted flies, or four colors for unweighted, front-weighted, rear-weighted, and fully-weighted flies. The two-color system is best, to avoid getting too complicated and forgetting your own marking method.

A third method is to use some sort of tying differentiation between weighted and unweighted. You might tie a throat on weighted flies and no throat on unweighted patterns, or use different color throats (assuming all your flies will have a throat; many shad patterns do not), paint a single dot on the head of weighted flies, or a similar system.

Casting Weighted Flies

Any type of weighted fly will usually be easier to cast than an unweighted fly fished with a series of split shot on the leader. I often fish with a lightly weighted fly and a sinking-tip line, or a lightly weighted fly with a mini lead head between the line and a short leader. It's not like casting a floating line and unweighted fly, but it's not bad.

Color-coding the heads of the flies helps to differentiate between weighted and unweighted flies. Here, the weighted fly has the black head and the unweighted fly of similar design has the white head.

FLY SIZE

Several years before this writing, Floyd Franke, an experienced shad fly fisherman and fly tier was fishing the Delaware with a friend. Franke offered him some of his Neon flies (see patterns at the end of the chapter; they are tied with colored monofilament line over a bright underbody for a translucent look). Franke's flies, as with most shad flies, are tied in sizes 8 and 6. The friend declined, first wanting to try smaller Neon flies that he had tied in sizes 10 and 12. The result was that the smaller size 10 and 12 Neon flies on that day with clear water outfished the standard 6 and 8 Neons by about six to one.

Franke states that with the clear water, he could see the shad and their reaction to the flies, and they shied away from his larger size 6 and 8 Neons, while readily taking the smaller size 10s and 12s fished in the same area. His conclusion, after other experiments, is that clearer water often requires smaller flies. Thus, tie some small examples of your favorite pattern—or of the Floyd Franke Neons—to try in clear water conditions.

STORING USED SHAD FLIES

After using your flies, put them in a "used" box for drying after the trip. Before returning flies to their right boxes, check them for any damage, loose thread, and dulled points such as might occur from hitting rocks. If you don't use a marking system, you can tell weighted from unweighted flies by tossing them in the air and catching them in your hand like a coin. Weighted flies will fall heavily.

FINAL THOUGHTS ON FLIES

In addition to the patterns of shad flies given below, there are perhaps hundreds more, locally or individually tied and used along the coasts. While we all enjoy tying specific patterns and experimenting with our own designs, color and size are more important than any specific pattern. The following are, however, some basic suggestions for fly tiers. These are not chiseled in concrete, but are generally consistent for proven shad flies.

- Hook size is critical. Use sizes 4 through 10 for hickory shad, with sizes 6 and 8 usually the best. For American shad, use sizes 8 through 1, with the best sizes usually 6 and 4. Best are hooks that are about 1X to 3X long, more like a heavy-shank nymphing hook than the longer-shank streamer hooks. Regular shank length hooks can also be used. But as noted above, it's best to use smaller flies for clear water. Experiment.
- Fluorescent colors work better than regular colors, but all colors should be bright. There are exceptions. Experiment.
- An exception to the above is that solid black flies also work both at night and during the day. Experiment.
- Tinsel or Mylar in a fly is good as long as there is only a little of it. Tinsel or Mylar is often used for the body of slim East Coast flies. Mylar or other flash materials, such as Flashabou, Krystal Flash, Kreinik's Flash-in-a-Tube, and other materials, should be used sparsely in wings and elsewhere on the fly. It does help to have some flies tied with more of this flash to try when fishing right at or before dawn, at dusk or night, or during very overcast days. Experiment.
- Tie or buy some flies that are made with glow-in-the-dark materials. These materials are available in different colors in body, ribbing, tail, and wing materials and might help when fishing on dark days, very early or late in the day, at night, or in turbid waters. Experiment.

Sometimes a completely different fly will work on shad. These solid black patterns both with and without a wing proved effective in some situations.

- Because of what appears to be short striking or slashing of shad at flies on some occasions, it helps to have short tails (if a tail is called for in the pattern) and short wings. Standard wing length for most trout and other streamers is about one and a half times the hook shank length. Most shad flies are tied with short wings that are either the length of the hook shank or no more than about one and a quarter times the shank length. Some wings are even tied shorter than the shank length. Experiment.
- Because of the occasional tendency of shad to strike short, some fly tiers and fishermen have tried other techniques. Years ago, angling author and fly fisherman Sam Slaymaker tried tying flies of regular size and wing length, but on long-shank hooks. This made them the shad-fishing equivalent of low-water salmon flies that are tied very sparsely and short on oversize hooks. The initial results seemed promising, but later continued research with these seemed to show that they were no more effective in attracting and hooking shad than standard shad fly patterns. Still, experiment a little.
- If developing your own patterns, stick to easy, simple designs, rather than getting caught up with the many materials and

possibilities available. Shad fishing can be fast and furious, and on some days, you can lose a lot of flies. A simple fly that produces well yet takes little time at the fly-tying bench is a real advantage here. Experiment.

- Another reason for a simple tie is that most shad anglers like to develop a pattern type and then tie this type of fly in many colors, varying the wing, body, and tail shades. This results in a "family" of flies that are all similar, easy to tie, and yet of different colors to match the various moods of shad when they might reject one or more colors. Experiment.
- For a translucent look to the body of your shad flies, consider overwraps of translucent materials on top of a tinsel body. This will come close to the original Pequea Quilby Minnow, a lead lure for spinning anglers. Possibilities for fly fishermen include wrapping the hook shank with a silver body material, then overwrapping it with translucent materials such as brightly colored monofilament line, plastic Larva Lace, and similar plastic wraps. Several anglers have done this with West Coast and East Coast patterns. On the East Coast, Floyd Franke has tied simple shad Neon patterns using colored mono wrapped over bright-colored thread on a double-point hook. On the West Coast, John Shewey used colored mono over silver or gold tinsel for his Red Devil and Yellow Devil, and Bill Schiffman did the same thing in designing his Pound Puppy Green and Pound Puppy Red. Another possibility is to tie flies with bodies of the new Gudebrod E-Z Dub. For example, white tied over a base of red thread will allow the red to show through when wet, making for a translucent lifelike effect. Experiment.
- Tie some bright, simple dry flies for use on shad. Past writings by several writers have noted that shad will take dry flies. This occurs primarily in the shallows at the end of the season when the fish are actively spawning, as opposed to just running upriver. While most shad are taken by fishing flies deep, dry-fly fishing offers a whole new aspect to the sport. Try heavily tied and hackled white and bright fluorescent flies on regular-shank dry-fly hooks, sizes 8 through 4. Bivisibles are great for this, for both flotation and visibility. For more strength in the hook, you can use regular-weight hooks (not the light wire used in most dry flies), provided that the fly has enough tail fibers and hackle to support it. You can also tie with a foam body or foam post wing for flotation. Dress standard ties with dry-fly dressing or floatant. Experiment.

EAST COAST SHAD FLIES

East Coast and West Coast shad flies can be used interchangeably on both coasts, but there are some subtle differences. Most of the East Coast patterns are a little plainer and slimmer than those used on the West Coast, which more closely resemble steelhead flies. Some of the most popular shad flies patterns, past and present, are given below. Where hook length was not stated in the original dressing, it is not given here. For all shad flies, a suggested length is a 2X to 3X long hook, unless otherwise specified by the originator. The most popular hook sizes for shad are 8, 6, and 4 for hickory shad and 6, 4, and 2 for American shad.

NEW ENGLAND/NORTHEAST SHAD FLIES

Connecticut River Shad Fly #1

Hook	Size 2–4, 2X–3X long.
Body	Silver tinsel, extended around the bend of the hook.
Wing	Red duck flight feather, tied full but short, about half the length of the hook.

Fished with a ¼-inch red glass or plastic bead ahead of the fly.

Connecticut River Shad Fly #2

Hook	Size 2–4, 2X–3X long.
Body	Gold tinsel, extended around the bend of the hook.
Wing	Orange or yellow, tied as above.
Bead	Orange or yellow, to correspond with wing color.

Joe Brooks, in his *Complete Book of Fly Fishing* (1958), describes similar patterns to the two above, but tied on size 1/0 hooks. This would generally be considered quite large for either American or hickory shad by today's standards.

Connecticut River Shad Fly #3

Hook	Size 2 or 4.
Body	Silver tinsel.
Hackle	Scarlet.

Connecticut River Shad Fly #4

Hook	Size 2 or 4.
Body	Silver tinsel.
Hackle	Orange fibers.

Enfield Dam Shad Fly

Hook	Size 2–3, 2X–3X long.
Body	Silver tinsel.
Wing	Yellow feather or hair.

Cole Wilde's Shad Fly

Hook	Stainless steel, size 1.
Body	Green fluorescent floss built up to cigar shape.
Ribbing	Embossed silver tinsel.
Hackle	White, tied in under the throat wet-fly style.
Head	Red thread.

A favorite of Cole Wilde, chief of the Fish and Water Life Department of the Connecticut Department of Environmental Protection, for shad on the Connecticut River.

Cole Wilde's Shad Flies—Other Patterns

Hook	Stainless steel, size 1 or 2.
Body	White, yellow, orange, or red fluorescent floss built up to cigar shape.
Ribbing	Embossed silver tinsel.
Hackle	White, red, orange, or yellow.
Head	Red or black thread.

Al's Shad Fly #1

Hook	Size 6 or 8, 3X long.
Tail	Pink Krystal Flash.
Body	Chartreuse braid wrapped around hook shank.
Collar	Chartreuse cactus chenille.
Eyes	Small silver bead chain.

This and the following four flies were designed by Albin J. Sonski, supervisor for the Kensington Fish Hatchery, Rhode Island.

Al's Shad Fly #2

Hook	Size 6 or 8, 3X long.
Tail	Red synthetic fibers.
Body	Wrapped silver braid or embossed tinsel.
Collar	Clear cactus chenille.
Eyes	Small silver bead chain.

Al's Shad Fly #3

Hook	Size 6 or 8, 3X long.
Tail	Copper Krystal Flash.
Body	Wrapped copper braid.
Collar	Copper cactus chenille.
Eyes	Small silver bead chain.

Al's Shad Fly #4

Hook	Size 4 or 6, 3X long.
Tail	Yellow hackle fibers.
Body	Yellow yarn.
Ribbing	Silver tinsel.
Hackle	Full yellow hackle collar.
Eyes	Medium silver bead chain.

Al's Shad Fly #5

Hook	Size 4 or 6, 3X long.
Tail	Silver Flashabou.
Tail addition	Small hammered silver willowleaf blade.
Body	Chartreuse chenille.
Hackle	Full yellow hackle collar.
Wing	Silver Flashabou, mixed in with the yellow hackle collar.
Eyes	Medium chromed dumbbell eyes.

Massachusetts Shad Fly

Hook	Size 4.
Tail	Golden pheasant tippet.
Body	Orange seal fur.
Ribbing	Silver tinsel, tied halfway down the body.
Hackle	Yellow, palmer tied, clipped to taper at the tail.

Attributed to Armans Courchaine of Somerset, Massachusetts.

Silver Yank

Hook	Size 6 or 8.
Body	Flat silver tinsel.
Wing	Red hackle fibers, tied short.

A northeastern pattern attributed to Ernie Clark. This fly is fished with ⅜-inch-diameter glass or plastic beads in front of it, placed in the order of red, yellow, red.

Shad Fly-Dart

Hook	Size 8.
Tail	Small tuft of yellow calf tail.
Body	White nylon floss.
Ribbing	Fine embossed silver tinsel.
Head	Red thread, tied large and lacquered.

Excellent for both American and hickory shad in eastern rivers.

The Jerk

Hook	Eagle Claw 119N, size 8.
Thread	Fire orange.
Tail	Fire orange fluorescent floss.
Rib	Flat silver.
Body	White fluorescent nylon "baby wool" yarn.
Eyes	Chrome bead chain, on top of hook (to make fly ride inverted, point up).
Head	Tying thread, well varnished.

Originated by Michael Jeavons, Toronto, Ontario, Canada, when fishing the West Branch of the Delaware in early June. This fly is fished on a sinking line, swinging the fly in front of shad holding in fast water.

Jelly Bean Shad Flies

Hook	Eagle Claw 1197N or 1197G.
Tail	Fake fur, calf tail, marabou, or other material.
Body	Underbody of floss, plastic strip, or thread. Epoxy coating, with or without glitter.
Head	Chenille, sparkle chenille.
Wing	Optional.

These flies, originated by Jack Denny of Belleville, New Jersey, are simple to tie and very durable as a result of the epoxied body. In finished appearance, they look like long, tapered jelly beans, thus their name. It is more a design than a pattern, since the tail, body, and head colors and materials can be varied widely. Marabou or fake fur will create more action in the water than will calf tail. The underbody is picked for color, and the epoxy coating adds sheen and translucency. Denny fishes his Jelly Beans in the upper Delaware River.

Neon Shad Fly

Hook	7287 double-point Mustad, size 4, 6, or 8.
Thread	Varies depending on desired body color with combined mono overwrap. For example, red thread with Golden Fluorescent Stren makes an orange body.
Body	25- to 30-pound color mono over thread to create translucent bright, neon color. Typical monos used include golden Stren, red Sunset Amnesia, or green Trilene XT Solar.
Wing	Few strands of Flashabou or Lure Flash, tied down and folded back.

Originated by fly tier and Delaware River shad fisherman Floyd Franke. The double-point hook is to aid in holding the stiff mono at the tail (pinch mono between the points at the bend) prior to wrapping it forward. Tying technique is to wrap the hook shank with thread, tie down mono at tail so that end is caught between the two hook bends, then wrap forward and tie off the mono, first capturing it between the double shanks that extend from the eye of the hook. Other variations Floyd has tried successfully are Neons tied on size 10 and 12 hooks to make miniature flies for fishing in clear water.

Thom Rivell Shad Fly #1

Hook	Mustad Viking 34007 stainless steel, size 4 or 6.
Body	Silver metallic chenille, wrapped on rear two-thirds of the hook shank.
Head	Fluorescent orange chenille, wrapped on forward third of hook shank.

Originated by fly fisherman and tackle shop owner Thom Rivell. The fly can also be tied with a gold body.

Thom Rivell Shad Fly #2

Hook	Mustad Viking 34007 stainless steel, size 4 or 6.
Tail	Few strands of chartreuse wool.
Body	Fine black chenille, wrapped on rear two-thirds of the hook shank.
Head	Chartreuse wool or chenille, wrapped on forward third of the hook shank.

Originated by Thom Rivell.

Bead Eye Shad Fly

Hook	Mustad gold or baitholder hook.
Thread	Red.
Tail	White Krystal Flash.
Body	White or pearl Diamond Braid Body material.
Eyes	Silver bead chain.
Head	Eyes wrapped and crisscrossed with red thread.

Originated by John Stercho, who with Mike O'Brien owns *Mid-Atlantic Fly Fishing Guide,* a monthly publication that in season has information on fly-rod shad fishing.

Gold Herring Fly

Hook	Size 6 or 8.
Thread	Red.
Tail	Frayed-out gold Mylar tubing from the body slipped onto the hook shank.
Body	Gold Mylar tubing slipped onto the hook shank.
Eyes	Gold bead chain.

Originated by Al Straub and tied for catching both herring and shad.

Larry Shortt Shad Fly

Hook	Mustad 3906B or 3666, size 6 to 12.
Thread	Fluorescent green; black for the head.
Weight	Lead wrapped in head area.
Tail	Fluorescent green marabou.
Body	Uni-Stretch green.
Rib	Flat gold, size 14.
Head	Fluorescent green chenille.

Developed and tied by Nova Scotia fly fisherman and fly tier Larry Shortt, and fished by him with a Sue Burgess extra-fast-sinking 7-foot leader. Can also be fished with great success when tied using orange as a substitute for the green.

Mysid Shrimp Shad Fly

Hook	Mustad 9671, size 8, with shank bent upward and with a swimming nymph hook.
Thread	Fine monofilament thread.
Antennae	Krystal Flash.
Eyes	Silver bead chain.
Tail	Krystal Flash, tied in to extend beyond eye of hook.
Tag	Pink chenille, tied in above shrimp eyes at bend of hook.
Weight	Lead wire, wrapped around hook shank.
Body	Body lace, wrapped over wrapped lead wire, with pearl poly tube tied in at bend of hook and folded over the wrapped body lace to form the shrimp carapace.

Developed by shad-fishing expert Brian Wiprud, who has researched the role of krill and mysid shrimp in the diet of shad and developed this pattern to closely imitate these ocean shrimp.

Wiprud Mysid

Hook	Mustad 9671 or equivalent, size 8 to 10, bent into the shape of a swimming nymph hook, barb bent down.
Thread	Fine monofilament thread.
Tail, antenna, and legs	Pearl Krystal Flash or equivalent.
Carapace	Pearl braid or tubing to match Krystal Flash.
Body	Small glass beads in pink, pearl, blue, and green.
Eyes	Small black bead chain.

Developed by shad fisherman and fly tier Brian Wiprud, this fly is tied by threading alternating pink and pearl beads onto the hook shank (about five), followed by blue and green beads (about three). Tie in bead chain at the underside of the shank and the bend, followed by Krystal Flash antennae and pearl braid, then tie off and cement. Tie in chain-eyes between the blue/green and pink/pearl beads. Fold over the braid, tie down, and tie off.

Jen Fly

Hook	Mustad 3906B or equivalent, size 6 or 8.
Thread	Fine monofilament thread.
Tag	Pearl braid, tied in over top of the Krystal Flash tail.
Tail	Pearl Krystal Flash.
Body	Pink and purple yarn, twisted together.
Eyes	Medium lead dumbbell eyes.

Developed by Brian Wiprud of New York, and said by him to be very effective for picky shad.

Pseudopod Shad Fly

Hook	Shrimp/caddis hook (Mustad 81001BR), size 8.
Thread	Fine monofilament thread.
Head	Small pink cone head in front of a 5⁄32-inch gold tungsten bead.
Tail	Six strands of pearl Krystal Flash, ½ inch or less in length.
Body	Pearl braid.
Weight	Lead wire wrapped around hook shank.

Designed by fly tier and shad fisherman Brian Wiprud, who developed this fly as an imitation of a copepod, one of the main foods of shad when they are in the ocean. The weight gets the fly deep for added effectiveness.

Bifulco Fly

Hook	Mustad 34007 or equivalent, size 6 or 8.
Thread	Fine monofilament thread.
Tail	Ten strands of yellow Krystal Flash.
Body	Purple glitter braid under a wrap of yellow Krystal Flash.
Eyes	Medium steel dumbbell.
Head	Purple glitter braid, wrapped and figure-eighted around eyes.

Developed by Brian Wiprud, New York shad fisherman and fly tier, and said to be particularly good with picky shad. Also effective in yellow and pink, which Brian thinks might suggest a copepod with egg sacs.

Zsa Zsa

Hook	1/32 to 1/16 ounce (size 6 or 8 hook) jig head with jig collar. If barb on collar, flatten with pliers. Buy painted or paint pink or chartreuse green with black dot for eye.
Thread	Fine monofilament thread.
Tail	Five to ten strands of pearl Krystal Flash, about 1/4 inch long.
Body	Pearl braid, wrapped around body and over collar to just behind the head, then a wrap of the pearl Krystal Flash over the braid, to just in back of the head.

Tied and developed by Brian Wiprud. He also suggests an alternative using a size 6 or 8 Mustad 3906B hook or equivalent, with a large beadhead painted hot pink, and then tied as above. The head can be painted with nail polish or bought in pink through Spirit River.

Smonig Flutter Fly

Hook	Mustad 38941 streamer hook, size 6.
Thread	Fine monofilament thread.
Spoon blade	Gold or silver peel-and-stick Mylar (available from craft stores in many patterns).

Developed by New York fly fisherman, shad enthusiast, and fly tier Brian Wiprud, who rates this as the fly fisherman's equivalent of the flutter spoon used by spin fishermen. Often used as a dropper with a weighted fly to get this fly deep. Rated as particularly effective for staging shad—those preparing to ascend rapids, not particularly active, and holding at the head of a pool. Shad can take their time in hitting these flies, but hit hard when they do, according to Brian. To make these "flies," cut a length of the tape about 1 by 1/2 inch, peel the protective backing, and push the hook point through the center of the sticky side. Fold the tape over on itself, and use scissors to trim into a slim oval shape and to expose the hook eye, if necessary. Thread a needle with sewing thread, and sew around the shank to fasten the tape securely to the hook shank. Tie off at the head, and cement with a superglue.

MID-ATLANTIC SHAD FLIES

Tom Loving's Shad Fly

Hook	Double-point salmon hook, size 2–8.
Body	Alternating bands of white and black wool.
Wing	White bucktail, tied short.
Head	Painted red.
Eyes	Painted on the red head, yellow with a black pupil.

One of the first flies developed specifically and exclusively for shad, and tied in two sizes, for the American and the hickory shad. Tom Loving developed it for shad fishing on the Susquehanna River in Maryland, and according to reports, it was first tied and fished about 1923. The larger sizes, 1 and 2, were used for the smaller hickory shad, while the smaller sizes, 4, 6, and 8, were used for the larger American shad.

While this was the most popular pattern, other variations of the same Loving style were also tied, including flies with a body of alternating bands of yellow and black. Wing variations included wings of solid yellow, white with a sparse red underwing, and black with a sparse yellow underwing. Some of the smallest flies that were used for American shad were tied on single hooks.

Examples of early shad flies tied in the 1920s by Tom Loving, used on American and hickory shad in the Susquehanna River area.

Burt Dillon's Shad Fly (also called the Chesapeake Bay Shad Fly)

Hook	Size 6 or 8, sometimes 10.
Tail	Fibers of golden pheasant tippet.
Body	White chenille.
Ribbing	Flat silver tinsel.
Wing	White calf tail or white saddle hackle feathers.
Head	White thread.
Eyes	Painted red on the white head.

This fly was developed in 1939 by Burt Dillon, then a Baltimore tackle shop owner. He tied the fly for fishing in the Susquehanna River, a popular shad river of the past that forms the head of the Chesapeake Bay. Conowingo Dam stopped shad from going upriver, although in recent years, shad have been trucked around the dam in an effort to restore this fishery. This is one of the few flies, and probably the first, developed exclusively for the smaller hickory shad that were, and still are, such a popular fly-rod fish in that area. When it was first tied over sixty years ago, the old-timers in the area told Burt that hickory shad could not be caught on flies, nor could they be caught in the small tributaries such as Deer Creek and Octoraro Creek, which since have become such popular spots for fly-rodding for hickory shad.

While any of these flies can be tied plain or weighted, this pattern was originally designed to be tied with lead wire to weight it. The turns of lead were bound down with tying thread, the lead was lacquered to prevent it from discoloring the body, and then the fly was tied as above.

Chesapeake Bay Shad Fly

Hook	Size 4.
Thread	White.
Tail	Golden pheasant tippet.
Body	White wool yarn.
Ribbing	Silver tinsel.
Wing	White bucktail.

Similar to Burt Dillon's Shad Fly, above, but with slightly different materials. This pattern is attributed to Tom Lentz.

Joobie

Hook	Size 6, 4X long.
Tail	Small segment of yellow duck quill.
Body	White silk floss.
Ribbing	Flat silver tinsel.
Hackle	Yellow saddle hackle fibers tied in at the throat, wet-fly fashion.
Head	Yellow.
Eyes	Painted red and black.

A shad fly originated by Tom McNally in 1952 when he was outdoor editor for the Baltimore *Evening Sun.* It has proved successful on a number of shad rivers in the Southeast.

According to McNally's instructions, this fly is tied with the hook shank lacquered, wrapped with 2/0 nylon thread, on top of which nine turns of soft lead wire are wrapped. The lead wire is then lacquered again to keep the lead from discoloring the floss, after which the fly is finished as above. This fly is similar in appearance, if not tying materials, to the California Shad Fly #4.

Maryland Shad Fly #1

Hook	Size 10; 3X, 4X, or 6X long.
Tail	Red hackle feather fibers.
Body	Silver tinsel.
Wing	Red hackle feathers.
Beard	Red hackle.

Maryland Shad Fly #2

Hook	Size 10; 3X, 4X, or 6X long.
Tail	Golden pheasant tippet.
Body	White chenille.
Ribbing	Silver tinsel.
Wing	White hackle streamer feathers.
Beard	Short white hackle fibers.
Head	White thread.
Eyes	Painted black with white pupil.

This fly is very similar in appearance to Burt Dillon's Shad Fly. It differs in the presence of the beard and the eye color.

Maryland Shad Fly #3

Hook	Size 10; 3X, 4X, or 6X long.
Tail	Lady Amherst pheasant tippet fibers.
Body	White chenille.
Ribbing	Silver tinsel.
Wing	Blue hackle feathers between two white hackle feathers.
Head	White thread.
Eyes	Painted black with white pupil.

Janet's Fancy

Hook	Size 6, 3X long.
Body	White silk floss.
Ribbing	Flat silver tinsel.
Tail	Red duck quill.
Hackle	Red duck quill, tied in at the throat, wet-fly style.
Wing	Short, sparse white marabou.

Originated, tied, and used by the late Lloyd Gerber, an avid Maryland fly fisherman and ardent conservationist.

Joe Zimmer/Irv Swope Shad Fly

Hook	Size 6 or 8, 3X long.
Body	Chenille body of white, red, orange, green, or yellow, or fluorescent shades of these colors.
Wing	Impala or calf tail, tied the length of the hook shank, of white, red, orange, yellow, or green, or fluorescent shades of these colors. Wing color to contrast with the body color.

Originated by Joe Zimmer and Irv Swope of Maryland, to imitate the colors and style of the popular shad dart or Quilby Minnow used by spinning shad fishermen. The most popular *original* colors of this fly include red wing with white body, white wing with red body, red wing with yellow body, yellow wing with green body, yellow wing with purple body, and white wing with fluorescent body. Today shad fishermen tie these flies almost exclusively with fluorescent materials. Other color combinations are also possible and effective.

Joe Zimmer's Shad Fly

Hook	Size 8, 3X long.
Tail	Short tuft of nylon monofilament wing material, or a synthetic such as Super Hair.
Body	Flat silver tinsel.
Wing	Nylon monofilament material or similar synthetic, tied the length of the hook shank.

This can be tied with any color wing and tail. It is a more recently developed shad fly, and a variation of the above, that has also proved successful over many seasons of use.

Irv Swope's Shad Fly

Hook	Size 6, 8, or 10, 3X long.
Tail	Fluorescent marabou of yellow, insect green, brown, claret, or red, tied short.
Body	Fluorescent wool of yellow, insect green, brown, claret, or red.
Wing	Fluorescent marabou, the same color as the tail.

This fly was originated by Irv Swope, an expert shad fisherman and fly rodder. It is tied with uniform body and wing colors, with five different patterns possible from the various colors used. Note that the insect green, claret, and brown are dark colors, similar to those of some of the flies used for shad early on in the 1800s.

The Silver Shad

Hook	Size 6 or 8.
Tail	Red gift-wrapping yarn tied short.
Body	Thin silver Mylar wound as tinsel.
Wing	White calf tail (yellow is an alternate color).
Head	Red thread.

Originated by the famous fly tier Poul Jorgensen, when he was living in Maryland. Poul and others fish it primarily on eastern streams.

The Royal Shad

Hook	Size 8, 4X long.
Thread	6/0 nylon nymph thread.
Tail	Sparse yellow calf tail tied short.
Butt	Red-orange fluorescent chenille.
Body	White floss.
Ribbing	Narrow flat silver tinsel.
Collar	Red-orange fluorescent chenille.
Wing	Yellow calf tail tied sparsely and reaching to end of tail.
Head	Black thread.

Originated by Baltimore fly tier and shad fisherman Wayne Grauer. This effective eastern pattern is also tied with pink or green fluorescent butt and collar.

Fli Dart

Hook	Size 8, 4X long.
Tail	Yellow calf tail.
Body	White floss tapered over 0.010 lead wire.
Ribbing	Embossed medium-width silver tinsel.
Head	Red-orange fluorescent floss.

Originated by mid-Atlantic fly fisherman Tom Cooney, and designed to imitate the darts used by spin fishermen. Note that in areas prohibiting lead, a non-lead substitute must be used for weight.

Green Dart

Hook	Size 8, 2X long.
Body	Fluorescent light green floss.
Ribbing	Embossed silver tinsel.
Wing	Green imitation polar bear.
Head	Light green with black dot painted on top.

Originated by Jess Harden of Maryland, and excellent for hickory shad.

Red Jasper Shad Fly

Hook	Size 4 or 6.
Tail	Yellow.
Body	Tinsel.
Head	Red fluorescent yarn.

Used in the Washington, D.C., area, fishing the Potomac River for American shad. An alternate tying method is to use a white tail.

Shad Queen

Hook	Size 8, 2X long.
Body	White fluorescent floss.
Ribbing	Silver tinsel.
Wing	Fluorescent dark pink imitation polar bear.
Head	White with black dot painted on the head.

The Red Screamer

Hook	Mustad 9672 streamer, size 6 or 8.
Thread	Black, 6/0.
Body	Silver tinsel.
Ribbing	Black thread.
Wing	Yellow marabou, topped with red marabou, equal in length to hook shank.

Mr. Baltimore

Hook	Mustad 9672 streamer, size 6 or 8.
Thread	Black, 6/0.
Body	Silver tinsel.
Ribbing	Black thread.
Wing	Pink calf tail, topped by white calf tail, equal in length to hook shank.

Pfeiffer's Braid Body

Hook	Size 6, 8, or 10, 2X long.
Thread	Red.
Body	Any bright-colored heavy Kreinik braid body material, or other bright braid material.
Wing	Calf tail or brightly colored and dyed hackle, contrasting with the body material color.

Any color combination can be used for this basic design. Popular color choices for the body/wing are red/white, orange/chartreuse, black/orange, yellow/red, purple/yellow, pink/yellow, gold/red, and silver/white. Any of the above body/wing colors can be switched for more variations.

The Simple One

Hook	Size 8, 2X long (hickory shad); size 6, 2X long (American shad).
Body	None.
Wing	White calf tail tied so that the wing completely encircles the hook shank when tied down at the head of the fly.
Head	Red.

Originated by the author as a simple saltwater pattern, and later revised for shad fishing on a smaller scale and on a smaller hook. The original also included a body of Mylar tubing or tinsel wound around the hook shank on the forward two-thirds of the shank, but this has since been discontinued in more recent versions. Also, while white works fine, popular variations are wings of red, pink, orange, bright green, blue, purple, yellow, and similar colors, all in fluorescent dyes, if available.

J. G. G.'s Deer Creek Special

Hook	Size 8, 4X long.
Weight	Lead fuse wire, wrapped on two-thirds of hook shank.
Overwrap	Cotton grocery cord or similar cotton cord to cover lead wire.
Body	Single coat of white acrylic paint.
Beard	Bright red hackle fibers.
Wing	Red saddle hackle tips (two pairs, faced concave side in).
Head	Black thread.

Tied and originated by Jack G. Goellner, for whom the fly is named, expert fly fisherman and aficionado of hickory shad on Deer Creek in Maryland.

Joe Bruce Spoon Fly

Hook	Size 6 or 8, bent slightly up at hook eye.
Thread	Red.
Frame	Surflon 15-pound-test braided fishing wire, tied on in back of the eye, then at the bend of the hook, to form a frame for the epoxy.
Body	Clear epoxy, spread between the frame and the hook shank, mixed with pearl or gold or silver glitter.
Eye	Stick-on prism eye.

Developed by Joe Bruce, Baltimore tackle shop owner, writer, and avid fly fisherman, this fly is made by crisscross tying the wire frame at the head of the fly, wrapping the thread back to the tail, then tying down both sides of the wire frame to make an outline of a spoon shape. The spoon itself is made by filling in the area between the frame with epoxy, then adding sparkle to the spoon and a prism eye on both sides of the spoon. Alternatives are to add the sparkle, glitter, or color to the epoxy during mixing to embed the finish into the spoon itself.

Joe Bruce White Shad Fly

Hook	Mustad 34007, size 1/0.
Thread	Fire orange flat waxed nylon.
Tail	Fire orange flat waxed nylon.
Body	Golden olive or pearl flash (cactus) chenille.
Head	Red medium chenille.

Developed by Joe Bruce, Baltimore fly shop owner, author, and avid fly fisherman.

Joe Bruce Hickory Shad Fly

Hook	Mustad 9672 streamer hook, size 8.
Thread	Fire orange flat waxed nylon.
Body	Wide flat silver or gold tinsel.
Wing	Red and yellow marabou.
Head	Fire orange flat waxed nylon.

Developed by Joe Bruce, Baltimore fly shop owner, author, and avid fly fisherman.

SOUTHERN COAST SHAD FLIES

Shad Slayer

Hook	Size 10, medium-length, heavy-gauge, wet-fly style.
Tail	Two yellow hen feathers, splayed apart 60 degrees horizontally.
Body	White chenille.
Head	Fluorescent orange.

Originated by Dean Havron, now of Okemos, Michigan, but who originated it while a medical student in Virginia to fish the Rappahannock River near Fredericksburg, Virginia. While he admits that it is a takeoff of a shad dart in color, he feels that the opposing yellow hackles work as swimmerets with more action in the water. He used it particularly for hickory shad.

Pink Shadillac

Hook	Size 6 or 8.
Wing	Pink over white Flashabou, tied bonefish style on hook shank and covering the hook point.
Eyes	Yellow painted lead dumbbell eyes (1/36 ounce), at head, but tied opposite the hook point so that the fly rides hook point up.

Originated by Capt. Phil Chapman, biologist for the Florida Game and Fresh Water Fish Commission and fishing guide on the St. Johns River in Florida.

Pfeiffer's Tube Shad Fly

Hook	Turned-up eye walleye bait hook, such as VMC 7299 or Eagle Claw L757, size 6 or 8.
Thread	Red.
Tube	⅛-inch-diameter plastic hydraulic tubing, or tubing sold for tube flies.
Body	Wrap of chenille, Kreinik braid, or silver or gold tinsel. Chenille or braid can be any bright color.
Wing	Stacked or veiled (wraparound) calf tail, any bright color and to contrast with body.

Developed by the author as an experiment with tube flies. This is completely different from other flies, in that the body and wing are tied on a small length of hollow plastic tubing with no hook. The tippet or leader is threaded through the tubing, and the tippet is tied to the hook eye. Thus, as with all tube flies, the hook and "fly" are separate.

WEST COAST SHAD FLIES

West Coast shad flies often are bulkier and have a lot more flash, cactus chenille, and other bright materials, in addition to the now-standard fluorescent colors. They also incorporate more use of collars, tags, tails, butts, and similar design features that are also typical of West Coast steelhead flies. Some good examples follow.

NORTHWEST COAST FLIES

Hayden Shad Fly

Hook	Size 6, 2X long.
Body	Medium oval silver tinsel.
Wing	A short hank of fluorescent red yarn tied on top of the hook behind the hackle.
Hackle	Yellow, tied sparsely.
Head	Red thread.
Eyes	Small gold bead chain, tied to the head.

Attributed to Brace Hayden of Seattle, Washington, and an effective fly all along the Pacific coast.

Shad Fly

Hook	Size 6, 1X long or 2X stout.
Thread	Red.
Tail	Paired red duck quills.
Body	Silver Mylar tubing or oval silver tinsel.
Hackle	White, tied sparsely around the hook shank.
Head	Large fluorescent red chenille ball.
Eyes	Larger silver bead chain eyes tied in front of the head.

Tied with lead wire wrapped around the hook shank under the body to weight the fly.

Russian River Shad Fly

Hook	Size 4.
Tail	Red hackle fibers.
Body	Oval silver tinsel.
Hackle	White.
Head	Red fluorescent chenille.

A variation tied by fly fisherman and expert caster Kay Brodney uses bright cherry red Christmas braid wrapping for the tail.

McCreadie Special

Hook	Size 2 to 4, regular shank.
Body	Red silk floss tied thickly.
Ribbing	Silver tinsel.
Wing	Black bear fur, tied high, long, and sparse.
Throat	Long, white imitation polar bear fur (real polar bear was used in the original).
Head	Black.
Eyes	Painted white with black pupil.

This fly is a popular West Coast pattern, especially in the Coos Bay, Oregon, region.

Victorine Shad Special

Hook	Size 4, 6, 8, or 10.
Body	Silver tinsel.
Hackle	White.
Eyes	Small red plastic beads, crisscrossed and tied in place in front of the hackle.

Developed some years ago by California tackle shop owner and fly fisherman Jim Victorine. The eyes differ from those of any other shad fly. They are made of small fluorescent beads threaded onto mono line, which is then flattened with a hot soldering iron on the ends to capture the two beads. The two beads on the mono make them the red plastic equivalent of a dumbbell eye.

The following nine patterns are from *Northwest Fly Fishing: Trout and Beyond,* by John Shewey.

Shewey Shad Shafter

Hook	Wright & McGill 1197N or similar, size 4 to 6.
Tail	Fluorescent chartreuse marabou mixed with chartreuse Krystal Flash and tied at midshank, extending about 1 inch beyond hook bend.
Eyes	Medium lead dumbbell or hourglass eyes.
Head	Chartreuse plastic chenille wrapped in back, front, and crisscrossed around the eyes.

This pattern can also be tied using fluorescent flame red materials. Originated by shad expert and author John Shewey for northwest river shad fishing.

Shad Master Marabou

Hook	Short-shank saltwater hook, size 6 to 10.
Body	Gold tinsel overwrapped with pearl Flashabou.
Wing	White marabou with a few strands of Krystal Flash.
Eyes	Small lead dumbbell or hourglass eyes with a large optic eye, red on yellow painted pupils.

Variations of the white can include yellow, chartreuse, and flame orange. Originated by John Shewey.

Yellow Devil

Hook	Gold down-eye, size 6 to 8.
Tail	Yellow Krystal Flash.
Body	Chartreuse monofilament over gold tinsel.
Wing	Yellow Krystal Flash.
Hackle	Yellow.
Eyes	Lead dumbbell or hourglass eyes with black-on-white painted pupils.

Originated by John Shewey.

Red Devil

Hook	Silver down-eye, size 6 to 8.
Tail	Fluorescent red Krystal Flash.
Body	Red monofilament over silver tinsel.
Collar	Fluorescent red Krystal Flash tied bullet style.
Eyes	Lead dumbbell or hourglass eyes with black-on-white painted pupils.

Originated by John Shewey.

Siuslaw Slayer

Hook	Gold down-eye, size 4 to 8.
Tail	Pearl Krystal Flash.
Body	Pearl diamond braid.
Collar	Pearl Krystal Flash and white hackle.
Eyes	Lead dumbbell or hourglass eyes with red-on-white painted pupils.
Head	Flame red chenille.

Originated by John Shewey.

Shad Master Red

Hook	Gold up-eye, size 6 to 8.
Thread	Fluorescent flame flat waxed nylon.
Tail	Pearl Krystal Flash.
Body	Pearl tubing.
Hackle	White.
Eyes	Lead dumbbell or hourglass eyes with red-on-white painted pupils.

Originated by Duaine Greyson.

Shad Master Green

Hook	Gold up-eye, size 6 to 8.
Thread	Chartreuse flat waxed nylon.
Tail	Pearl Krystal Flash.
Body	Pearl tubing.
Hackle	White.
Eyes	Lead dumbbell or hourglass eyes with green-on-white painted pupils.

Originated by Duaine Greyson.

Pound Puppy Red

Hook	Gold up-eye, size 6 to 8.
Thread	Fluorescent red flat waxed nylon.
Tail	Pearl Flashabou and pearl Krystal Flash.
Body	Bright red monofilament over silver tinsel.
Wing	Pearl Flashabou.
Hackle	White.
Eyes	Lead dumbbell or hourglass eyes with red-on-white painted pupils.

Originated by Bill Schiffman.

Pound Puppy Green

Hook	Gold up-eye, size 6 to 8.
Thread	Chartreuse flat waxed nylon.
Tail	Fluorescent green Krystal Flash.
Body	Chartreuse monofilament over silver tinsel.
Wing	Pearl Flashabou.
Hackle	White.
Eyes	Lead dumbbell or hourglass eyes with green-on-white painted pupils.

Originated by Bill Schiffman.

Diamond Shad

Hook	Alec Jackson Spey, size 7, nickel.
Thread	White, 8/0.
Body	One large silver-lined red bead followed by four medium silver-lined diamond beads.
Tail	White marabou and pearl Krystal Flash.
Hackle	White.
Eyes	Small silver chain bead.

From *Tying Glass Bead Flies,* by Joe J. Warren.

Marigold Shad

Hook	Alec Jackson Spey, size 7, gold.
Thread	Orange, 6/0.
Body	Four large silver-lined orange beads.
Tail	Pearl Krystal Flash.
Eyes	Large silver chain bead.
Beard	Pearl Krystal Flash.

From *Tying Glass Bead Flies,* by Joe J. Warren.

Sunshine Shad

Hook	Alec Jackson Spey, size 7, nickel.
Thread	Yellow, 6/0.
Body	Four large silver-lined yellow beads.
Tail	Rainbow Krystal Flash.
Eyes	Large silver chain bead.
Beard	Rainbow Krystal Flash.

Shad Shrimp Fly

Hook	Size 6 or 8.
Thread	Fluorescent lime green.
Body	Lime green chenille.
Wing	Insect green hackle dressed with lime green Krystal Flash.

Sunshine Shad

Hook	Alec Jackson Spey, size 7, nickel.
Thread	Yellow, 6/0.
Body	Four large yellow beads.
Tail	Rainbow Krystal Flash.
Eyes	Large silver chain bead.
Beard	Rainbow Krystal Flash.

CALIFORNIA SHAD FLIES

California Shad Fly #1

Hook	Size 6.
Thread	Black.
Tail	Orange hackle fibers.
Body	Flat silver tinsel.
Hackle	Orange hackle fibers, tied in wet-fly fashion under the throat.
Wing	Light brown calf tail.

This and the following ten California shad flies are from the booklet *How to Catch, Bone and Cook a Shad,* from the California Department of Fish and Game.

California Shad Fly #2

Hook	Size 4.
Thread and head	Yellow.
Tail	Yellow calf tail.
Body	Yellow chenille.
Ribbing	Oval silver tinsel.
Throat hackle	Yellow.
Wing	Yellow calf tail.

California Shad Fly #3

Hook	Size 4, 3X long.
Thread	Red.
Body	Embossed silver tinsel.
Wing	Red calf-tail fibers.

California Shad Fly #4

Hook	Size 4.
Thread	Yellow.
Tail	Yellow calf tail.
Body	White floss.
Ribbing	Oval silver tinsel.
Throat	Yellow calf tail tied in wet-fly fashion.
Wing	Red calf tail.
Eyes	Red, painted on the yellow head.

California Shad Fly #5

Hook	Size 4.
Thread	Yellow.
Tail	Red calf tail.
Body	Oval silver tinsel.
Hackle	White.
Collar	Red chenille, tied in with the hackle.

California Shad Fly #6

Hook	Size 4.
Thread	Red.
Tail	White calf tail.
Body	Oval silver tinsel.
Butt	Red chenille.
Hackle	White.
Wing	White calf tail.
Collar	Red chenille.

California Shad Fly #7

Hook	Size 4.
Thread	Red.
Tail	White hackle fibers.
Body	Oval silver tinsel.
Butt	Red chenille.
Hackle	White.
Collar	Red chenille.

California Shad Fly #8

Hook	Size 4.
Thread	Red.
Tail	Yellow calf tail.
Body	Oval silver tinsel.
Butt	Red chenille.
Throat	Yellow calf tail.
Collar	Red chenille, tied in behind head.

California Shad Fly #9

Hook	Size 4.
Thread	Orange.
Tail	Orange calf tail.
Body	Oval silver tinsel.
Hackle	Orange, tied in at throat wet-fly style.
Wing	White calf tail.
Eyes	Bead chain, tied in at head.

California Shad Fly #10

Hook	Size 4, 3X long.
Thread	Red.
Tail	Red hackle fibers.
Body	Embossed silver tinsel.
Hackle	White hackle fibers.
Eyes	Bead chain, tied in at head.

California Shad Fly #11

Hook	Size 4.
Thread	Red.
Tail	White hackle fibers.
Body	Oval silver tinsel.
Hackle	Long white hackle fibers, tied in at throat wet-fly style.
Eyes	Bead chain, tied in at the head.

All flies on all plates are identified left to right, top to bottom.

PLATE 1: Northeast coast shad flies

Row one: Connecticut River Shad Fly, Connecticut River Shad Fly (Variation), Cole Wilde Shad Fly
Row two: Al's Shad Fly #1, Al's Shad Fly #2, Al's Shad Fly #3
Row three: Al's Shad Fly #4, Al's Shad Fly #5, Massachusetts Shad Fly
Row four: The Jerk, Jelly Bean, Mini Neon
Row five: Bead Eye Shad Fly, Gold Herring Fly, Mysid Shrimp
Row six: Wiprud Mysid, Zsa Zsa, Smonig

PLATE 2: Mid-Atlantic shad flies
Row one: Tom Loving Shad Fly, Burt Dillon Shad Fly, Joobie
Row two: Maryland Shad Fly #1, Maryland Shad Fly #2, Maryland Shad Fly #3
Row three: Janet's Fancy, Zimmer/Swope Shad Fly, Irv Swope Shad Fly
Row four: Silver Shad, Royal Shad, Fli Dart
Row five: Red Jasper, Simple One, J.G.G.'s Deer Creek Special
Row six: Joe Bruce Spoon Fly, Joe Bruce Hickory Shad Fly, Joe Bruce White Shad Fly

PLATE 3: Southern, Northwest coast and miscellaneous shad flies

Row one: (Southern shad flies) Shad Slayer, Pink Shadillac, (Northwest coast shad flies) Hayden Shad Fly

Row two: Western Shad Fly, McCreadie Special, Jim Victorine Shad Fly

Row three: Shewey Shad Shafter, Shad Master Marabou, Red Devil

Row four: Shad Master Red, Siuslaw Slayer, Shad Master Green

Row five: Pound Puppy Red, Pound Puppy Green, (Miscellaneous shad flies) Pfeiffer's Shad Tube

Row six: Frittery #1, Frittery #2, Metallic Eye Diver

PLATE 4: California shad flies

Row one: California shad Fly #1, California Shad Fly #2, California Shad Fly #3
Row two: California shad Fly #4, California Shad Fly #5, California Shad Fly #6
Row three: California shad Fly #7, California Shad Fly #8, California Shad Fly #9
Row four: California shad Fly #10, California Shad Fly #11, Craig's Kryptonite Shad Fly
Row five: Chartreuse Riffle Bug, Orange Riffle Bug, Orange Rock Pupfish
Row six: Red Header Dolly (Red), Red Header Dolly (Yellow), Red Headed Dolly (Pink)

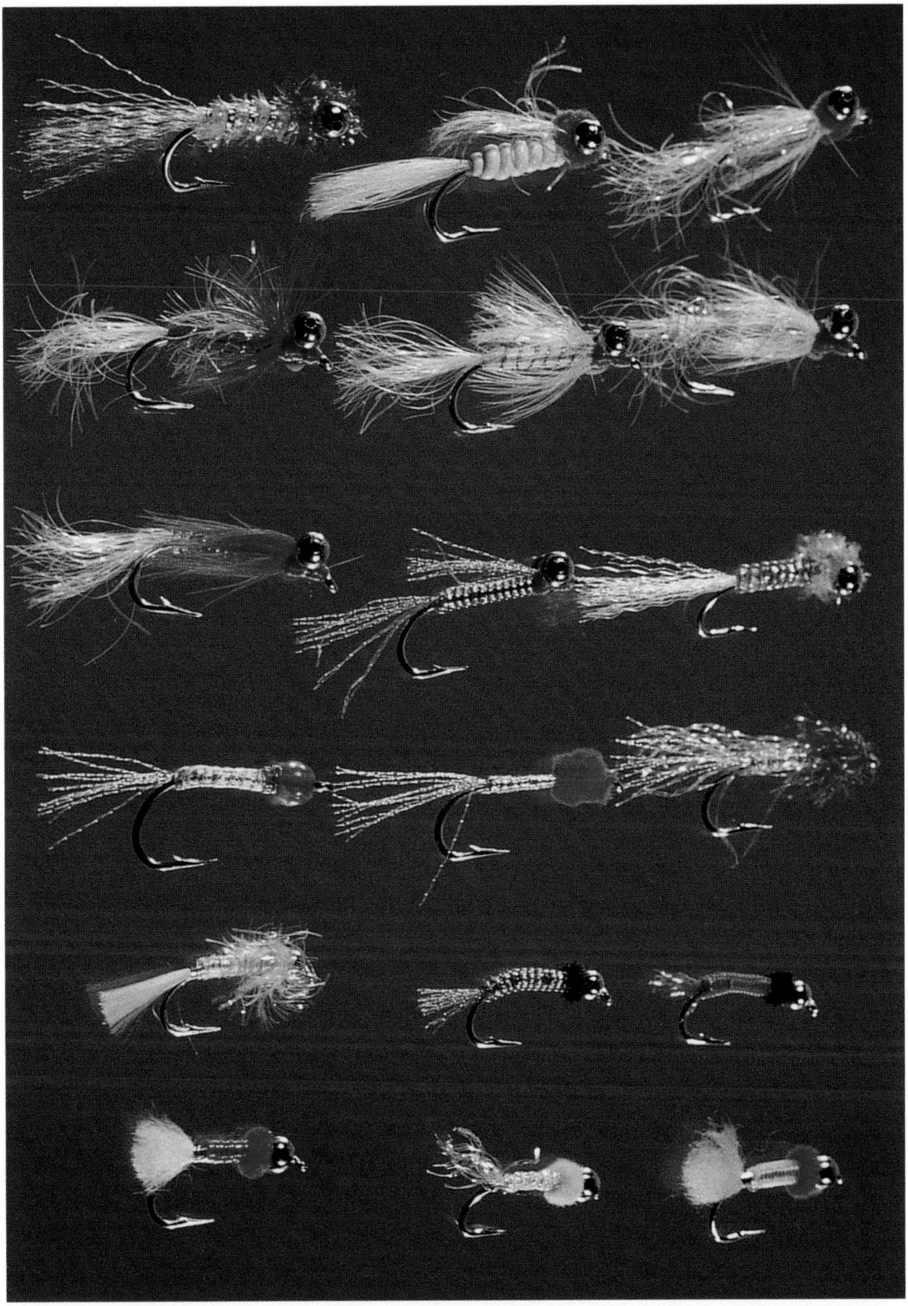

PLATE 5: California shad flies

Row one: Rick's Red Headed Comet, Red Headed Dolly (White), Red Headed Pearl Comet

Row two: Red Comet, Yellow Comet, Orange Comet

Row three: Electric Orange Comet, Orange Kryptonite Fluorescent Comet, The Iceman

Row four: '99½ Benton Fly, Blind Egg Head, Nuclear Green Death

Row five: Chartreuse Larva, Orange Larva, Merthiolate Larva

Row six: Carl's Hot Red, Carl's Pearl Death, Carl's Amnesia

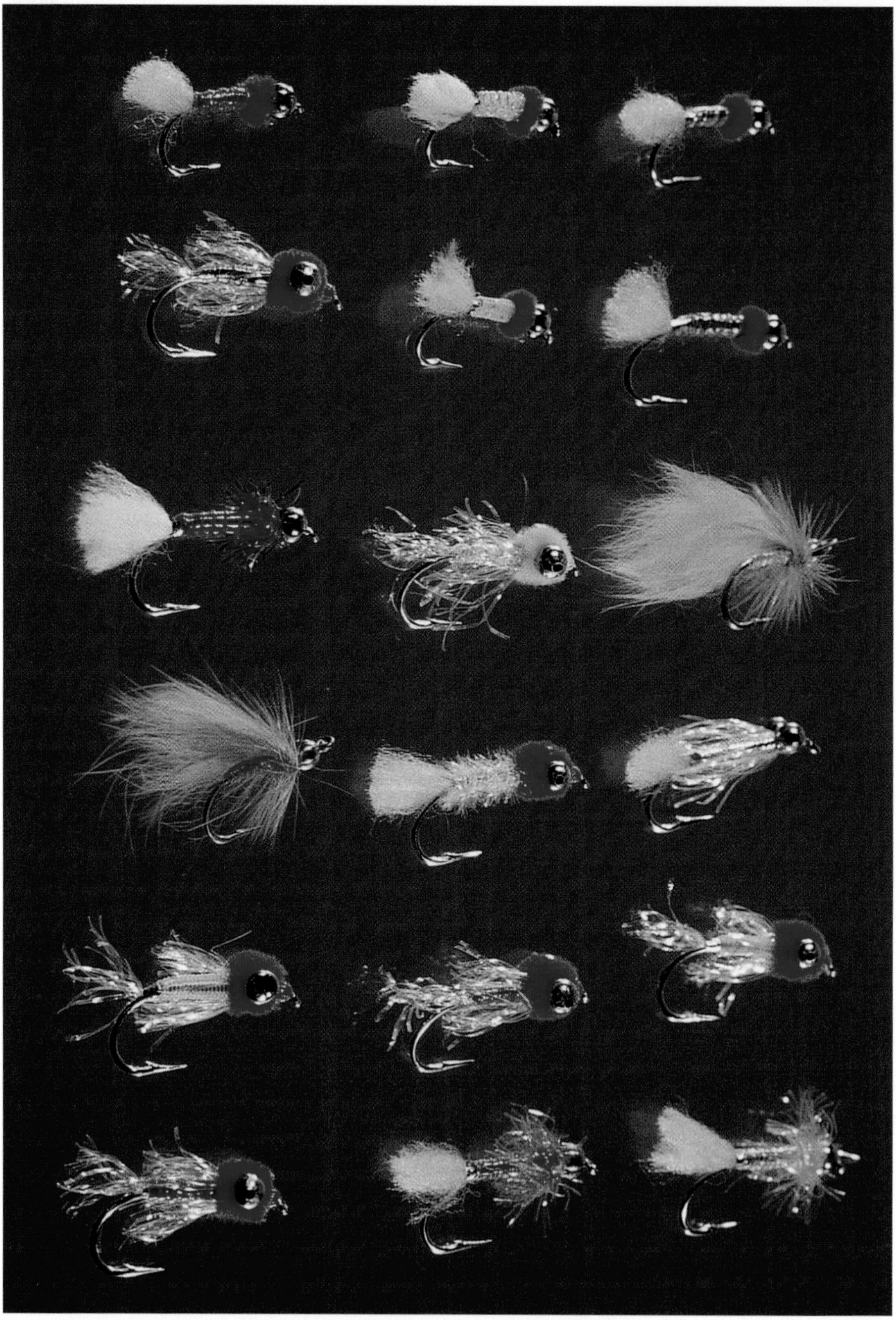

PLATE 6: California shad flies

Row one: Carl's Hot Pink, Carl's Pearl & Red, Carl's Hot Green
Row two: Carl's Ultimate Green Death, Carl's Stren, Carl's Neon Green
Row three: Candy Apply Red, Carl's Pearl Death Ultimate, Carl's Green Rabbit
Row four: Carl's Pink Rabbit, Carl's Red & White, Carl's Chrome Death
Row five: Carl's Green Amnesia Ultimate, Carl's Pink Ultimate, Carl's Stren Ultimate
Row six: Carl's Red Ultimate, Carl's Hot Pink, Carl's Hot Green

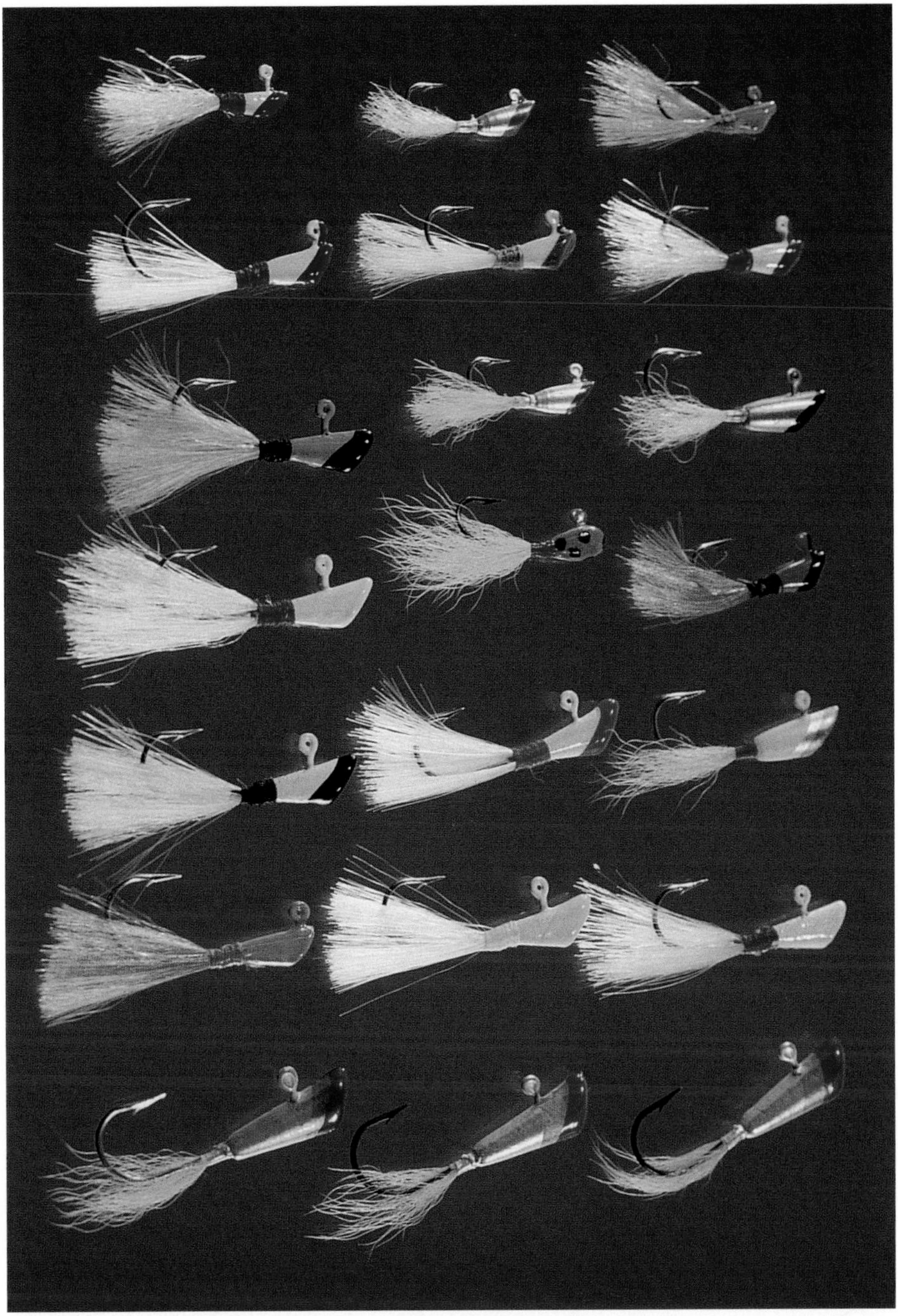

PLATE 7:
Assorted shad darts in various sizes and colors

PLATE 8: Assorted shad spoons

Rows one through four: Assorted shad spoons for casting
Row five: Typical spinners used for shad fishing
Rows six and seven: Flutter spoons as used for fishing off of a downrigger or cast with additional weight or as a tandem rig with a dart

Craig's Kryptonite Shad Fly

Hook	Eagle Claw 1197, nickel finish, size 6 or 8.
Thread	6/0, chartreuse green Monocord.
Tail	Twelve strands of chartreuse Krystal Flash, topped off with frayed-out chartreuse Mylar tubing.
Underbody	Medium 1⁄32-inch holographic tinsel.
Body	Chartreuse Edge Bright or craft lace, coated with Dave's Flexament.
Underwing	Twelve strands of chartreuse Krystal Flash.
Overwing	Medium chartreuse Mylar, frayed out.
Eyes	Medium silver bead chain.
Head	Chartreuse Estaz or cactus chenille wrapped over and around the eyes and tied off.

Originated by northern California Feather River shad and fishing guide Craig Bentley. Also rated good for trout, chinook salmon, and striped bass.

The following twenty-one patterns were originated by Carl Blackledge, Santa Rosa, California, guide and fly tier, principally for fishing in California's shad waters.

Carl's Hot Red

Hook	Size 6.
Tail	White wool.
Underwrap	Chrome tinsel.
Body	Red Edge Bright.
Collar	Red chenille.
Head	Chrome bead.

Originated by Carl Blackledge, Santa Rosa, California, guide and fly tier, principally for fishing in California shad waters.

Carl's Pearl Death

Hook	Size 6.
Tail	Mylar.
Body	Pearl Diamond Braid.
Collar	Green chenille.
Head	Chrome bead.

Originated by Carl Blackledge, Santa Rosa, California, guide and fly tier, principally for fishing in California shad waters.

Carl's Amnesia

Hook	Size 6.
Tail	Green wool.
Underwrap	Chrome tinsel.
Body	Green Amnesia (monofilament line).
Collar	Red tinsel.
Head	Chrome bead.

Originated by Carl Blackledge, Santa Rosa, California, guide and fly tier, principally for fishing in California shad waters.

Carl's Hot Pink

Hook	Size 6.
Tail	Green wool.
Underwrap	Chrome tinsel.
Body	Pink Edge Bright.
Collar	Red chenille.
Head	Chrome bead.

Originated by Carl Blackledge, Santa Rosa, California, guide and fly tier, principally for fishing in California shad waters.

Carl's Pearl & Red

Hook	Size 6.
Tail	White wool.
Body	Pearl Diamond Braid.
Collar	Red chenille.
Head	Chrome bead.

Originated by Carl Blackledge, Santa Rosa, California, guide and fly tier, principally for fishing in California shad waters.

Carl's Hot Green

Hook	Size 6.
Tail	Green wool.
Underwrap	Chrome tinsel.
Body	Light green Edge Bright.
Collar	Red chenille.
Head	Chrome bead.

Originated by Carl Blackledge, Santa Rosa, California, guide and fly tier, principally for fishing in California shad waters.

Carl's Ultimate Green Death

Hook	Size 4.
Thread	Red, 6/0.
Tail	Mylar.
Underwrap	Chrome tinsel.
Body	Dark green Edge Bright.
Wing	Mylar.
Eyes	Chrome bead chain.
Head	Red chenille.

Originated by Carl Blackledge, Santa Rosa, California, guide and fly tier, principally for fishing in California shad waters.

Carl's Stren

Hook	Size 6.
Tail	Green wool.
Underwrap	Chrome tinsel.
Body	Yellow Stren (monofilament line).
Collar	Red chenille.
Head	Chrome bead.

Originated by Carl Blackledge, Santa Rosa, California, guide and fly tier, principally for fishing in California shad waters.

Carl's Neon Green

Hook	Size 4 or 6.
Tail	Green wool.
Underwrap	Chrome tinsel.
Body	Dark green Edge Bright.
Collar	Red chenille.
Head	Chrome bead.

Originated by Carl Blackledge, Santa Rosa, California, guide and fly tier, principally for fishing in California shad waters.

Candy Apple Red

Hook	Size 4.
Tail	White wool.
Underwrap	Chrome tinsel.
Body	Red Edge Bright.
Hackle	Red cactus chenille.
Head	Chrome bead.

Originated by Carl Blackledge, Santa Rosa, California, guide and fly tier, principally for fishing in California shad waters.

Carl's Pearl Death Ultimate

Hook	Size 4.
Thread	Light green, 6/0.
Tail	Mylar.
Underwrap	Chrome tinsel.
Body	Pearl Diamond Braid.
Wing	Mylar.
Eyes	Chrome bead chain.
Head	Green chenille.

Originated by Carl Blackledge, Santa Rosa, California, guide and fly tier, principally for fishing in California shad waters.

Carl's Green Rabbit

Hook	811 S Tiemco.
Thread	Green, 6/0.
Underwrap	Chrome tinsel.
Body	Light green Edge Bright.
Wing	Green rabbit fur.
Hackle	Green, three wraps.
Head	Chrome bead.

Originated by Carl Blackledge, Santa Rosa, California, guide and fly tier, principally for fishing in California shad waters.

Carl's Pink Rabbit

Hook	811 S Tiemco.
Thread	Pink, 6/0.
Underwrap	Chrome tinsel.
Body	Pink Edge Bright.
Wing	Pink rabbit fur.
Hackle	Pink, three wraps.
Head	Chrome bead.

Originated by Carl Blackledge, Santa Rosa, California, guide and fly tier, principally for fishing in California shad waters.

Carl's Red & White

Hook	Size 4 or 6.
Thread	Red, 6/0.
Tail	Green wool.
Body	Pearl Crystal Chenille.
Eyes	Bead chain.
Head	Red chenille.

Originated by Carl Blackledge, Santa Rosa, California, guide and fly tier, principally for fishing in California shad waters.

Carl's Chrome Death

Hook	Size 4 or 6.
Thread	Red, 6/0.
Tail	Green wool.
Body	Mylar.
Wing	Mylar tubing.
Eyes	Chrome bead chain.

Originated by Carl Blackledge, Santa Rosa, California, guide and fly tier, principally for fishing in California shad waters.

Carl's Green Amnesia Ultimate

Hook	Size 4.
Thread	Red, 6/0.
Tail	Mylar.
Underwrap	Chrome tinsel.
Body	Green Amnesia (monofilament line).
Wing	Mylar.
Eyes	Chrome bead chain or chrome dumbbell.

Originated by Carl Blackledge, Santa Rosa, California, guide and fly tier, principally for fishing in California shad waters.

Carl's Pink Ultimate

Hook	Size 4.
Thread	Pink, 6/0.
Tail	Mylar.
Underwrap	Chrome tinsel.
Body	Pink Edge Bright.
Wing	Mylar.
Eyes	Chrome bead chain.
Head	Pink chenille.

Originated by Carl Blackledge, Santa Rosa, California, guide and fly tier, principally for fishing in California shad waters.

Carl's Stren Ultimate

Hook	Size 4.
Thread	Red, 6/0.
Tail	Mylar.
Underwrap	Chrome tinsel.
Body	Yellow Stren (monofilament fishing line).
Eyes	Chrome bead chain.
Head	Red chenille.

Originated by Carl Blackledge, Santa Rosa, California, guide and fly tier, principally for fishing in California shad waters.

Carl's Red Ultimate

Hook	Size 4.
Thread	Red, 6/0.
Tail	Mylar.
Underwrap	Chrome tinsel.
Body	Red Edge Bright.
Wing	Mylar.
Eyes	Chrome bead chain.
Head	Red chenille.

Originated by Carl Blackledge, Santa Rosa, California, guide and fly tier, principally for fishing in California shad waters.

Carl's Hot Pink

Hook	Size 4 or 6.
Thread	Pink, 6/0.
Tail	Pink wool.
Underwrap	Chrome tinsel.
Body	Pink Edge Bright.
Hackle	Pink cactus chenille.
Head	Chrome bead.

Originated by Carl Blackledge, Santa Rosa, California, guide and fly tier, principally for fishing in California shad waters.

Carl's Hot Green

Hook	Size 4 or 6.
Thread	Green, 6/0.
Tail	Green wool.
Underwrap	Chrome tinsel.
Body	Light green Edge Bright.
Hackle	Green cactus chenille.
Head	Chrome bead.

Originated by Carl Blackledge, Santa Rosa, California, guide and fly tier, principally for fishing in California shad waters.

Chartreuse Riffle Bug

Hook	Eagle Claw 1197N, size 6 or 8.
Thread	Chartreuse, 6/0 UNI-thread.
Tail	Twelve strands of chartreuse Krystal Flash married with chartreuse Permatron or equivalent.
Rib	Fine silver wire.
Body	Chartreuse Permatron or equivalent.
Underwing	Twelve strands of chartreuse Krystal Flash.
Overwing	Chartreuse Permatron or equivalent.
Eyes	Medium silver bead chain.
Head	Chartreuse cactus chenille.

Originated by Feather River guide Craig Bentley. A subdued version of the Kryptonite Comet for clear water or when shad are spooky or selective.

Orange Riffle Bug

Hook	Eagle Claw 1197N, size 6 or 8.
Thread	Orange, 6/0 UNI-thread.
Tail	Twelve strands of orange Krystal Flash.
Rib	Fine silver wire.
Body	Orange Permatron or equivalent.
Underwing	Twelve strands of orange Krystal Flash.
Overwing	Orange Permatron or equivalent.
Eyes	Medium silver bead chain.
Head	Orange cactus chenille.

Originated by California fishing guide Craig Bentley.

Orange Rock Pupfish

Hook	Eagle Claw 1197N, size 6 or 8.
Thread	Orange, 6/0 UNI-thread.
Tail	Orange bucktail, length of hook shank.
Body	Orange vinyl piping.
Eyes	Medium hourglass, nickel finish.
Head and shoulders	Cactus chenille, two turns behind eyes, then figure-eighted around eyes.

Originated by Craig Bentley to imitate shrimp when fishing for shad. Craig notes that the body should resemble a grublike shape when properly tied, tapered to the head.

Red Headed Dolly (Red)

Hook	Eagle Claw 1197N, size 6 or 8.
Thread	Red, 6/0 UNI-thread.
Tail	1/8-inch-diameter bunch of white FisHair, length of hook shank.
Body	Red vinyl piping.
Wing	Medium pearl Mylar tubing, frayed.
Eyes	Medium silver bead chain.
Head	Medium fluorescent red chenille, figure-eighted around the eyes.

Originated by Craig Bentley and so named because the vinyl body has the feel of a child's doll. Developed in an attempt to mimic the soft-bodied grubs used by spin fishermen to take shad. The FisHair tail gives the fly a tail like the western favorite, the Flea Fly. Other Red Headed Dolly patterns include yellow, pink and white, tied the same way except that the vinyl piping color of the body matches the suffix name (in parentheses). The head remains red on all of the patterns.

Rick's Red Headed Comet

Hook	Eagle Claw 1197N, size 6 or 8.
Thread	Red, 6/0 UNI-thread.
Tail	White marabou.
Rib	Embossed flat silver tinsel.
Body	Pearl cactus chenille.
Wing	Medium pearl Mylar tubing, frayed.
Eyes	Medium silver bead chain.
Head	Red cactus chenille, figure-eighted around the eyes.

Developed by Rick Thompson of Grass Valley, California, and found to be deadly on the Yuba River when fishing shallow riffles with a weight-forward floating line and long leader.

Red Headed Pearl Comet

Hook	Eagle Claw 1197N, size 6 or 8.
Tail	Medium pearl Mylar tubing, frayed.
Body	Pearl Firebrite braid.
Wing	Medium pearl Mylar tubing, frayed.
Eyes	Medium silver bead chain.
Head	Medium fluorescent red chenille, figure-eighted around the eyes.

Red Comet

Hook	Eagle Claw 1197N, size 6 or 8.
Thread	Red, 6/0 UNI-thread.
Tail	Medium pearl Mylar tubing, frayed.
Rib	Fine silver wire.
Body	Red Permatron or equivalent.
Wing	Medium pearl Mylar tubing, frayed.
Hackle	Red saddle hackle, three turns.
Eyes	Medium silver bead chain.
Head	Red thread.

Yellow Comet

Hook	Eagle Claw 1197N, size 6 or 8.
Thread	Yellow, 6/0 UNI-thread.
Tail	Medium pearl Mylar tubing, frayed.
Rib	Fine silver wire.
Body	Yellow Permatron or equivalent.
Wing	Medium pearl Mylar tubing, frayed.
Hackle	Yellow saddle hackle, three turns.
Eyes	Medium silver bead chain.
Head	Yellow thread.

Orange Comet

Hook	Eagle Claw 1197N, size 6 or 8.
Thread	Orange, 6/0 UNI-thread.
Tail	Medium pearl Mylar tubing, frayed.
Rib	Fine silver wire.
Body	Orange Permatron or equivalent.
Wing	Medium pearl Mylar tubing, frayed.
Hackle	White saddle hackle, three turns.
Eyes	Medium silver bead chain.
Head	Orange thread.

Electric Orange Comet

Hook	Eagle Claw 1197N, size 6 or 8.
Thread	Orange, 6/0 UNI-thread.
Tail	Medium pearl Mylar tubing, frayed.
Underbody	Medium 1⁄32-inch silver holographic tinsel.
Body	Orange Larva Lace or equivalent.
Hackle	Orange saddle hackle, four turns.
Eyes	Medium silver bead chain.
Head	Orange thread.

Orange Kryptonite Fluorescent Comet

Hook	Eagle Claw 1197N, size 6 or 8.
Thread	Orange, 6/0 UNI-thread.
Tail	Dozen strands of orange Krystal Flash.
Underbody	Medium 1/32-inch silver holographic tinsel.
Body	Orange Larva Lace or equivalent.
Wing	Dozen strands orange Krystal Flash.
Eyes	Medium silver bead chain.
Head	Orange thread.

The Iceman

Hook	Eagle Claw 1197N, size 6 or 8.
Thread	White, 6/0 Monocord.
Tail	Medium pearl Mylar tubing, frayed.
Underbody	Medium 1/32-inch holographic tinsel.
Body	Clear sparkle vinyl piping.
Eyes	Medium silver bead chain.
Head	Pearl ice chenille or pearl Estaz.

Originated by Feather River, California, guide Craig Bentley at the suggestion of guide Jerry Sitton, who noted to Bentley that shad would often take a clear fly when they would not take anything else.

'99½ Benton Fly

Hook	Eagle Claw 084F, size 4 to 8.
Bead	5mm fluorescent red, countersunk on one side.
Thread	Red, 6/0 UNI-thread.
Tail	Dozen strands of chartreuse Krystal Flash.
Underbody	Medium 1/32-inch silver holographic tinsel.
Overbody	Chartreuse Edge Bright or craft lace.

Originated by California guide Craig Bentley in 1993, with this pattern evolving from the original in June 1999. So named because Craig's middle name is Benton and also because Yakima tackle has a drift rig for steelhead called the Fenton Fly, made of two corks on mono with a strand of yarn tied to the accompanying hook. The Fenton Fly is designed to imitate a single egg, as is this Benton Fly for fly rodders.

Blind Egghead

Hook	Eagle Claw 1197N.
Thread	Red, 6/0 UNI-thread.
Tail	Dozen strands of chartreuse Krystal Flash.
Underbody	Medium 1/32-inch silver holographic tinsel.
Body	Chartreuse Edge Bright or craft lace.
Head	Medium fluorescent red chenille.

Craig Bentley's soft-head version of the beadhead '99-1/2 Benton Fly for those situations when the shad spit out the hard-head version.

Nuclear Green Death

Hook	Eagle Claw 1197N.
Thread	Red, 6/0 UNI-thread.
Tail	Chartreuse medium Mylar tubing, frayed.
Underbody	Medium 1/32-inch silver holographic tinsel.
Overbody	Chartreuse Edge Bright or craft lace.
Wing	Chartreuse medium Mylar tubing, frayed.
Head	Medium fluorescent red Estaz.

A very bright or loud version of the Blind Egghead, designed for fishing shad when the water is cloudy or off-colored.

Chartreuse Larva

Hook	Size 4 to 8.
Bead	5mm silver or brass.
Thread	Chartreuse, 6/0 UNI-thread.
Tail	Chartreuse FisHair.
Underbody	Medium 1/32-inch silver holographic tinsel.
Overbody	Chartreuse Edge Bright or craft lace.
Collar	Peacock herl, five turns.

Orange Larva

Hook	Size 4 to 8.
Bead	5mm silver or brass.
Thread	Orange, 6/0 UNI-thread.
Tail	Dozen strands of orange Krystal Flash.
Underbody	Medium 1/32-inch silver holographic tinsel.
Overbody	Orange Edge Bright or craft lace.
Collar	Peacock herl, five turns.

Merthiolate Larva

Hook	Size 4 to 8.
Bead	5mm silver or brass.
Thread	Cerise, 6/0 UNI-thread.
Tail	Dozen strands series Krystal Flash.
Underbody	Medium 1/32-inch silver holographic tinsel.
Overbody	Merthiolate or hot pink Edge Bright or craft lace.
Collar	Peacock herl, five turns.

MISCELLANEOUS SHAD FLIES

Frittery Shad Fly #1

Hook	Size 8, 2X long (hickory shad); size 6, 2X long (American shad).
Tail	Yellow calf tail.
Body	Fluorescent white chenille or Ultra chenille.
Head	Fluorescent red chenille or Ultra chenille.

Originated as a fly-tying design style by the author, this fly closely resembles a typical original-color shad dart, with the yellow tail, white body, and red head. Its main feature is that it is easy to tie, since it involves tying from the tail forward, tying off the white body at the same point at which the red head is tied down. The red head is then wrapped up and back again, to be tied off in midsection of the fly. This makes for a very dartlike appearance. Variations include any colors of tail, body, and head. Typical tail colors are white, yellow, chartreuse, cerise, and pink. Typical body/head combinations include white/red, yellow/red, pink/red, chartreuse/red, red/yellow, red/white, pink/red, yellow/purple, black/red, and white/black. Experiment.

Fritter shad flies, like these developed by the author, can be tied with or without wings. They are tied off behind the bulky chenille head instead of just behind the hook eye.

Frittery Shad Fly #2

Hook	Size 8, 2X long (hickory shad); size 6, 2X long (American shad).
Tail	Yellow calf tail, tied short.
Body	White chenille or Ultra chenille.
Wing	Short tuft of yellow calf tail.
Head	Red chenille or Ultra chenille.

The method of tying this is the same as for the Frittery Shad Fly, above, except that a short wing is tied in about one-third the length of the hook shank back from the eye, at the same point where the body is tied off and the head begun. Thus the wing protrudes from just forward of the center of the body, not at the true head end of the fly immediately in back of the hook eye. The patterns and color combinations are the same as for the original Frittery, with the addition of the wing. Wing colors should contrast with the body. Typical colors are white, yellow, pink, purple, red, cerise, chartreuse, orange, green, and lavender.

Metallic-Eye Diver—Red and White

Hook	Size 6 or 8, 2X long.
Thread	Bright red.
Tail	Red Flashabou, ten to twelve strands.
Body	Pearl braid.
Wing	Red calf tail with topping of red Flashabou.
Eyes	1/50-ounce metallic eyes, painted red with black pupil.
Head	Red.

The following four patterns were originated by Lefty Kreh and designed for both American and hickory shad. Tied with dumbbell eyes to give them weight to sink in the fast shad rivers.

Metallic-Eye Diver—Yellow and Chartreuse

Hook	Size 6 or 8, 2X long.
Thread	Yellow.
Tail	Silver Flashabou, ten to twelve strands.
Body	Small chartreuse chenille.
Wing	Dark yellow calf tail.
Eyes	1/50-ounce metallic eyes, painted yellow with black pupil.

Originated by Lefty Kreh.

Metallic-Eye Diver—Hot Orange

Hook	Size 6 or 8, 2X long.
Thread	Bright orange.
Tail	Red Flashabou, ten to twelve strands.
Body	Orange chenille.
Wing	Orange calf tail.

Originated by Lefty Kreh.

Metallic-Eye Diver—Black and Green

Hook	Size 6 or 8, 2X long.
Thread	Black.
Tail	Copper Flashabou, ten to twelve strands.
Body	Small green chenille.
Wing	Black calf tail with ten to twelve strands of copper Flashabou.
Eyes	1/50-ounce metallic lead eyes, painted red with black pupil.

Originated by Lefty Kreh.

The following two patterns are from *Fly Patterns of Umpqua Feather Merchants,* by Randall Kaufmann.

Shad Fly, Orange

Hook	TMC 5263, size 6.
Thread	Fluorescent fire orange single strand nylon floss.
Tail	Fluorescent fire orange floss.
Body	Fluorescent fire orange floss.
Eyes	Silver bead chain.

Shad Fly, Green

Hook	TMC 5263, size 6.
Thread	Fluorescent green single strand nylon floss.
Tail	Fluorescent green floss.
Body	Fluorescent green floss.
Eyes	Silver bead chain.

The following miscellaneous shad flies are from Terry Hellekson's excellent two-volume compendium of fly patterns, *Fish Flies.* Hook sizes and styles are not listed, although in his text, Hellekson notes that his research found that the Tiemco TMC3769 and the Daiichi DAI1530 in sizes 4 through 10 were currently the most popular. He also notes that the eyes included in most patterns are optional. He also likes certain synthetic materials such as Crystal Hair, Crystal Chenille, and Fly Brite, and uses them in many of his patterns. Other similar materials in similar colors can be used to tie these, usually without affecting your catch ratio.

Abomination

Thread	White.
Tail	White calf tail.
Body	White chenille.
Ribbing	Flat silver tinsel.
Hackle	CH30 silver Crystal Hair spun on as a collar.
Eyes	Silver bead chain.

Ardin

Thread	Fluorescent red.
Tail	Tuft of red marabou.
Body	Dubbed with blends of #57 fluorescent chartreuse lamb's wool and FB23 chartreuse Fly Brite.
Hackle	Chartreuse hen hackle tied on as a collar and tied back.
Eyes	Gold bead chain.

Originated by Eric Sumpter of Rancho Cordova, California, for use on the American River, California. The tail should be tied long and pinched back until the fish actively hit it.

Black Knight

Thread	Black.
Body	Black monofilament wrapped over a well-tapered underbody of black floss.
Underbody	Black floss.
Hackle	Black tied on as a collar and tied back.
Eyes	Silver bead chain.

Black N' Black

Thread	Black.
Tail	Black calf tail.
Body	Dubbed with a blend of #1 black lamb's wool and FB02 black Fly Brite.
Hackle	Black hen hackle tied on as a collar and tied back.
Eyes	Silver bead chain.

Boomer

Thread	White.
Tail	Tuft of white marabou.
Body	Wrapped silver diamond braid.
Wing	CH01 pearl Crystal Hair.
Hackle	White tied on as a collar and tied back.
Eyes	Silver bead chain.

Copper Shad

Thread	Orange.
Tail	CH23 copper Crystal Hair.
Body	Copper diamond braid.
Hackle	Fire orange tied on as a collar and tied back.
Eyes	Gold bead chain.

Delaware Special

Thread	Red.
Tail	Yellow marabou.
Body	Yellow mono over an underbody of flat silver tinsel.
Underbody	Flat silver tinsel.
Eyes	Silver bead chain.
Head	Red chenille wrapped through and around eyes.

Designated Hitter

Thread	Fluorescent fire orange.
Tail	CH23 chartreuse Crystal Hair.
Body	CH23 chartreuse Crystal Hair wrapped over an underbody of yellow floss.
Hackle	Fluorescent fire orange hen hackle tied on as a collar and tied back.
Eyes	Nickel-plated lead dumbbell eyes.
Head	Fluorescent green chenille wrapped through and around eyes.

Echo

Thread	Red.
Tail	CH03 red Crystal Hair.
Body	Dubbed with FB03 Fly Brite.
Hackle	Red tied on as a collar and then tied back.
Eyes	Silver bead chain.

Executioner

Thread	Black.
Tail	FB07 fire orange Fly Brite.
Body	Dubbed with a blend of #9 orange lamb's wool and FBO6 orange Fly Brite.
Hackle	Black tied on as a collar and tied back.
Eyes	Gold bead chain.

Fitzgerald

Thread	Fluorescent blue.
Tail	CH13 blue Crystal Hair.
Body	Silver diamond braid.
Hackle	Blue hen hackle tied on as a collar and tied back.
Head	Silver bead.

Full Moon Fever

Tail	CH03 red Crystal Hair.
Body	CH02 black Crystal Hair wrapped over underbody of black floss.
Thorax	Red Glo-Brite chenille.
Head	Black nickel bead.

Golden Girl

Thread	Yellow.
Tail	FB31 gold Fly Brite.
Body	Clear 20-pound monofilament over an underbody of gold diamond braid.
Underbody	Gold diamond braid.
Hackle	Fluorescent fire orange hen hackle tied on as a collar.
Eyes	Gold bead chain.

Golden Shad

Thread	Orange.
Tail	CH31 gold Crystal Hair.
Body	Dubbed with FB31 gold Fly Brite.
Hackle	CH31 gold Crystal Hair spun on as a collar.

Green Death

Thread	Fluorescent green.
Tail	Frayed-out silver Mylar piping from body.
Body	Fluorescent green 20-pound Amnesia monofilament over an underbody of silver Mylar piping.
Underbody	Silver Mylar piping.
Eyes	Silver bead chain.
Head	Fluorescent green chenille wrapped through and around the eyes.

Howdy

Thread	Fluorescent orange.
Body	Fluorescent orange chenille.
Hackle	Fluorescent fire orange tied on as a collar and tied back.
Eyes	Gold bead chain.

Judge

Thread	Black.
Tail	CH02 black Crystal Hair.
Body	Black chenille.
Hackle	Black hen hackle tied on as a collar and tied back.
Eyes	Silver bead chain.

Juror

Thread	White.
Tail	FB01 pearl Fly Brite.
Body	White chenille.
Hackle	White hen hackle tied on as a collar and tied back.
Eyes	Silver bead chain.

Log Hole

Thread	Black.
Tail	Fluorescent pink glow-in-the-dark Flashabou.
Body	Fluorescent pink glow-in-the-dark Flashabou over an underbody of white floss.
Hackle	Blue dun tied on as a collar and tied back.
Head	Silver bead.

Lolo

Thread	Fluorescent chartreuse.
Tail	FB23 chartreuse Fly Brite.
Body	Fluorescent green chenille.
Hackle	Fluorescent chartreuse tied on as a collar and tied back.
Eyes	Gold bead chain.

Mac's Black

Thread	Black.
Tail	Black calf tail.
Body	Dubbed with a blend of #1 black lamb's wool and FB01 pearl Fly Brite.
Hackle	Black hen hackle tied on as a collar and tied back.
Head	Large black.
Eyes	Painted red dots.

Marta

Thread	Yellow.
Tail	CH04 yellow Crystal Hair.
Body	Yellow chenille.
Hackle	Yellow tied on as a collar and tied back.
Eyes	Gold bead chain.

Orange Death

Thread	Fluorescent orange.
Tail	Frayed-out pearl Mylar piping from body.
Body	Fluorescent orange 20-pound Amnesia over an underbody or silver tinsel.
Hackle	Frayed pearl Mylar piping.
Eyes	Silver bead chain.
Head	Fluorescent white chenille wrapped through and around the eyes.

Paradise Beach

Thread	Red.
Tail	Dyed red grizzly marabou.
Body	Black diamond braid.
Eyes	Silver bead chain.

Tied and designed to fish for shad early in the morning at the Paradise Beach area of the American River.

Pat's Prince

Thread	White.
Tail	Clear (white) Miclon or Z-lon.
Body	Chartreuse plastic lace wrapped over an underbody of flat silver tinsel.
Hackle	White tied on as a collar and tied back.
Eyes	Silver bead chain.

This fly can also be used as a design for tying similar patterns using a red or orange body.

Porker

Thread	Yellow.
Body	Dubbed with #6 yellow African Angora goat, tied full and fat.
Hackle	Yellow tied on as a collar and tied back.
Eyes	Gold bead chain.

Princeton Plus

Thread	White.
Tail	Mixed white calf tail and FB01 pearl Fly Brite.
Body	White chenille.
Hackle	Red tied on as a collar and tied back.
Eyes	Silver bead chain.

Royal Shad

Thread	Red.
Butt	Dark olive chenille.
Body	Red floss.
Hackle	Red tied on as a collar and tied back.
Eyes	Silver bead chain.

Rosy

Thread	Red.
Tail	Red calf tail.
Body	Dubbed with a blend of #4 red lamb's wool and FB03 red Fly Brite.
Hackle	Red tied on as a collar and tied back.
Eyes	Silver bead chain.

Shad Buster

Thread	White.
Tail	White calf tail.
Body	Dubbed with a blend of #2 white lamb's wool and FB01 pearl Fly Brite.
Hackle	Orange tied on as a collar and tied back.
Eyes	Silver bead chain.

Silver Shad

Thread	White.
Tail	CH30 silver Crystal Hair.
Body	Silver diamond braid.
Hackle	CH30 silver Crystal Hair spun on as a collar.
Head	White.

Silverado

Thread	White
Tail	CH30 silver Crystal Hair.
Body	Wrapped with fine silver Mylar piping.
Hackle	CH30 silver Crystal Hair spun on as a collar.
Eyes	Silver bead chain.

Stan's Orange

Thread	Fluorescent orange.
Tail	CH06 orange Crystal Hair.
Body	Fluorescent orange chenille.
Hackle	CH06 orange Crystal Hair spun on as a collar.
Eyes	Gold bead chain.

Timbuctoo

Thread	Chartreuse.
Tail	Clear (white) Miclon or Z-lon.
Body	Chartreuse chenille.
Ribbing	Oval gold tinsel.
Hackle	Chartreuse tied on as a collar and tied back.
Eyes	Gold bead chain.

Ugo

Thread	Blue.
Tail	White marabou.
Body	Dubbed with a blend of #30 purple lamb's wool and FB19 purple Fly Brite.
Hackle	Purple hen hackle tied on as a collar and tied back.
Eyes	Silver bead chain.

Verdict

Thread	Black.
Tail	FB11 green Fly Brite.
Body	Dubbed with FB21 claret Fly Brite.
Hackle	Black hen hackle tied on as a collar and tied back.
Eyes	Silver bead chain.

Veronafly

Thread	Fluorescent green.
Tag	Fluorescent green yarn.
Body	Well-tapered fluorescent green yarn.
Hackle	White tied on as a collar and tied back.
Eyes	Gold bead chain.

Wet Pinky

Thread	Fluorescent pink.
Tail	White marabou.
Body	Fluorescent white chenille.
Ribbing	Oval silver tinsel.
Eyes	Gold bead chain.

Developed by Dave Howard of Roseville, California.

White's Light

Thread	White.
Tail	White marabou mixed with CH01 pearl Crystal Hair.
Body	CH01 pearl Crystal Hair wrapped over an underbody of white floss.
UnderBody	White floss.
Eyes	Silver bead chain.
Head	Fluorescent white chenille wrapped through and around the eyes.

Yuba Special

Thread	White.
Tail	Black marabou.
Body	Dubbed with FB02 black Fly Brite.
Hackle	White hen hackle tied on as a collar and tied back.
Eyes	Silver bead chain.

CHAPTER 5

Spinning, Casting, and Trolling Tackle

While fly-fishing for shad is increasing in popularity, spinning is also undeniably a great way to take both American and hickory shad. For shad fishing, this means light rods capable of casting the small darts, spoons, and jigs taken by shad. The light tackle also provides more fun in the fight, without tiring you. For shad, light tackle—soft-action rods, small reels, and light lines—is the ultimate. Don't go *too* light, however. Shad—whether American or hickory—are strong fish that have ocean-run stamina to fight hard, run the distance, and battle with head-shaking throbs. The smaller hickory shad lack the size and strength of the larger American shad cousins but more than make up for it with their above-water acrobatics.

You should also avoid going too heavy. The upper jaw of a shad's mouth is soft, and often they are hooked in the upper jaw. Tackle too heavy or fighting them too hard can pull the lure free or risk losing the fish. You may find that you want to use slightly different types of equipment for the two species and for different fishing conditions.

The best tackle for American shad is something slightly lighter than the medium freshwater gear used for lake bass fishing, but heavier than the light or ultralight tackle best for the smaller hickory shad, though sometimes used for American shad. Such outfits make it easy to cast the lures that are usually no more than ¼ ounce, and often only ⅛ ounce or less, something that would be more difficult with a heavier outfit.

There are some situations where you might want a heavier outfit, however, such as when trolling for shad or fishing downriggers (either trolled or from an anchored boat). A heavier rod here will prevent an excessive bow in the rod when trolling or from the force of the river current against the line, lure, and sinker when anchored and still fishing. River currents exert great force against the line and lures, particularly with the sinkers that are often used to get the lures deep and keep them deep. In this, as in trolling, sometimes sinkers from 1 to 3 ounces are necessary to get the lures to the right depth, particularly on the larger West Coast rivers. Here, standard freshwater bass gear or even heavier tackle is ideal. Use an outfit consisting of a medium freshwater reel, 8- to 10-pound-test line, and a 6½- to 7½-foot rod built for ⅜- to ¾-ounce lures. Even heavier tackle is required to handle the sinkers up to 8 ounces that are a must to get deep enough when fishing below some West Coast dams.

RODS

The fiberglass rods with which I started shad fishing years ago were great, but the graphite sticks of today offer far better sensitivity, allowing you to feel what the lure is doing, more readily detect strikes, tick the bottom when shad are deep, and feel more of the fight of the shad on the line. Most graphite rods have a much stiffer action than past fiberglass rods, and this can be detrimental when fishing for soft-mouthed shad. Get a graphite rod with sensitivity, but with an even or parabolic action, in which the rod bends well down toward or into the handle. Rod length and rod types vary on the East and West Coasts.

Typical casting rods for shad fishing. The two at the bottom are long handled and are excellent for placing in rod holders when boat fishing.

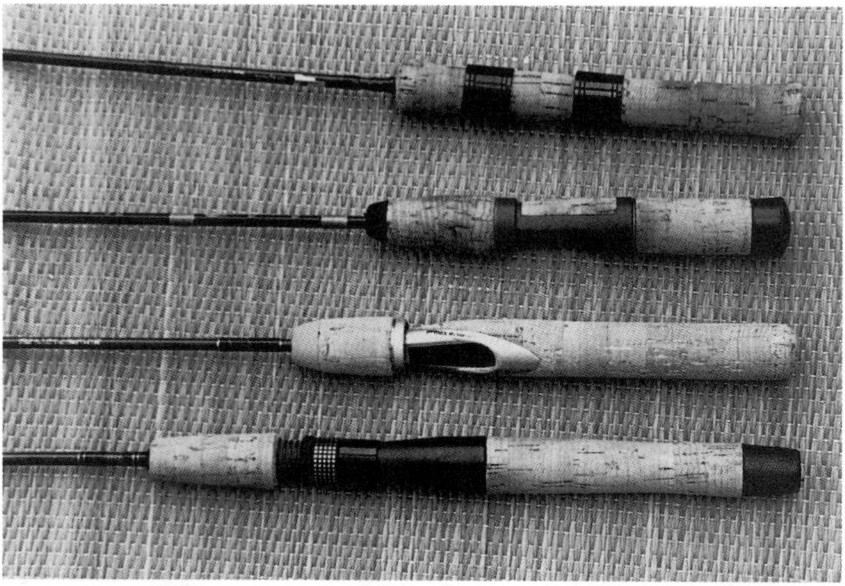

Examples of spinning rods for shad fishing. *Top:* Two light rods for fishing with light reels for hickory shad. *Bottom:* Larger, more typically freshwater rods for fishing with standard-size reels for American shad. Note the lack of a reel seat and the two sliding bands on the top rod—typical of very light outfits.

Rod Length

While everyone has his or her own preference in rod length, I like rods of about 5½ to 6½ feet, very light or ultralight, when fishing for hickory shad, and 6 to 7 feet for casting, river anchoring, and trolling for American shad.

On the West Coast, which has only American shad, these rods lengths are also popular for most fishing. Some anglers like longer rods, however, more like the models used in the same waters for the steelhead that run at similar times. These are particularly popular around dams, where long casts are often necessary. These long rods are often 8 to 9 feet long, with 8½ feet a good compromise. For boat fishing, many anglers use the same 6- to 7-foot-long rods favored by East Coast anglers.

On the East Coast, rod action varies with the species, since both American and hickory shad are sought. For hickory shad, pick a rod designed for casting 1/32- to 3/16-ounce lures. For American shad, choose a rod that will cast from 1/16- to 3/8-ounce lures. If you plan to cast spoons with an in-line sinker for weight to get the spoon deep, you will have to go with heavier tackle. Try a 6½-foot rod with a lure range equal to the sinker weight you are casting. This will be the same as, or similar to, your rod for trolling. For trolling, get a stiff rod with a casting range of 3⁄8- to 3⁄4-ounce lures. I like a rod of about 6 to 6 1⁄2 feet in length, with what might be called a parabolic action, and slightly on the soft side.

Stiffness

Just how soft a rod should be depends not only on the fishing, but also the type of terminal tackle to be trolled. Get a trolling rod that can handle the sinker weight and current force, but not one so stiff that it might tear the lure out of the shad's mouth during the fight. Realize, however, that you can't effectively use these rods for just casting a single or even tandem dart rigs when tiny darts are used. You will be able to cast some of the larger 1⁄4- to 3⁄8-ounce darts, especially if rigged in tandem.

It might be argued that heavy sticks with a light tip (like some bass-fishing "worm" rods) would be the answer. In theory, they should provide stiffness in the butt for trolling, yet a light tip to cope with the action of the fighting shad. But it just doesn't work that way. I'll admit that I do not like fast tip rods for any fishing, so it can be argued that I am prejudiced. In my experience and that of many others, although stiff-butt rods might be fine for trolling the shad lure or holding it in place in a current when anchored, all the theory goes down the drain when a fish hits. The light tip completely collapses and does not provide the bowing and cushioning effect required to cope with the long runs and soft mouths of shad. The light tip on most rods is only about 12 to 18 inches of the tip section, so in practice, you end up with an 18-inch whippy rod on the end of a stiff broom handle of a butt section. And this short "action" portion of the rod makes fighting any fish difficult. The stiff butt section can threaten to tear the lure free. For the same reason, very short rods (under 5 feet) are seldom good with light or ultralight tackle. The short rods have fine leverage for fighting big fish with heavy tackle, but unless extremely soft, they lack the shock absorbency for fighting soft-mouthed shad on a light line.

Because of the additional shock absorbency of longer, soft, flexible rods, noodle rods had gained some slight favor with shad anglers, particularly on the West Coast. Currently, that popularity is in decline, with only a few anglers using them. These rods range up to 10 1⁄2 feet long and are very soft, almost spongy. They are designed for very light lines, such as 2-pound-test, but can be used with 4- and 6-pound-test line for shad fishing. In many cases, they are almost too soft and long for easy control or handling of shad. In addition, they are not good boat rods.

The longer the rod, the more difficult it is to control the fish at the boat and to effect a smooth landing or netting. Even when shore fishing or wading, you often need a buddy to net the fish, or at least a smooth, shallow shoreline so you can slide the fish into the shallows for landing and hook removal. If choosing a noodle rod for boat fishing, get one no more than 8 to 9 feet long, and consider this length for wading and bank fishing also.

Local Conditions

Rod choice must be dictated by local conditions also. On the West Coast, shad make their runs in rivers at about the same time as salmon, and these larger fish are often hooked while fishing for shad. As a result, anglers there often pick a rod that is a compromise—a standard-length rod that is medium-action and a little heavy for shad, but a little light for the larger salmon. Longer steelhead rods are also used, particularly from the shore or while wading. These typically 8½-foot-long steelhead rods are generally used on the small streams of the West Coast, but are also used by a minority of anglers (about 25 percent) fishing big rivers like the Columbia. Other shad fishermen fishing below dams on these larger rivers typically use level-wind gear. Typically this includes a 7½-foot-long popping-style rod, according to West Coast shad aficionado Bruce Holt, press relations representative for G. Loomis. He suggests, naturally, something like the G. Loomis HSR 9000 rod. Similar rods from other manufacturers work quite well also, although heavy rods are a must to deal with the 2 to 8 ounces of lead sometimes necessary to get spoons and darts down deep in the current where the American shad travel.

Grips

Grips can be foam or cork. Foam is a little warmer and more comfortable for this often chilly early-season fishing, but foam is heavier (about five times) than cork. If wading, that extra weight might be a consideration. For boat fishing, it won't be. Get a rod with a straight grip if fishing from a boat, so that the grip will fit into a rod holder. Pistol or other swelled-grip rods just won't fit into the tubular holders, although they can be held by a bracket or clamp-style rod holder.

A butt cap is nice. The best ones are of rubber, to better prevent the rod from slipping when propped at an angle.

Reel Seats

Reel seats on modern rods are usually skeletal style—skinny seats built right on the blank or with part of the blank exposed. This is ideal for shad fishing, since it provides maximum sensitivity from the line, through the rod, to the grip and to your hand. Just pick one that locks the reel easily

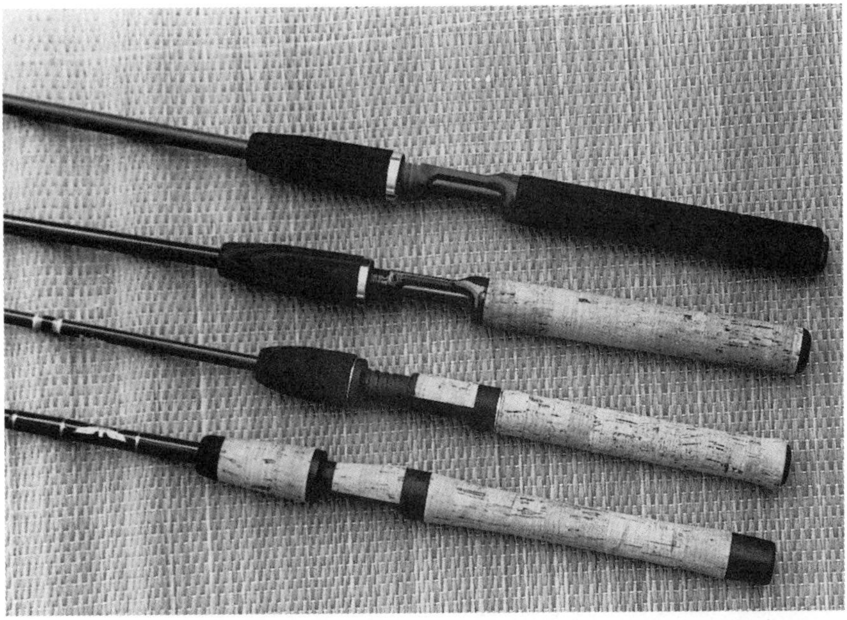

For trolling or anchored fishing in rivers, slightly longer handles are needed to fit into the rod holders. These are still light rods that are ideal for shad fishing and will work well with the rod holders on any boat.

and securely in place. Double-locking collet nuts are nice but not necessary. When buying new equipment, check the rod and reel before leaving the store. While rare today, in the past some reel feet have not fit onto some reel seats, even when both were made by the same manufacturer.

Some very light shad rods might have sliding rings on a cork or foam grip in place of a reel seat. These are rarer today than in the past, particularly with the development of plastic/graphite reel seats and the lightweight skeletal styles that have little more weight than a couple of metal rings. When used, sliding rings are usually found on the tiny ultralight panfish and crappie rods of 4½ to 5½ feet in length.

Guides

Almost all guides today are made of a ceramic ring fitted into the metal guide ring. Avoid the white ring guides. They are inexpensive, soft, and in time will groove. All the best ones, of a harder material such as Hardloy, aluminum oxide, silicon carbide, or silicon nitride, will not groove. Unless they are damaged, they will last a lifetime. Make sure that the rod has enough guides to evenly distribute the stresses of casting and fighting fish. As a general rule, you want one guide for each foot of rod length. The trend today is for a high frame and smaller ring guides. The high frame reduces the possibility of line slap against the rod blank, while the smaller ring reduces weight without affecting casting performance. This is particularly important in light shad rods.

It also helps to have a keeper ring or hook holder of some type to hold the dart or lure when not fishing. If your rod lacks one, a simple homemade device is easy to add. Simply fold over a small loop (about 1½ inches folded) of 50- to 100-pound mono, then use rod wrapping or heavy fly-tying thread to carefully wrap the ends of the loop to the rod. Complete with a whip finish, and seal with epoxy rod finish or clear fingernail polish to protect the wraps. The mono loop will hold any size lure. Another possibility is to tape or wrap, whip, and seal a 1-inch length of ¼-inch-diameter PVC tubing (available in hobby shops) to the butt end of the rod for securing a lure.

Casting Rods

The same general rules for grips, guides, and other appointments apply to casting rods, with the exception of the guides. You still want good ceramic guides, but won't need the high frames or large rings of spinning. Usually a butt guide ring size of 16 to 12 millimeters is fine, going with smaller guides up the rod. Double-foot, low-frame guides are best here. You want a straight handle to drop easily into a rod holder. Also, you won't find an ultralight casting rod. Casting rods are used primarily for trolling and downrigger fishing, even though spinning rods are used for this purpose also.

Spincast Rods

Spincasting rods are very similar to casting rods. Most have the exact same features, although some have shaped-cork or molded pistol grips that are not good for boat fishing for the above described reasons. Often they are a little lighter or softer than standard bass-style casting rods and thus are ideal for shad fishing.

Other Considerations

Spinning, spincast, and casting rods come in one-, two-, and multipiece models. Most of the smaller rods up to about 6 feet are one-piece, while longer rods are generally two-piece, sometimes three-piece. If storage or travel is a problem, choose a two-piece or multipiece rod if available.

With the wealth of rod manufacturers marketing rods today, you can find plenty of shad rods at local tackle shops. If they are not familiar with shad fishing, ask about rods for panfish, crappie, and trout (for hickory shad) or rods for smallmouth bass, light largemouth bass, heavy trout, and general freshwater fishing (for American shad).

Rod Choices

My personal preferences for rod types for shad are as follows:

American shad trolling

- Spinning tackle
  —East Coast: Medium-action blank, relatively soft parabolic action, 6 to 6½ feet long, two-piece, center-ferruled, fixed reel seat, high-frame hard ceramic guides, straight grip, rubber butt cap, and keeper ring.
  —West Coast: Consider the same rod style, or perhaps a longer rod such as an 8- to 9½-foot-long steelhead type, with a long rear grip for leverage when fighting a fish.
- Casting tackle
  —East Coast: Medium-action blank, soft to fast action, 6 feet long, one- or two-piece, through-the-handle blank, hard ceramic ring guides, straight foam or cork grip, fixed reel seat, and rubber butt cap.
  —West Coast: Use the same rod or a longer soft rod, 8 to 9 feet in length, with long rear grip. Steelhead casting rods are often ideal for American shad on these larger rivers. Go with a 7½-foot popping-style rod for handling heavy sinkers on big rivers.

American shad casting or hickory shad trolling

- Spinning tackle
  —East Coast: Soft, medium-action blank, 6 to 6½ feet long, one- or two-piece, fixed skeletal reel seat, straight cork grip, lightweight high-frame small-ring hard ceramic guides, rubber butt cap, and keeper ring.
  —West Coast: American shad only. Similar to the above. Consider also an 8- to 9-foot-long rod, similar to those used for steelhead, which can usually be found in the same rivers.

Hickory shad casting

- Spinning tackle
  —East Coast only: Very soft and light blank, 5 to 6 feet long, capable of handling tiny 1/32-ounce lures, one-piece, short cork grip, skeletal fixed reel seat, high-frame small-ring hard ceramic guides, keeper ring, and rubber butt cap.

REELS

For trolling for shad, you can use the same spinning reel that you use for freshwater bass fishing. Use a standard freshwater spinning reel spooled with lighter line than you would normally use for bass or other popular freshwater species. For casting with spinning tackle, a slightly lighter reel is best. Most tackle manufacturers build reels in a series of three to six sizes. These usually range from ultralight through light, medium fresh water, fresh water/light salt water, and so on. For hickory shad, you can go with the light or ultralight. When spinning for American shad, use the light model. In any case, pick a good-quality reel with a full bail, smooth roller guide, instant antireverse, easy-to-grip handle, and smooth drag.

Since accuracy is important when casting to specific spots for shad, feathering the cast to slow the line with your index finger is an important trick. With this, you can control a cast that is going too far by dropping your index finger close to, or lightly touching, the spool as line is going out. This will slow the line and reduce casting distance. For right-handed casters, the line should spool onto the reel clockwise when facing the reel. This means that the line will come off counterclockwise, making it easy to

Spinning tackle's ability to cast the small lures needed to take shad has made this the most popular way to fish. Ideal reels for shad fishing include smaller reels spooled with light line for hickory shad fishing in small streams (top), and medium-sized freshwater reels for fishing American shad in major rivers.

feather the cast as it brushes against your index finger dropped into place for this purpose. If you are left-handed, you will end up using the same reel, since almost all reels made today have interchangeable handles for right- or left-hand conversion. In this situation, feather the line by dropping your index finger to the top of the spool so that the line will brush against the back of your finger. Some reels are made with line spooling the reverse of this; if so, reverse the above instructions for right- and left-handers.

Buy the best-quality reel you can afford, since quality will pay off and make it the least-expensive reel in the long run. Important features in a shad reel include brass, bronze, or stainless gearing; a large ball-bearing bail roller; instant antireverse; front or center drag; large, smooth drag washers; comfortable grips; and fold-down reversible handle.

Quality and Capacity

Most of the better spinning reels of today have the following features: full bails, almost indestructible bail springs, reversible right- or left-hand drive, and smooth drags. Capacity is important, particularly for American shad, which use the current to make long downstream runs. Pick a reel with at least a 100- to 150-yard capacity for American shad, and at least an 80-yard capacity for hickory shad. Even the smallest ultralight reels will have this much capacity of 4-pound-test line for the hickory shad fishing, and the larger reels used for American shad will usually hold about 100 to 150 yards of 6- to 8-pound-test mono. If in doubt, more line capacity is better than less, since the fish of a lifetime might be hooked in fast currents or a location where a lot of line is a must to prevent a breakoff.

Gear Ratio and Retrieve Speed

Gear ratio, which translates into speed of retrieve, can be important even though shad usually hit while the lure is still or swinging in the current. In some cases after being hooked, shad will immediately run upstream, since this is their natural tendency when spawning. In these cases, it is important to retrieve line as rapidly as possible to prevent the shad from throwing the hook. This is a greater possibility when using shad darts or spoons than with flies, since the weight of the dart gives them some leverage to throw the lure.

If you have a choice, pick a reel with a high-speed retrieve. Fast-retrieve gear ratios are especially important in smaller reels, such as the ultralight models used for hickories or if you are going really light for the American shad. Fast-retrieve reels will make it easier and quicker to get the line back in for the next cast.

As a test, I checked a few reels for line retrieval rates. A standard freshwater spinning reel with a 4:1 gear ratio and a 2-inch-diameter spool will retrieve about 24 inches of line with each turn of the handle. A miniature, or ultralight reel with a 1½-inch-diameter spool and the same 4:1 gear ratio will only retrieve about 18 inches of line with each turn of the handle—a 25 percent reduction over the larger reel. The answer is a faster gear ratio. A small reel with a 1½-inch-diameter spool and a gear ratio of 5.5:1 will retrieve line at a rate of 24¾ inches per handle turn. But even this does not help the very tiny ultralight reels. The smallest currently available spinning reel in my collection has a spool diameter of 1 3/16 inch and a 5.2:1 gear ratio. Thus, considering that a spinning reel is filled only to within about ⅛ inch of the spool lip, and that this reel holds a 1-inch-diameter coil of line, this means that it will retrieve about 16 inches of line per handle turn.

Realize also that the small diameter of the spool on these tiny reels also limits the pound-test of line that you can use. The tiny reel mentioned above is rated for 90 yards of 4-pound-test line and 160 yards of 2-pound-test line. There would not be enough line capacity for heavier line, such as 6-pound-test, which might coil or twist anyway on the small-diameter spool.

Even with sufficient line capacity, these small spool diameters tend to spool line in very tight coils, which makes it difficult for the line to straighten out until it gets wet and stretched by fishing. Ideally, a small, light reel with a large-diameter spool would be great for shad—or any light-tackle fishing—but these do not seem to be in vogue at the present.

Antireverse

The instant antireverse feature found on most modern spinning (and casting) reels is a good feature, since it eliminates any slack in the reel when setting the hook or when a fish strikes. Lacking that, there was always some backslap of the rotor until a pawl caught a gear to stop the back turning of the rotor and bail. This created strain on the pawl and gear, and also created slack, which could allow enough time for a shad to throw the hook or cause it not to get hooked solidly.

Drag

A smooth drag is important, particularly with the fragile mouths of shad and the fact that you can't pressure or horse them and that they do have the current to help in their fight. Spinning reel drags are located in the front—under the spool—or in the rear, in the gear housing. A recent third alternative is the center drag, introduced in 1999 by Abu Garcia, with large drag washers outside of the housing but directly in back of the spool. The front and center drag systems are best, since the smaller washers that have to be fitted into the rear will heat up on long runs and do not have the same drag surface area. With any reel, assuming good, smooth, soft washers, the more surface area, the better. It's important to back off the drag after each fishing trip to reduce the constant pressure on the soft washers. Constant pressure can in time deform them and make the drag stiff, sticky, or rough.

Bails

Bails must completely flip over when you turn the handle to close the bail and engage the line. Most companies today use a system of unbreakable bail springs that have eliminated the bail problems of the past. Larger bail rollers on a ball-bearing race have also lessened the possibility of sticking bail rollers. This improves reel function and also lessens line wear and abrasion—particularly important with the light line used for shad fishing.

Casting Reels

Level-wind casting reels can be used for trolling or paying out lures when still-fishing from an anchored boat. They can also be used if casting with a long rod when using heavy darts, jigs, or a dart-sinker rig. Regular or narrow-width reels are fine. A very few ultralight casting reels are made by companies such as Shimano, Mitchell, Pinnacle, and Silstar. Choose

Casting reels are ideal for both trolling or still fishing from an anchored boat and fishing with downriggers and flutter spoons. These are typical American shad fishing reels. The top row of reels are small casting reels; the bottom reels are more typically used for freshwater bass fishing.

a casting reel with a good drag, easy thumb-bar or push-button spool release, good brass and/or stainless steel gearing, comfortable handle knobs, and good level wind. The line capacity of any freshwater casting reel is usually sufficient for shad.

Spincast Reels

Spincasting reels, which fit onto standard casting rods, are seldom used in shad fishing because most have limited line capacity and lack the smooth drags of spinning and casting reels. They can be used for hickory shad, but I would hate to trust one in a fast river when hooked to an American shad.

LINES

Monofilament Lines

Monofilament lines are best for most shad fishing. Choose 4- to 6-pound-test for hickory shad and 6- to 10-pound-test for American shad. Since this is early-spring, and often cold-weather, fishing, choose the limp, soft, or specific "cold-weather" lines. Since most fishing is in the mid-depths of a river, with few obstructions or snags to catch or abrade the line, special abrasion-resistant lines are seldom required. If this is a problem where you fish, you might want to go with a heavier pound-test or line rated for abrasion resistance. Keep in mind, however, that the limp lines ideal for cold-water fishing are never as abrasion resistant as other lines or as lines specifically made to withstand abrasion.

Gel-Spun and Thermal-Fusion Lines

Some anglers are now trying the newer gel-spun braid and thermal-fusion lines, and they do have their place. They are far thinner than mono for the same pound-test (or far stronger for the same diameter), with far less stretch and greater sensitivity than mono. This means that by using gel-spun or fusion lines for shad fishing, you can go with the same pound-test, but the thinner diameter creates less bellying of the line with the current than you would have with mono, while having more sensitivity to strikes. Conversely, you could use the same diameter but have a stronger pound-test line. The strength ratio for lines of the same diameter is about 5:1 for gel-spun braids to mono and about 4:1 for thermal-fusion lines to mono.

As with any braided line, knots are a problem with gel-spun lines. The best solution for the many lure changes required in shad fishing is to tie a Bimini twist in the end of the line, then tie this doubled line to a slightly heavier nylon mono using a blood knot. Clip the knot closely. With a mono leader of about 6 feet, it's possible to quickly and easily change lures using a Palomar or improved clinch knot. Another possibility is to tie a single Palomar directly to the lure, although this puts the opaque braid directly in contact with the lure, whereas a mono leader would be slightly less visible.

Fluorocarbon Lines

For most anglers, the jury is still out on the use of the fluorocarbon lines for shad fishing, as well as a lot of other fishing. These lines—expensive, so formerly just sold as leader material—are said to be less visible, since they have a refractive index that is closer to water than that of nylon mono lines. But it's not that simple. The refractive index does not make them invisible, since that of water is 1.33, while that of fluorocarbon is 1.45 to 1.50 and that of mono nylon is only a little more, about 1.60.

Also, knots tied in fluorocarbon are not as strong as knots tied in nylon mono. For example, a nylon mono line tied with a Trilene (double) knot or improved clinch knot will test at about 90 to 95 percent of the line strength, while the same knot tied in fluorocarbon line will test at about 70 to 75 percent of the line strength. This means that you would have to use 14-pound-test fluorocarbon mono to get the same ultimate strength in a rigging as you would with 10-pound-test nylon mono, and the thicker diameter will cause the loss of some of the advantages of the better refractive index of the fluorocarbon. Considering that shad are usually caught in the murky, milky waters of spring runoff, when the water is stained and high, there seems to be little advantage to using fluorocarbon lines when shad fishing.

Line Choices

My lines choices for shad fishing are as follows:

American shad

- Casting: 6- to 12-pound-test mono line with spinning tackle, or 10- to 15-pound test thermal-fusion line with revolving spool tackle, a 6-foot mono leader tied to the end of the line for easy lure change.
- Trolling: 8- to 10-pound-test mono line with spinning tackle, or 10- to 20-pound-test braided line with revolving spool tackle.

Hickory shad

- Casting: 4- to 6-pound-test mono line with spinning tackle.
- Trolling: 6- to 8-pound-test mono line with spinning or revolving spool tackle.

CHAPTER 6

Casting and Trolling Lures and Rigs

Though a wide variety of lures will take shad, almost all of them have two characteristics in common—they are small and brightly colored.

Just to show how simple a lure will take shad, one of the most popular lures for years on the Northeast Coast was a single gold hook with a red bead on the leader just above the hook. In spite of its sparse appearance, it takes shad and is a well-known if somewhat unusual shad lure.

Another simple and more recent discovery in shad lures from the West Cost is that of using a brass swivel as a lure. Here, a swivel or snap swivel, usually a size 3, is attached to a ringed-eye hook. That's it. No dressing, no paint, no nothing. Anglers are using brass swivels, although nickel-plated or black might also work, considering that shad do hit nickel-plated spoons and black darts and flies.

Conventional lures for shad were first designed for the baitcasting tackle that was in use before spinning came into being and popularity. For this, some of the early lures for shad were larger than the lures we use today, or were fished in tandem to give some casting weight to the rig. Also, early small lures were used with sinkers for the same reasons we do so today—for casting weight and also to help get and keep the lure down with the shad. Despite this, most lures fall into one of two categories: spoons and jigs or jig style (darts come into this category). Just which lure was used first is probably lost in the history of the early days of shad sportfishing or may, as I suspect, have varied in different locations.

SPOONS

Considering the highly regional, and even local, conditions of shad fishing, just who used which lure first, or which river system spawned a popular lure type or color, is probably the subject of many a hot-stove argument. On the Mid-Atlantic Coast, several small lures have long been popular for shad. Buddy Grucela thinks that his father was the first person to take shad by sportfishing methods on the Delaware River in the 1930s, using a silver spinner-spoon no longer manufactured.

In the same area in the 1940s, the popular lure was the double O (00) Drone, a small single-hook spoon then made in Annapolis, Maryland. It became instantly popular in a several-state area, as far south as Virginia. At about the same time in the same area, a spoon made by the Nungesser Company of Arlington, Virginia, was also very popular for shad. In North Carolina, a size 1 Reflecto spoon became popular, often fished in tandem with a shad dart.

On the West Coast, small but thick and heavy spoons and wobblers became popular, often fished with lead weight to help get the spoons deep in the fast rivers holding shad. Gold Hildebrandt spoons are also popular.

With the variety of metal lures available, each part of the two coasts has its favorite spoon, but almost any spoon will work almost anywhere. The many models of spoons made by the West Coast–based Luhr Jensen Company are popular there, since many of their spoons are designed a little thicker and heavier for the strong flow of West Coast rivers. Luhr's

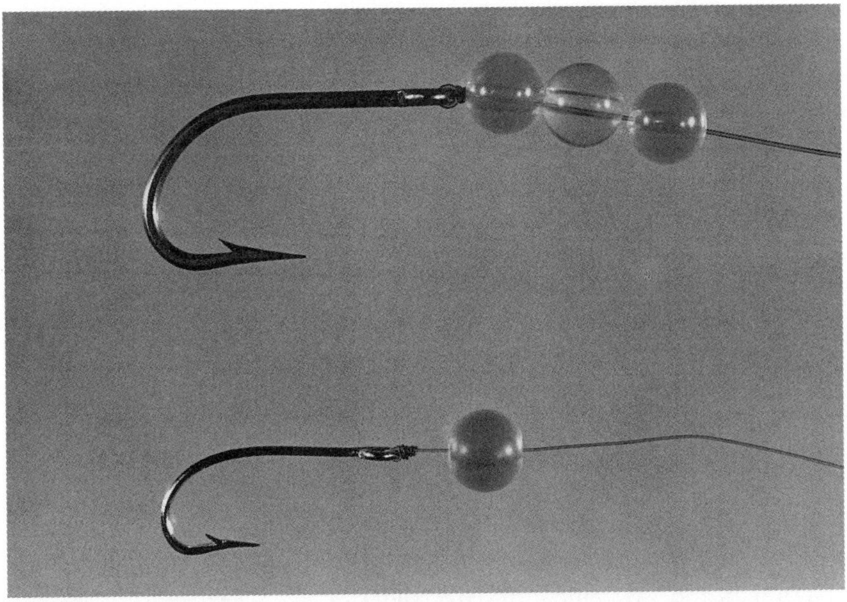

One of the earliest lures used was nothing more than a colorful glass bead or two threaded onto the line above a bare hook. This is a modern example, with plastic beads of fluorescent red and green.

Casting spoons that are typically used for shad.

Wobbler, Kokanee King, Knobby Wobbler, Krocodile, size 2 McMahon, and the Tom Mack are all good shad lures for both coasts.

South Bend lures such as the Super Duper, Trix Oreno, and Flip-It are popular and are sold under the Luhr Jensen label now that they have obtained the company. Hopkins spoons, widely known for their effectiveness on everything with fins in salt water, are also effective lures in small sizes. The smallest Shorty spoons (1/8 ounce) in both gold and chrome are the most popular size and finishes for shad. Another popular shad spoon is the Barracuda in sizes 00, 0, 1, and 2.

The Eppinger Dardevle series of spoons in small sizes and fixed single or swinging treble hook styles are also good. Those suitable for shad fishing include the Dardevle Spinnie (1/4 ounce and 1 3/4 inches long), Dardevle Midget (3/16 ounce and 1 3/8 inches long), Dardevle Skeeter (1/32 ounce and 15/16 inch long), Dardevle Skeeter Plus (1/16 ounce and 15/16 inch long), and the Lil' Devle (1/8 ounce and 1 1/8 inches long). All of these lures come in dozens of colors and finishes, with chrome, gold, nickel, brass, red/white, and red/yellow the best colors.

Any spoon for shad fishing should be small, ranging from about 3/4 to 1 1/2 inches in length. Weight is less important, since most are trolled or cast with a sinker weight or with a downrigger. In some cases, the very small, lightweight spoons used by ice fishermen, and generally available in locally popular brands in the northern parts of the country, will also work well on shad.

The finish on a shad spoon is a subject for endless debate. Nickel, chrome, and gold-plated are the most popular. Popular painted finishes include red/white, red/yellow, solid orange, solid fluorescent orange, solid fluorescent green, and solid fluorescent red. It pays to have a wide assortment of colors and metallic finishes, since some days the shad will hit only one color, and in some cases they even seem to change color preferences hourly. For casting a spoon without lead, or to get a spoon deep in fast current, you must use a thicker spoon, such as several models available from Luhr Jensen, Hopkins, or Eppinger (Dardevle).

I like all of my spoons, for shad as well as other types of fishing, to have a split ring, welded jump ring, or small swivel attached to the eye. I don't like to tie my line directly to the lure through the hole punched in the spoon blank, for two reasons. I find that the separate ring gives the spoon more action in the water, and more importantly, even with stringent quality controls of the manufacturing companies that do not provide their spoons with a separate line-tie ring, the line can fray on the edges of the metal or on a rough paint or finish job, causing lost lures and fish. For those lures lacking a ring or swivel, it's easy to add one or to tie a tiny snap or snap swivel to the end of your line for lure changes.

Though certainly not a complete list, some typical spoons and major manufacturers are listed below. Many of these spoons come in a wide range of sizes, and usually the smallest sizes—no more than about 1½ inches long—are best for shad.

EGB: Blinker
Lucky Strike: Half Wave
Blue Fox: Pixee
Acme: Little Cleo, Kastmaster, K. O. Wobbler, Fiord Spoon, Phoebe, Sidewinder, Wob-L-Rite, Kamlooper, Thunderbolt
Luhr Jensen: Krocodile, Kokanee King, Hus-Lure, Super-Duper, Crippled Herring, Cast Champ, Pet, Kwikfish, Canadian Wonder
Hopkins: Shorty
Nungesser
Dardevle (Eppinger Co.): Spinnie, Midget, Skeeter, Skeeter Plus, Lil' Devle
Cather
Huntington: Drone
Clark
Williams
Swedish Pimple

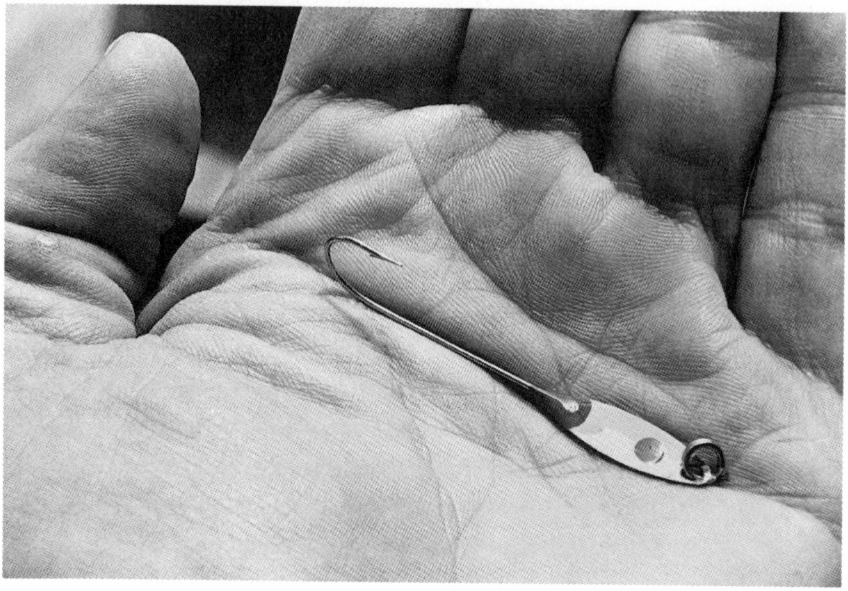

A flutter spoon.

Flutter Spoons

One new form of spoon is the small flutter spoon, first fished by Ron Bauer and Gary Conner on the Delaware River. They use them in conjunction with downriggers to get the spoons deep to where the American shad run and to hold the spoons deep in the current. Flutter spoons are fished from an anchored boat. The flutter spoons are mostly homemade and consist of a willowleaf blade on which is soldered a long-shank hook. Most are small, ¾-inch-long (size 1 or 2) blades, metallic on the concave side, painted on the convex surface, and have a long-shank size 2 Aberdeen hook soldered in place and a split ring added to the blade for a line tie. Bauer and Conner also believe in dipping the spoons in WD-40 lubricant. WD-40 has been used as a fish attractant in other types of fishing. The advantage of the blades is that they flutter (thus the name) in the water in back of the downrigger clip, rather than just hanging motionless, as would a dart or jig. Being very lightweight, they have lots more action than other spoons.

Bauer and Conner also suggest experimenting with color. They have found that different colors work best as the water warms and the season progresses. They start with a dark chartreuse/hammered gold finish, then switch in turn to light chartreuse/plain gold, red and white/hammered nickel, and red and white/plain nickel.

JIGS

Small jigs and bucktails, often refined and specialized to the point where they are called shad darts, are the other main shad-fishing lure. They share equal popularity with spoons.

Though jigs and bucktails come in a wide variety of shapes and sizes, only the small ones will work for shad. This means fishing lures about ¼ ounce and under for American shad and ⅛ ounce and under for hickory shad. Stay with simple shapes, such as small ballhead or bullethead styles. These are commonly available for all types of fishing, work well, and are less expensive than more exotic shapes that are also available.

The small, so-called crappie jigs work well for shad. These are ballhead jigs that usually have a short marabou tail, chenille body, and hackle collar. Variations include those with no collar, but a palmered hackle spiraled around the chenille body; those with a marabou tail and simple chenille body; those with spiky, cactus chenille bodies and marabou tails; and those with shiny mylar bodies and tails. Those with the shiny mylar are best primarily in murky waters or when fishing during very low light levels, at dawn or dusk. In addition, there are jigs with soft plastic bodies and marabou tails, as originated by the Lindy Fuzz-E-Grub and since copied by some other companies.

DARTS

The specialized shad dart began with the Quilby Minnow, as originated by the Pequea Works of Strasburg, Pennsylvania, in about 1940. Today similar molded, leadhead lures with the typical tapered body and colored calf tail are standard along all shad waters. The turkey-quill lures have faded to obscurity or become tackle collectibles, whereas the lead shad darts have remained popular on both coasts in colors that would rival the NBC peacock. In addition, larger sizes of shad darts have become popular as a lure for most species of fresh- and saltwater game fish.

Though shad darts come in assorted sizes, the most productive ones for shad fishing are those of about ⅛ ounce or less. In these smaller sizes, they are made in ⅛-, 1/16-, 1/32-, and 1/64-ounce weights. At various times, either larger or smaller lures produce best, so most anglers carry an assortment of sizes as well as a painter's palette of colors. Today almost any color is available, most of them in bright fluorescent colors of white, red, orange, yellow, green, lavender, purple, pink, and so on. Considering the many solid and two-tone combinations that you can get, most shops in shad areas carry a few dozen color combos. There are slight variations of favored darts on the East and West Coasts. On the East Coast, most of the darts have a short, often yellow calf tail that contrasts with the bright-

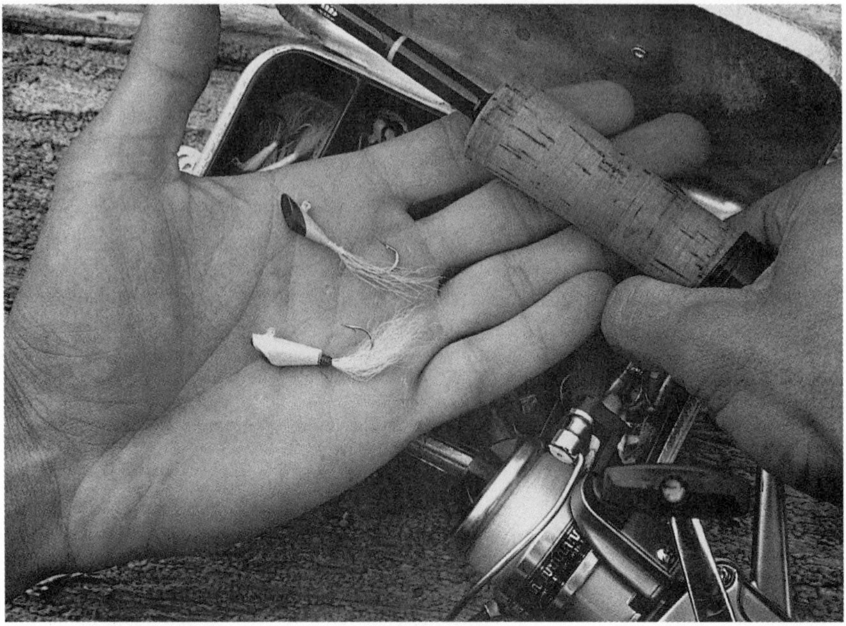

Typical shad darts.

colored body. In some areas of the West Coast, the most popular dart is one of chartreuse color, with no tail such as might be used for crappie or East Coast shad.

If making your own shad darts from molds such as those by Hilts and Do-It, you have a choice of mixed sizes of darts in one mold or all cavities of a single size. Be careful in buying paint. Acrylic is perhaps the easiest to use of the liquid paints. Be sure to first coat with a base of white, since fluorescent colors will lose their brilliance if not over a white base. Powder paints are also easy to use. These are in a fine powder form, almost like talcum powder. The lead lure is coated by heating it with a torch (but not enough to melt the lead), then stirring it in the powder paint and removing. Curing is instant, and two-tone finishes (body/head) are possible by two heat and dipping procedures. Tie the tail on last to avoid burning the tail or thread. (For more details on making shad darts and other lures and tackle, refer to *The Complete Book of Tackle Making,* by C. Boyd Pfeiffer.)

SPINNERS

Other lures for shad are also used and popular in some areas, including spinners. The Mepps Aglia, C. P. Swing, June Bug spinners, Panther Martin, Blue Fox Vibrax, Rooster Tail, Luhr Jensen Shyster, Manns Winger, and other spinner lures are all effective for shad. The advantage of a spinner—revolving blades—is also its disadvantage. The blades will presumably attract shad, but too bright or shiny a blade might also scare the fish away. They are best in stained or murky water or under low light levels, such as a very overcast day or at dawn or dusk. Dull-, painted-, and copper-finish blades are also good when fishing for shad, and sometimes can be better than the more prevalent gold- and silver-finish blades.

MISCELLANEOUS LURES

Almost any lure that is small and bright can be used for shad, and this leads to some unusual and interesting possibilities. Examples are the East Coast colored plastic or glass beads on a leader above a plain gold hook, mentioned earlier. The same technique has caught on for shad fishing the West Coast, specifically the Columbia River (Washington/Oregon). Another West Coast shad-fishing method uses a brass swivel attached to a hook as the only attractant. Angler and shad fisherman Brian Wiprud feels that the translucent-colored beads might closely mimic the bioluminescence of krill, copepods, and other natural oceanic shad food, and thus help to trigger strikes.

Some anglers occasionally use a shad scale, hooked at the edge and drifted in the current. Early records point to some anglers even scaling caught shad to create a "chum" of scales that are supposed to attract shad and produce more hits. Since the scales are relatively loose, this is not beyond reason. To further confirm this as a valid, although unusual, way to fish is the fact that some researchers have found scales in the stomachs of shad. Of course, it is not known whether the scales had been ingested accidentally or on purpose.

Realize that in some areas and states, fishing with fish parts is (or has been) illegal. Check local regulations before chumming with scales or fishing with a scale on a bare hook.

Though not widely popular, small plastic-tailed jigs have also been used for shad fishing. These come with bright-colored heads, and the tails come in colors to rival a rainbow. Plain straight-tail, buttontail, and curly sickle-shaped-tail soft plastic jigs have all been used, with at least some success. Best sizes, as with other jigs and shad darts, are under ¼ ounce and down to about 1/32 ounce. Since the plastic tails are often translucent and are available in bright and fluorescent colors, these might mirror the concept of the translucent look of the original Pequea Quilby Minnow shad darts of sixty years ago. The Fuzz-E-Grubs from Lindy do the same thing, but with a marabou tail in a short plastic body that slides onto the hook shank of the jig.

Other possibilities, especially for deeper waters or coping with fast currents, are small sizes of blade baits. Blade baits are primarily used for largemouth and smallmouth bass, but in small sizes they are ideal for fishing deep for shad. Typical blade baits include the Silver Buddy, Heddon Gay Blade, Heddon Sonar Flash, and Cicada. All will work in their smallest size available, with the best blade baits for shad under 2 inches, preferably under 1½ inches. Similarly, small crankbaits of about the same size will also work, with the best of these fluorescent or bright colors without being shiny. Lures in the fluorescent colors used for walleye and steelhead/salmon are often best for shad.

TANDEM RIGGINGS AND RIGGING WITH SINKERS

There are no right or wrong ways to rig shad lures, provided they get to the fish and do the job. Both sinker riggings and tandem lure rigs without sinkers are used for casting, anchored-boat fishing, and trolling.

A wide variety of sinkers can be used, based on the rigging planned. For in-line sinker riggings, consider pinch-on sinkers, which have ears on each end to pinch over the sinker after the line is wrapped once or twice around the body of the sinker; rubber-core style, with a rubber core in the slotted body that is twisted to hold the line in place; or egg or bullet sinkers, which slide onto the line and require a swivel or stop on the line to keep the sinker above the lure. For drop-style sinker riggings, consider bell, dipsy, bass-casting, bank, or similar-style sinkers. You can also use pencil lead (primarily used on the West Coast) but must have the swivel and rubber tubing sleeve into which the lead fits. The West Coast pencil lead rigs consist of a T-shaped three-way swivel, with the line and leader tied to the two upper T eyes, and a sleeve of surgical hose wire-wrapped to the vertical T swivel. The pencil lead is cut to length for the weight desired and held in place by the elastic surgical hose sleeve. Some of the more popular riggings are described below.

In-Line Sinker Rigs (Mostly for Casting)

- Use an egg, bullet, or other hollow lead sinker. Slide the sinker on the line, then tie on a swivel. To the other swivel eye, add 18 inches (approximately) of mono line and tie to a shad lure (dart, jigs, spoon, or spinner).
- Same as above, but instead of cutting the line to tie in a swivel as a sinker stop, use a Carolina Keeper stopper. These are slit plastic buttons that are easy to open with pliers to thread the line through, then close to grip the line. Thread the sinker on first, then the Caro-

lina Keeper, then tie the lure to the end of the line. The Carolina Keeper can be positioned anywhere on the line.

- Use a pinch-on sinker. Position the sinker on the line. Run the line around the ear at one end, then around the body of the sinker once or twice, then around the ear. Close the ears to hold the line. Tie the shad lure to the end of the line.
- Use a rubber gripping sinker. Position the sinker on the line, holding the line against the rubber core, and then twist the core to securely hold the line. Tie the shad lure to the end of the line.

Drop Singer Rigs (Mostly for Anchored-Boat Fishing)

- Use a three-way swivel, and tie the line to one eye. Tie an 18-inch length of mono to the second eye, and tie the shad lure to the end. Tie a short length of mono (about 6 inches) to the third eye, and tie a drop sinker to the end. Since the lure, particularly a spoon, will trail out behind the bottom-bouncing sinker, you can adjust the position of the lure by the length of the sinker line if bouncing the sinker on the bottom. Note that on this or any similar rigs, you can use a lighter mono on the sinker so that you will break the line and lose only the sinker in case the sinker snags.
- Use the above rig, but with two three-way swivels to fish two different lures. This is the equivalent of a two-hook bottom bait rig used in surf fishing. If you don't have three-way swivels, you can use a standard swivel (two eyes) and tie the lure dropper and line to one of the eyes, the sinker dropper line to the other eye. For the upper dropper and lure, tie the line and dropper to the upper eye and the line going to the second swivel to the other eye.
- Slide the eye of a snap swivel on the line, then tie the end of the line to a standard barrel swivel. Add 18 inches of line to the second swivel eye, and tie the lure to the end. Use the snap of the snap swivel to hold and easily change sinker weight.
- For a no-swivel alternative to the above, cut the line where you wish the sinker to be, and tie a blood knot with one long tag end. Tie the lure to the end of the line and the sinker to the tag end of the dropper. You can also do this with two knots to run two lures and a sinker.

Tandem Lure Rigs (for Casting or Boat Fishing)

Tandem riggings for shad lures will vary slightly based on whether the lures are cast, trolled, or still-fished. Any of the basic methods described can be interchanged, provided they work for you and your fishing style.

- Use the same no-swivel alternative as above to tie one lure to the end of the line and a second to the long tag end of the dropper knot.
- Use a three-way swivel as above for the sinker rigs, only use two lures in place of a lure and sinker.
- An alternative to the above is to tie an in-line dropper loop in the line where you want to run the second lure. This dropper loop can be cut close to the knot to make a single-strand dropper for tying a second lure. An alternative to this is to use the dropper to interconnect a lure separately tied to droppers (like a snelled hook) with a loop in the end. This also allows you to prepare lures on short, looped droppers for instant changing without tying knots. This is particularly useful with cold hands or in low light levels at dawn or dusk.

CHAPTER 7

Other Equipment and Gear

BOOTS AND WADERS

Unless fishing from a boat or from shore, boots are a necessity in shad fishing. Although wet wading can be done later in the season for trout and smallmouth, the early-spring water temperatures during shad season require some protection. You might start fishing for shad with the water temperature in the fifties, whereas optimal spawning temperature for shad is generally in the low sixties.

Boots come in two styles: hip boots and waders. If you know you're only going to be fishing in shallow water or wading a short distance from shore in a shallow river, then hip boots are OK. For maximum versatility in all fishing, I fish only waders, since they work in both shallow and deep water.

Hip boots fit up to the crotch and fasten to the belt with straps. Waders are usually chest-high (armpit height is best) and used with suspenders. For safety, be sure to get a belt to fit around the outside of the waders, high up on the chest. Should you fall in, the belt tight around your chest will help slow water intake into the waders and make it easier to recover your footing and get out safely. Some waders come with belts and loops through which to fit the belt on the outside of the waders.

Waders and hip boots come in several thicknesses of neoprene and also in light travel or breathable styles. Those fishing cold waters for trout, salmon, and steelhead in addition to shad might want to consider the insulated neoprene boots for warmth. If you'll be using your waders for a variety of fishing conditions or for travel, there is another option: Buy the lightweight or travel waders, and in cold weather, wear longjohns or other flannel or insulated undergarments under your regular pants for warmth, as well as extraheavy boot socks to keep your feet warm. I use this arrangement with a pair of lightweight boot-foot waders that are also easy to pack for travel.

Waders and hip boots come in stocking-foot styles, which require separate heavy wading shoes, and boot-foot styles, with the boot foot built into the hipper or wader. Both styles have their fans. I like the boot-foot style, since there is nothing else to carry or put on at the stream. Those who like the stocking-foot waders or boots worn with separate wading shoes correctly point out that the separate shoes provide better foot and ankle support. Both the separate boots and boot-foot style waders and hippers come with regular rubber lug soles or felt soles, and sometimes have metallic cleats or studs fastened to the sole. As a general rule, the felt soles are better, since they grip slippery rocks far better than the rubber lug soles. The metal cleats are usually not necessary and make the boot stiffer and more difficult to walk in. If desired, you can also buy separate add-on grippers of chain, felt sandals that fit over regular boots and shoes, and various cleated and metal-studded slip-on and strap-on additions. I like felt soles yet use chain grippers for those times when cutting through heavy algae growth might be required. Usually this is necessary later in the season, when fishing for smallmouth, not early in the spring for shad before the algae has bloomed.

SAFETY AND PFDS

Personal flotation devices—PFDs for short—are required for any person in any style of boat, but generally not for wade fishing. Check local and state regulations on this, however. Wearing a PFD is highly recommended for any wading, and especially so for high water, early-spring runoff, and on any waters that you have not waded before or with which you are unfamiliar. This can even apply to waters that you waded in years past, since winter conditions and storms can change the bottom of any river any time.

Fortunately, PFDs come in very comfortable styles, including ones with several pockets, which can double as a fishing vest. Since the pocket requirements for shad fishing are far less than those required for bass, trout, or salmon, a few pockets in a PFD are often enough to hold a box or two of flies, leader tippet spools, stream thermometer, clippers and nippers, mini lead heads, and similar gear.

If you don't like the bulk of the standard PFD vests, consider SOSpenders, now approved by the Coast Guard. These look like wide suspenders that fit over your chest, but they have mouth-inflatable and CO_2 cartridge-inflatable flotation pockets. A number of different models are available; check your local fly-fishing store or fly-fishing catalog house for information and the right model for your use.

WADING STAFF

Thirty years ago—even ten years ago—I waded rivers without worrying about falling in. But with a few more years on me, and after an incident two years ago, I have since always carried a wading staff. I was shad fishing in the early spring and had waded out into fast, waist-deep water to take some photos of several fly anglers who were regularly catching shad. After jockeying for the best photo location and then finishing up with the photos, I suddenly realized that I had gotten into a position where it was almost impossible to back up, impossible to go farther, and impossible to easily turn around. With two Nikons equipped with long lenses around my neck, I was in an awkward position, as well as one that could have been financially disastrous had I fallen in. Fortunately, one of my subjects saw my predicament. He waded over and came to my rescue, giving me a hand to get back into slower, safer water. I felt like the old lady being escorted across the street by the Boy Scout, but losing my

A wading staff is highly recommended for wading fast shad streams and rivers. This one, by Folstaf, will fold down and fit into a belt holster, yet will instantly snap into a usable staff when removed from the case.

pride was better than losing a few thousand dollars in Nikons. The next day I ordered a Folstaf. This wading staff comes in two lengths and several styles, all of which fold up into a 9-inch package that fits into a sheath that now rides all the time on my wader belt. Bungee cord keeps the sections together, so that all you have to do for instant use is grab the handle and pull it out of the sheath for it to unfold. For shad fishing—or other wading—I would never again be without it. Other manufacturers, such as Sports Tools and W. W. Grigg, make similar fold-up wading staffs.

CLOTHING

The secret of clothing choices for shad fishing—or for any fishing, for that matter—is to plan on it getting hotter than you think, colder than you think, and that it is sure to rain. The cold and the rain are more likely than heat in shad fishing, but there can be some hot spring days. In some climates, such as when shad fishing the St. Johns River in Florida in late November, the temperature can be quite variable. You might have hot days, but in the morning and evening, when the shad fishing is best, you could even have some frost.

Since most shad fishing is done in early spring—which varies with latitude—dress warmly and in layers. The best protection for your legs and body is insulated or neoprene waders, or travel waders over long-johns or long insulated underwear. For your body, try layers consisting of insulated underwear, heavy shirt, vest or fleece pullover, light jacket, and an outer shell of a rain jacket or nylon windbreaker. Rain jackets are particularly good even if there is no sign of rain, since they will block the wind, which otherwise can rob you of body heat and lessen the insulation value of your other garments. While natural fabrics such as cotton are good next to the skin for wicking away moisture and perspiration, consider also some of the modern synthetic insulated fibers, which are warm and retain some insulation even if wet. These fibers can be found in fleece pullovers, jackets, shirts, and sweaters. Wool and down are ideal for warmth but must be used under a rain parka during inclement weather, since down in particular is a poor insulator once wet.

Rain gear is also a must, for rainy days and the drizzle that often accompanies spring, and to protect from wind. The insulation of any fiber can be tremendously increased with rain gear by eliminating the loss of heat from the wind. Choose a parka style that will fit over your waders if wading, or a long style if boat fishing. Look for tight cuffs, an attached hood, and a storm flap over the front zipper in any purchase.

Up to 30 percent of body heat can be lost through the head. The answer for this is a hat or hood to keep your head warm. Balaclavas are neck-and-head hoods, most with adjustable drawstrings that allow a snug fit around the face on really cold days. They also keep your neck warm. Most fishermen like a baseball-style cap (you can wear it under a rain parka hood or balaclava). Get one with a dark underbrim, which will absorb light reflected from the water, rather than a light or white underbrim, which will bounce light back into your eyes.

I always seem to get cold around my neck first. For this, consider a neck collar that is like a dickey but without the chest and back flaps. Often these are sold as skiers' headbands. Check that the collar will fit over your head and fit your neck comfortably before buying. Balaclavas can be pulled down as neck protection and are also great for this.

Consider also fingerless gloves. The several styles include those without any finger ends, which allow you to tie knots and adjust flies, or those in a mitten style in which the end of the mitten flips back to expose the bare fingers when you need to tie a knot or adjust tackle.

FISHING VESTS

Fishing vests come in many styles, lengths, colors, and with various pocket quantities and configurations. If you already have a fishing vest for your other fishing needs, it will undoubtedly work fine. Vest requirements for shad fishing are not too demanding. If you are buying a vest

Since shad fishing requires only simple gear, some anglers opt for shoulder packs in place of fishing vests. These over-the-shoulder bags (both sides) and the chest bag (center) are ideal for carrying the flies or lures and accessory equipment needed for shad fishing.

for shad fishing, consider a shorty style, since you'll probably be wearing it outside of your waders. A standard or long vest might get wet if you wade too deep. If fishing in hip boots, either a shorty or standard length is fine, since neither will come close to the tops of your hip boots.

You will need enough pockets for a few items, but not nearly the number of fly boxes normally carried by trout anglers. A large pocket in the back for a spare sweater or raincoat (or to carry one you remove if it becomes too warm in late morning) is very handy. Some vests have special pockets for sunglasses, stream thermometer, hemostats, leader tippet spools, and the like. These are handy, but not mandatory.

Before buying a vest, consider those things that you might carry in it to check for the type, size, and number of pockets. Many are now made with a neck yoke for comfort—an important consideration for the long hours spent standing in one spot while shad fishing. A possible complete list of contents for shad fishing with both fly and spinning gear, though you won't want or need all of this, might include the following:

- Several fly boxes for standard and weighted shad flies.
- Several boxes of darts and spoons, along with a few sinkers.
- Box or boxes of split shot.
- Packet of twist-on lead wire.
- Leaders.
- Leader spools and leader tippet spools.
- Mini lead heads (for making a sinking-tip line when added to a floating line).
- Stream thermometer.
- Polarizing sunglasses.
- Flashlight.
- Flex Light or cap clip-on light for tying on flies and lures.
- Rain jacket.
- Fingerless gloves.
- Spare reel spool, filled with line (spinning or fly).
- Spare reel (needed more for fly fishing where different sink-rate lines are required).
- Hemostats, Ketchum Release, or other dehookers, for removing hooks from shad.
- Hook hone.
- Magnifiers (to fit over glasses for tying on flies).
- Camera (small point-and-shoot, stored in a waterproof zipper-lock bag or small waterproof box such as those by Otter).
- Fishing pliers.
- Fishing knife.
- Snacks and water bottle.

LURE BOXES

You'll need some way to carry your darts and spoons. The best are those with separate compartments by which lures can be separated by type, size, and color. The large flat boxes with multiple compartments or dividers for making compartments are ideal for boat fishing. For shore and wade fishing, pick smaller boxes that will fit into your vest pockets. Alternatives are boxes with foam strips into which hooks can be fixed, or bag systems that have zippered or zipper-lock closures on tough, individual plastic pockets that keep lures separate. If fishing from a boat, the larger, single-side satchel boxes or the similarly large lure boxes with lots of compartments are ideal for separating out colors, sizes, and styles of darts, spoons, other lures, and sinkers. If you need a waterproof lure box, both Otter Box and Mangrove make several lure boxes with either ripple foam or divided compartments.

FLY BOXES

Fly boxes and wallets come in many sizes, but most fall into one of the following categories:

- Individual compartment boxes (like the DeWitt).
- Those with clips or a spring sleeve to hold fly hooks (like the Perrine).
- Wallets in which the flies are hooked into a lamb's wool patch.
- Boxes with foam ridges or bars in which to hook flies.
- Boxes with slots or plastic buttons to hold the bend or point of a fly.
- Boxes with microslit foam, the flies fitting in the slits with the foam, grabbing and holding the hook by the bend. The only company with this system is C & F Design. Some of these are waterproof.

Everyone has a preference, but I don't like those with the foam bars or ripple foam in which to hold flies. Once a hole in the foam is made, it gets larger in time and the flies fall out. This new idea takes an old problem—one of fly storage—and makes it worse. Those by C & F Design that have slits in the foam to hold the fly by the bend or hook point are exceptions to this. They work well.

The lamb's wool patches work fine, but if you put wet flies back into the wallet, they can rust hooks—not only the wet flies, but also others in the same wallet. I like the Perrine boxes that have clips or a spring bar for holding hooks, although the spring bar can dull or even break hooks, if you're not careful. I also like the DeWitt lightweight plastic compartment boxes, and other lightweight brands like them, since these allow separating flies by color, style, or size for easy access while fishing. The boxes with the plastic buttons or molded slots to hold flies by the bend and point are OK, although those with preformed slots do limit the fly selection to the number of slots available in each box. Those with the buttons are more flexible. Consider the Otter Box for a waterproof box for flies.

Regardless of the type of fly box used, *don't* put wet flies back into the box, for the rust reasons mentioned above. The best solution here is to carry a small separate plastic box into which you place wet shad flies once they have been in the water. You can use any size or style of box, since you are just throwing them in there—not arranging or storing them. One easy solution is to punch some holes or windows into the side of a plastic 35-millimeter film can, line it with plastic window screen, and attach the can and lid to a lanyard that is attached to your vest. Then place the flies in this can, where the open mesh windows will allow the flies to dry out. As an alternative, use a zipper-lock bag. Then, when you get home, empty this box or bag as one of the *must dos* (along with cleaning your rod and backing the drag off of the reel), rinse the flies if necessary, and allow to air dry completely before returning them to their rightful storage fly box.

Similarly, if you fall in or if a fly-box pocket of your vest dips beneath the waves, be sure to open up this box, empty the contents, and allow the flies to air dry completely before refilling and closing the box for the next trip. Failure to do this can result in dozens of rusted, ruined shad flies. I know, since I've been there and done that!

LEADER SPOOLS

Some vests have special pockets for leader tippet spools. This makes it easy to use and to pull out any size of mono you might need for rebuilding a leader. In any case, carry spools that you think you might need for making any leader repairs on the water. You will need various tippet sizes, likely 4-, 6-, 8-, and 10-pound-test, depending on conditions and the species you seek. If you think you'll need heavier pound-tests for rebuilding a taper, carry spools of those sizes also. I usually carry small spools of 12-, 15-, 20-, and 25-pound-test to tie into the basic butt section of 30- or 40-pound-test that is loop-connected to the line.

SPARE REEL SPOOLS OR SPARE REELS

If you are not sure if you will be fishing the shallows for spawning shad or fishing deep pools for shad running upstream, it helps to carry a second reel or spare spool for the reel you are using. This is more important for fly fishermen, for the variety of lines necessary to get deep, than for spin fishermen, who only need to add weight. Most often, you might plan on fishing deep with a sinking or sinking-tip line, but find that some of the fish are frisky and just under the surface or moving into the shallows to begin spawning. This occurs more often late in the season and in upriver locations where the shad typically spawn.

Carrying a spare fly reel, or spare spool, for alternate conditions is just good sense, and it's smart to have it in your vest so that you can change on the water without going back to the car, losing time and possibly a good shad-fishing position.

Similarly, spinning anglers should carry a spare spool or two filled with the correct pound-test of line. Spinning reel spools are easy to switch by either popping them off or removing the drag knob (front drags) and changing spools. If you are wading as you do this, just be sure to not drop the drag knob in the water!

LEAD: MINI LEAD TIPS, SPLIT SHOT, WRAP-ON WIRE

Lead, if not in the fly or lure, is a way of getting down deep to the shad on big rivers. I'll use the term "lead" here, but as more and more agencies are becoming concerned about the toxic environmental effects of lead and banning its use in some areas, you might need to use one of the nontoxic substitutes being developed by the tackle industry. In any case, you can use weight in several ways, and each has its pros and cons.

The mini lead heads are 2- to 5-foot lengths of lead-core line, with a loop in each end. You can buy them or make them as described in chapter 3. They are ideal when loop-interconnected between the fly line and leader or in the middle of a leader. As such, they are easier to cast than split shot or other kinds of weight and yet still help get and keep a fly deep without affecting the action or swing of the fly, such as might occur with heavy weight tied into the fly.

Split shot can be used in one large shot or several smaller shot spaced along the leader or leader tippet. Spacing the shot is best for casting, but a single larger shot, about 12 to 18 inches above the fly, will work best to get the fly down. Split shot is also the ideal way to add a little weight to a spinning dart or spoon rig, using one or more split shot on the line about 18 inches above the terminal tied lure. Often larger split shot are best to add sufficient weight to be a real aid in casting or sinking the lure.

Lead twist wire is least effective, since it is thin and does not have much weight. Even if several are used, it usually does not have the desired sinking effect required for shad fishing.

SINKERS

Depending on your method of fishing lures, you may or may not need sinkers. For casting darts from shore, while wading, or from a boat, sinkers are generally not necessary. Where they are necessary, such as fishing

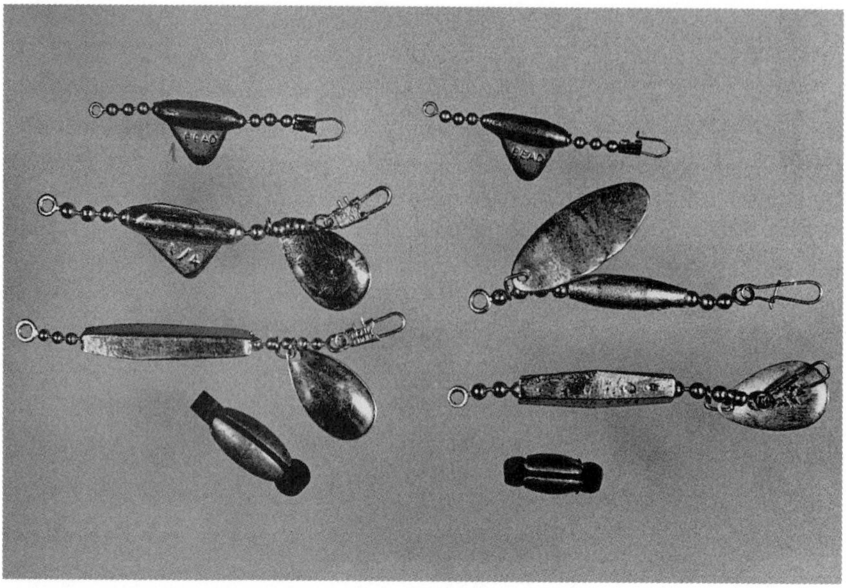

Various types of sinking rigs, including keel sinkers (top row and middle left), to sink shad darts and spoons in fast current when slow trolling.

the Columbia on the West Coast, upstream and cross-stream casts with a drifting line require less sinker weight than when fishing from an anchored boat. Here, 1- to 3-ounce sinkers are usually fine, casting and allowing the sinker to bounce along the bottom as the line drifts, taking the lure deep. Typical rigs include a sinker on the line (egg, rubber core, pinch-on); a dipsy, bell, or bank sinker attached to the snap of a snap swivel, with the line and leader attached to the swivel eyes; or a sliding sinker rig in which a snap swivel is placed on the line above a swivel between the line and short leader. If casting spoons, you will want sinkers ahead of the spoon for casting weight.

If fishing from an anchored boat and drifting lures downriver, sinkers are often necessary to get the lure—even shad darts—down to the shad. You can use egg sinkers on the line above a barrel swivel (almost like a bass-fishing Carolina rig), with the spoon or dart at the end of the line. You can also use the easy on-off rubber-core type or pinch-on sinkers. Another possible rig involves a three-way swivel with the line tied to one eye, the leader ending in the lure tied to the second, and a short dropper or leader tied to a sinker fastened to the third eye. It's easy this way to make your own rigs, even adding a second three-way swivel up the line to add a second lure on a leader, almost like a two-hook bait bottom rig. Using such rigs, it's possible to add any amount of lead. For fishing the fast waters of Columbia below Bonneville Dam or even farther downriver, up to 8 ounces of sinker are used to hold bottom and get the lures deep. Use basic ball or bank sinkers for this fishing.

For trolling, consider a regular torpedo sinker, crescent sinker, or bead-chain keel sinker. If using spoons, which might twist the line, use a crescent, banana-shaped, or keel sinker to prevent line twist. If fishing a tandem rig with a spoon and dart, place the spoon on the point or tail end of the line, since spoons will often tangle as they twist and wobble if placed up the line on a dropper.

STRIPPING BASKETS

Stripping baskets are plastic or framed, mesh-bag baskets that fit by straps to the waist to hold the fly line as it is stripped in. As such, they prevent line from falling in the water, where surface tension would make it difficult to shoot the line on the next cast. Originally they were made to fit in front, until some innovative soul figured out that you strip to the side (left side for right-handed casters), which is a better location for it. You can make your own from a small, open-weave plastic laundry basket or a plastic dishpan with holes cut into the bottom to drain water. Some companies make knobs or pins that can be fastened into the bottom of a homemade basket to keep the line from tangling. In addition, special line-holding hooks that fit onto the belt are sold as a simple substitute for the stripping baskets.

Commercial stripping baskets for boats include the FlyLine Tamer (several other companies sell similar products), which resembles a tall, narrow, 36-by-12-inch trash can that sits on a boat deck and into which the angler strips line to keep it from tangling with other tackle. A homemade equivalent is a tall, plastic mesh laundry bin weighted with a little concrete, the concrete covered with outdoor artificial turf.

THERMOMETERS

Stream thermometers determine water temperature, which in turn helps you determine what the shad might be doing during their spawning run. A stream thermometer is like an oral thermometer, with a cap on one end and a protective sheath for carrying in your vest.

A better idea might be one that Capt. Norm Bartlett uses to check temperatures when he's fishing for shad or anything else. He uses a battery-operated electronic indoor-outdoor thermometer that, with a small switch, will measure both air and water temperatures (the latter with a small probe on a long wire) and will show degrees in both Fahrenheit and Celsius. You can carry the dial in your vest pocket or pin it to your vest, let the wire probe hang in the water, and switch back and forth to measure both air and water temperatures. The big digital dial makes it a lot easier to read than the glass thermometers, and most of these are illuminated for low light levels. Try Radio Shack or similar electronic stores for these. Some boats and depth-finder riggings include a surface temperature reading, which is another simple way to check on shad conditions.

POLARIZING SUNGLASSES

You should have polarizing sunglasses for shad fishing. Though you may or may not be able to see shad in the water, it's good to have that option. Best are polarizing glasses with side shields to cut out glare and reflection from the side. While each angler may have personal preferences as to the lens color, most experts agree that for early-season river conditions, the lighter colors, such as yellow or amber, usually provide the best visibility of fish in the water. These light-colored lenses not only give maximum contrast to spot fish against the bottom, but also provide maximum light transmission. For example, Hobie, a maker of premium polarizing glasses, rates light transmission of its lenses as follows: gray, 12 percent; copper, 17 percent; and yellow Sightmaster, 25 percent. Action Optics rates the transmission of its lens colors as follows: brown, 12 percent; gray, 12 percent; copper, 13 percent; and yellow, 32 percent. The company also makes photochromic polarizing lenses that change in shade with light levels. These have variable light transmission; the photochromic amber lens, for example, ranges from 23 to 38 percent. All the polarizing glasses from Costa del Mar have 15 percent light transmission, with the exception of the Sunrise lens, which has 29 percent. This is the best choice for sunrise or sunset shad fishing.

With the glasses of most companies, for eye protection on a bright day, gray is best and copper second. If you'll be shad fishing during bright midday conditions as well as at dawn and dusk, carry two pair of sunglasses with different-colored lenses for the different light conditions.

In very low-light situations you'll want to remove your sunglasses. Having a lanyard for them to hang around your neck allows you to keep them at hand for when you do need them, or for a quick look beneath the water.

The angle of the sun affects how and what you see and how you are able to peer through the glare of the water. One way to test for the best view is to angle your head left and right to see if this makes a difference in underwater visibility.

LIGHTS

Often shad fishing is best at low light levels. This means fishing not only on overcast cloudy days, but also the periods from before dawn to just after sunup in the morning, and from late afternoon until well after dark. For safe wading and fishing, this requires a flashlight. I recommend two: a bright one for finding your way safely into or out of the river, and a small, low-beam, clip-on style for tying on flies, checking hook points, unhooking fish, and so on.

A small, two-cell (AA or C), waterproof flashlight will give you maximum visibility while walking the bank, wading, getting into and out of a boat, unloading tackle, and reloading tackle at the end of the trip. There are many popular brands in either aluminum or high-impact plastic and sealed with an O-ring to keep them watertight. Get one in a bright color so that you can find it if you drop it under low-light conditions. Popular brands include MagLight and Pelican. For light when tying flies, there are smaller flashlight options. For any of these consider also the possibility of a red lens or light that will prevent night blindness and yet will provide sufficient light for tying flies.

Headlamps are also good. These fit over your cap and on your head so that your hands are free. This is particularly good if you're carrying a wading staff in one hand and a fly rod in the other.

Flex-Lite is the big name in the pocket-carried flexible neck lights used by fly fishermen. While widely known to fly fishermen, they, or a similar light, are equally important for spin anglers for tying on a new shad dart after a breakoff or when changing colors when it's otherwise too dark to see. These are not really bright enough for lighting your way in the dark, but they are ideal for tying on flies, tying darts, unhooking fish, adding or removing split shot, and making up sinker rigs. They take two AA batteries and fit into a pocket with a clip to secure them, just like a pen or pencil. The flexible neck allows you to position the light in any direction.

Other possibilities are clip-on lights, which hold a small, one-cell waterproof flashlight. Some mount on the center brim of a cap, others to the side. All are small and practically weightless.

DEHOOKERS

Dehookers help you unhook shad that you want to release without the necessity of handling or picking up the fish. Releasing shad in the water not only is quicker, but it's also better for the fish, since you are not handling them. Several dehooker tools are available, as follows:

- Ketchum Release. This tool, by Waterworks, consists of a short length of open-side tubing molded into a long-angled handle. To

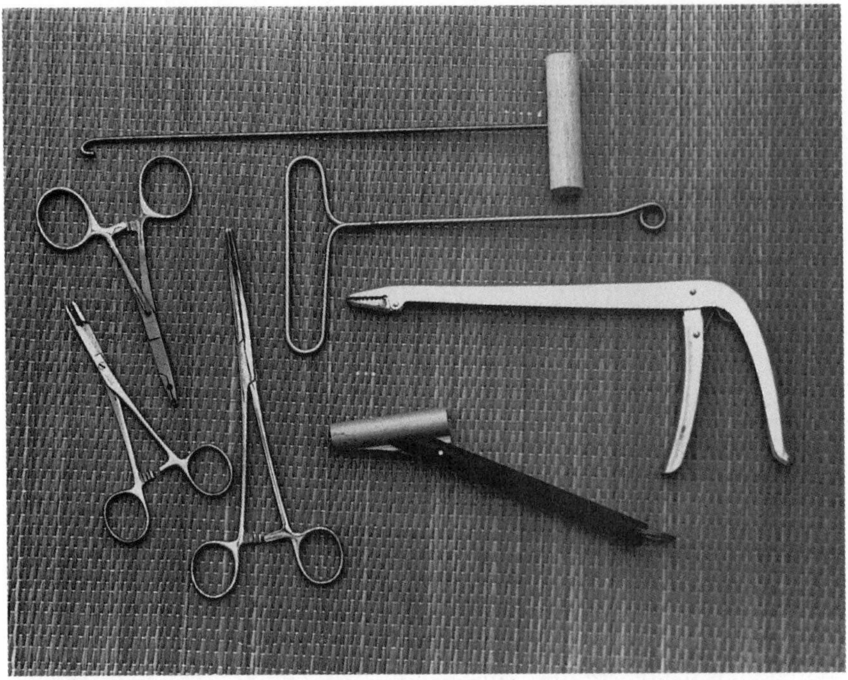

Hemostats (far left—three models) are ideal for removing hooks from shad. Other hook removers include simple wire devices (top two), the Baker Hook-out and the Ketchem Release (lower right), for fly fishing.

use, you hold the handle, slip the open tube over the leader, and slide it down over the fly. Push against the hook bend to back out the hook, and release the fish. Overall fly size will determine the usefulness of these tools. Several sizes are available. The best for shad fishing is the "big bug" model, designed for flies approximately size 10 and larger. A saltwater model is available with end tubes of 5⁄16, 1⁄2, and 3⁄4 inch diameter that are all interchangeable on 6-, 10-, and 36-inch shaft handles. For these, pick the 6- or 10-inch handle for wade fishing or the 36-inch handle for boat fishing. If you choose one large enough to fit over a dart, these are also ideal for spinning anglers to remove darts.

- Baker Hookout. These plierlike, right-angled tools come in two lengths and in plated and stainless steel models. Gripping the plierlike handle closes jaws by which you can grab the fly or lure and release it. Just be careful that the jaws do not damage the fly body. These same jaws can also damage the painted finish on a dart, but will not appreciably hurt a spoon.

- Hemostats. These fly-fishing versions of surgical tools work like straight pliers but have finger-hole scissor handles and lock in a closed position once the fly is gripped.
- Hook disgorger. These are simple molded plastic or metal sticks with a V notch at one end. Position the V notch against the hook bend, give a quick push, and the hook will usually back out. This may require holding the fish to prevent it from backing up with the fly.

NET

If you release all your shad, you won't need a net. If you plan to and are legally allowed to keep shad, then a net comes in handy. For wading, use a short-handled net sufficient to hold a fish that might reach in excess of 24 inches. Many models are available, either with wood or aluminum handles and with mesh, knotted, or rubberized bags. The simplest way to carry them is with some sort of snap that allows fastening them to the back of the fishing vest. I like a French snap on the net for hooking into a vest D-ring. French snaps open in the middle for quick release without looking. Several other similar quick-release snap systems are also available. I am also experimenting with, and like so far, the zinger-style Gear Keepers by Hammerhead. These are like zingers on steroids, and they come in several pull strengths and with different fastening rigs. One with a snap on each end can be snapped into the D-ring on the back of your vest, with the other end snapped into the net handle. To use it, reach in back of you to swing the net and lanyard cord over your shoulder to land the fish.

If fishing from a boat, you will want a long-handled net. Sometimes shad don't want to swim upstream or resist coming to the boat, and a long-handled net makes it possible to reach out safely and still land the fish. Get a net with a 30-inch ring size and as long a handle as you can store easily on your boat.

FISHING LOG

A fishing log is a personal thing. Some people like them and record everything about their fishing trips; others could not be less interested. Many are sold; probably few are used properly. If you do use one, or make up your own, important information to include is the date, place fished, times fished, times when fish are caught, success ratios in different parts of the river, light conditions (light level, overcast or sunny), rain or other weather conditions, water flow, water turbidity, air temperature, water temperature, any noted presence of shad, fly colors or patterns used, dart colors and sizes used, success on each fly dart pattern and color, and overall catch success. You may also want to include any observations, names of fishing friends on the trip, personal experiences, or other thoughts.

If kept religiously, logs or records can be handy. Some years ago (before my first book on shad fishing), I fished with Wahob Edwards, who began keeping records in 1953 on his shad fishing in the Tar River near Rocky Mount, North Carolina. He was a retired accountant when I met him, and such record keeping was natural for him. While his records showed nothing remarkable about the fishing, they did provide him with a seasonal input into shad fishing in his area. For example, by charting the season, he pretty well established the timing of the shad run and its length in the Tar River. With this information, he knew when he was likely to catch his first shad of the season and when the fishing was about over. By keeping records of the numbers of fish caught each month, he narrowed down the best times to April or May. But if he wanted a high percentage of roe fish, his records showed June as the best month to fish. Any angler could do the same thing, making such records as complete or basic as desired.

BOAT ACCESSORIES

Anchors

It's important to know your river and to have the basic equipment. This includes not only the required safety equipment, as mandated by the Coast Guard or state or local agencies, but also equipment necessary for your fishing. You will need a boat capable of safely navigating the river. In some rivers this might be a 14-foot johnboat, while in others you might need a 16-foot V-bottom aluminum. On the Columbia River, Lenox Dick, author of *Experience the World of Shad Fishing,* says an 18- or 20-foot boat is the smallest that can be used safely on the 6-mile stretch below Bonneville Dam on the Columbia. And even then, a special modified anchoring system is required. Local West Coast companies make special wide fluke anchors capable of holding bottom. To avoid wearing out arms or backs, most anglers use a crank or motorized anchor retrieval system to raise the anchor. In addition, you must have enough anchor rope. As a general rule, an anchor rode—the amount of line required based on depth ratio—is about 7:1 to 10:1. Thus if you are anchoring in 10 feet of water, you should have 70 to 100 feet of rope; in 20-foot depths, 140 to 200 feet; and so on.

Anchoring in midriver is a favorite way to fish for shad. On some slow rivers, you might be fine with less rope or anchor rode using a standard mushroom, Danforth-style or navy-style anchor. But check first and know your river, your boat, and your boating capability.

Downriggers and Depth Finders

Downrigger fishing to put lures deep using depth finders to help locate shad is practiced on both the East and West Coasts. To the best of my knowledge, downrigger fishing for shad on the East Coast was originated and developed in about 1990 by two Pennsylvania fishing buddies, Ron Bauer of Bethlehem and Gary Conner of Horsham. Gary Conner bought some new flutter spoons made and sold by Dave's Sport Shop in Doylestown, Pennsylvania. They first tried them at Dingman's Ferry, but not by fishing with downriggers. They found them to be more effective than the traditional shad darts or other spoons and continued using them.

The next year they fished again at Dingman's Ferry. Ron had by then bought a downrigger, attached it to his boat, and tried it on a whim. It was a downrigger left over from some fishing they had done on Lake Erie, when Ron lived farther west in Pennsylvania. "That's the first time I had seen a downrigger used on the river for shad," Ron told me about five years after that first trip for shad. "I also had my locator [fish finder] with me." The results were phenomenal, using the combination of the Humminbird LCD depth finder to locate the depth of the shad run and the downrigger weight and downrigger clips to hold the fishing line in order to place the flutter spoons right at that depth. The result was that they caught a lot more fish than traditional-fishing anglers, sometimes catching shad when others caught nothing. Using this system, the two have had eighty-shad days during a time when this is just not considered possible by most anglers.

If you are interested in trying this system for fishing flutter spoons, but want to use it only occasionally or don't wish to make a major investment in equipment, there are some simple substitutes. One simple way to do this is to use a heavy, short boat rod and reel, and spool the reel with heavy line—wire cable or 200-pound-test mono. If you can't get mono this heavy locally, try a saltwater catalog or buy some heavy weed-cutter line. You won't need much of this line, so capacity is not a concern. Tie the line, being careful with the knots, to a heavy downrigger weight or substitute molded lead weight. You can make weights by pouring molten lead into empty food cans of different sizes and adding a bolt fixed with a nut for a line tie. Do this outside, following all lead-handling safety precautions and with the can in a bucket of sand, as the hot lead will sometimes melt the solder holding the can together. Then use standard outrigger or downrigger clips to hold the fishing line, or a loop of separate line through which the fishing line runs. Setting of these clips is important; too strong a setting may break the line or pull the lure out of the shad's mouth, and too light a setting might pull free before a shad hits. If you want to save more money, experiment with clips made of spring clothespins, with extra rubber bands on the clothespins for a stronger setting, if desired. Mount the short boat rod in a securely clamped rod holder, and clip the fishing line to the line clips.

Another way to fish flutter spoons or willowleaf spoons and blades is the "dead-sticking" method, as described by Albin J. Sonski, hatchery supervisor of the Connecticut Kensington Fish Hatchery and an avid shad fisherman. In this method, the line is tied to one eye of a three-way swivel, with a 2- to 3-foot leader ending with the willowleaf spoon lure tied to the second swivel eye, and a 1- to 3-foot leader ending with a 2- to 5-ounce bank sinker tied to the third eye. Casting or spinning outfits rigged with 8- to 20-pound-test line are used, fishing from an anchored boat and casting the rig downstream. Lightweight saltwater rods and downrigger rods are favored for this fishing. The sinker hits bottom, holding the fluttering willowleaf spoon above the bottom and in the current where the shad will find it. The sinker weight of 2 to 5 ounces varies based on the river current.

Rod Holders

Rod holders of many styles are available to hold rods when still-fishing from an anchored boat, when trolling, or when just wanting a rest from holding the rod. Some are permanent mounts on boats, but usually these are on larger boats only. Many clamp-on styles are available. Check for the best type for your fishing. You want one that will securely hold your tackle (casting or spinning style), yet will allow easy and quick release for striking and fighting the fish. For best results, clamp one or more on each side, positioning them to place the lures as far apart as possible.

If using two rod holders, clamp them on the transom or rear gunwale area, 180 degrees apart to position the rods far apart. If using four rods and rod holders, position two on the transom facing rearward but at a slight outward angle, and two farther forward straight out from the boat at right angles to the boat axis.

CHAPTER 8

Basic Shad-Fishing Techniques

STANDARD SHAD FISHING

The standard method of shad fishing is to cast across and slightly downstream, allowing the fly or lure to drift with the current in an arc until it ends up directly below you. Then retrieve slowly in short jerks and lifts, allowing the fly or lure to swing up and then sink back down. Often this technique is enough to entice a strike. Shad will frequently hit just as the fly or lure ends the swing in the current, and just before you begin retrieving the fly or lure.

Often it is possible to feel the fly or lure (easier with a lure) as it swings through the drift arc. Hold the rod up and at a high angle to do this. This will keep the current from bellying the line and gives you more direct contact with the lure when the shad hits. If the fly or lure is deep, this may also allow you to feel it tick along the bottom as it hits rocks. If the fly or lure tends to ride up when pulled by the bellying line, give a brief upward lift of the rod to create some slack line, then drop the rod to allow the fly or lure to sink again. Do this several times throughout a cast or swing if necessary, to help the lure or fly get deep to the shad.

DEEP FISHING

For even deeper fishing, cast the lure upstream. You can cast almost directly upstream or at a 45-degree angle. Either way, this gives the lure more time to sink in the water column before coming against the resistance of the line and swinging around downstream and planing up from the current. To feel any hits, it's vital to maintain contact with the lure by reeling just enough line to prevent slack from developing. Do this by timing and matching the speed of the current as the lure bounces along the bottom.

CAST LENGTH AND CASTING ANGLE

You can control just how deep the lure sinks and swims by the length of the cast and the casting angle. Of course, it will also depend upon the river depth and the current speed. With a long cast, the lure will have more time to sink in the current and get down to the shad. Also, the greater the upstream angle of the cast, the more slack there will be in the line, again allowing the lure to sink deeply.

Another strategy can be used alone or with any of the above tricks. This is to make a cast and then leave the bail of the spinning reel open while the lure sinks in the current. Leave the bail open for only a few seconds or so. This is most often used in across-stream casts to give the line slack and to allow the lure to sink. But it can also be used with either the long cast or the upstream angle cast as well. And by counting off while the bail is open, you can experiment with different fishing depths and make identical repeat casts once shad are hooked with a certain casting technique. You can also count the number of line coils coming off of the reel for each drift or cast to time the "open bail time."

Because it's usually necessary to get your lure far out into the river, the best cast to make from the shore is across or slightly upstream, sometimes coupled with the open bail technique to allow the lure to sink. Too sharp an upstream angle may bring the lure down in front of you. Usually this is futile, unless fishing a fast river system with a deep channel next to the bank.

OTHER SPECIAL RETRIEVES

The standard drift-and-swing method of fishing with the upstream straight retrieve does not always work. Other possible retrieves for both spinning and fly fishing include the following:

- Dry-fly fishing. This is not so much a fly-rod retrieve as it is creating a drag-free drift of the dry fly so that the shad will take it. In this sense, dry-fly fishing for upriver shad late in the season, when they are surfacing and taking dry flies, is just like trout fishing. The secret here is to use a longer-than-normal tippet, and to make a fly-rod cast with lazy S's in the line that will wash out before the bellying line starts to drag the fly or put it down. It also helps to make a slightly upstream cast to allow some slack in the line and to prevent premature line bellying. Use a high-rod, high-line technique to further reduce the possibility of line drag and to get the maximum float from the dry fly through the current. At the end of the drift, or when the fly starts to drag, lift the line from the water to make a backcast, change direction on the next false cast, and get the fly out again to the same drift or a new drift.

- Nymph fishing. Nymph fishing with the fly rod is little different from dry-fly fishing. Most of it involves fishing subsurface nymphs for shad that are surface feeding or cruising and taking surface insects late in the season. For this, make the same slight upstream or cross-stream cast used for dry-fly fishing. Throw some lazy S's into the line to prevent early line bellying, and use the high-rod, high-line technique described above until the nymph starts to drag, then repeat the cast.
- Deep nymph retrieves. Deeper nymph fishing is accomplished the same way, but using a weighted nymph to get down in deep pools or to deep shad. Because of the strong currents often found in shad rivers, this is best from a boat or using as short a line as possible to prevent the fly line from being caught by other currents and causing the nymph to make an unnatural drift.
- Fast retrieves. Fast, straight-in retrieves are possible with spinning, casting, and fly tackle. With spinning and casting tackle, they are easy, since this involves nothing more than a straight cranking retrieve. With a fly rod, this becomes more difficult. Since the rod is held with one hand and the other used for line retrieve, the natural tendency of the fly is to move in a jerky, twitchy motion. To achieve a straight retrieve, grip the rod under one arm and use both hands—hand over hand—to retrieve the fly line as smoothly and evenly as possible. When a shad hits, loosely grab the line to let the line slide after the strike, as the fish starts to make its first run. At the same time, grab the rod with the other hand (rod hand) to raise the rod, get a high angle and shock absorbency into the outfit, and begin to fight the shad normally.
- Twitching, jerky retrieves. Twitching, jerky retrieves are typical for shad fishing if not using the drift technique, but they are accomplished in completely different ways based on the tackle used. If using a casting, spincast, or spinning outfit, alternate a twitch of the rod with each turn of the reel handle. Hold the rod low and pointed toward the line and lure when doing this. Often this will make the lure twitch every 18 inches or so on the retrieve, enough to attract any shad in the neighborhood. Once a shad hits, it's easy to strike, raising the rod high to fight the fish. With a fly rod, hold the rod low and with the tip pointed toward the line. Keep the rod and rod tip steady. With the line hand, make strips to retrieve the

fly. Realize that each strip of the line will cause the fly to move, alternating with a pause as you move your line hand forward to make the next strip. These strips can be short or long, depending on how much line you pull in with your line hand between each pause. The pauses can be short or long in duration, depending on the length of time between strips of the fly. With fly gear or spinning, spincast, or casting gear, it's possible to vary this to make erratic jerky retrieves or to keep the retrieve regular and steady with even strips and pauses.

- Downstream line mending. This is a method of whipping the lure or fly back and forth in front of the noses of shad that are holding in a riffle or tail of a pool. Usually it is done after making a cross-stream cast to allow the fly or dart to drift through the pool to the position directly below you, where the shad often hit it. This does not work as well with a spinning outfit as it does with a fly outfit. The heavy lure and light line make it difficult to get the dart to whip or swing back and forth. In contrast, with the thick fly line, light leader, and fly, it's an easy technique.

  Hold the rod straight downstream, and then flip the rod tip to one side of the current. With a fly rod, the current will catch the line and cause it to mend, pushing it downstream and, at the end, causing the fly to whip or swing away from its previous holding position. This is alternated with a flip of the rod to the other side to allow the current to again catch the line, push it downstream, and cause the fly to whip back to the original position. This can be done repeatedly to flip the fly back and forth in front of the shad until one takes, or until you tire of it and decide to try a different color fly or different spot or technique. This same method can be used while shortening or lengthening the line to allow the fly to swing in different parts of the pool or to different members of the same pod of shad. It's not fly fishing in the traditional sense, but it does work when repeatedly used after each cross-stream cast. You should try it at least once or twice at the end of each cast.

SPLASHING SURFACE SHAD

Sometimes shad are splashing on the surface. Depending on where you fish, this is sometimes called "washing" or "breaking." Often this possibility increases as you fish farther upstream in shallower water as the fish ascend the river. Thus it is far more likely at the headwaters of a river than near the mouth. It is also more likely late in the season, while or after the shad are spawning, than with the first early runs. In any case, you don't have to get deep. And if you're fishing for hickory shad, you generally do not have to get as deep as for American shad. In these cases, fishing with a high-rod, high-line technique will work fine for drifting a shad dart. If fishing flies, you can try the high-line technique, but because of the weight and bulk of the line, this will be more difficult. A long rod (9 feet) helps. You still might need a weighted fly, or some split shot or other weight on the leader, to keep the fly down a few inches or more rather than just skimming across the surface.

MULTIPLE-LURE RIGS

The size, type, and number of lures (as with tandem rigs) that are fished will also determine how deep the lures get and how they are presented to the shad. Most casting anglers like to fish a single lure—usually a small dart or heavy spoon—tied directly to the end of the line. But tandem rigs can be used when casting as well as trolling, provided that the lures are close together—usually no more than about 18 inches to 2 feet apart.

The two-lure rig is a little harder to cast, but it will get deeper than a single lure. You can't use the sharp back-and-forward "snap" cast that works so well with a single lure. A better technique when casting tandem rigs and lures is to use a "bait-style" cast, in which you bring the rod over the shoulder, stop or pause, and then smoothly cast the rod forward, releasing the line as usual. This cast keeps the lures from snapping off the line, minimizes casting dangers, and keeps the lures from tangling.

It's also possible to add weight to the outfit to get down by adding a rubber-core, split-shot, or similar in-line sinker. If the heavier sinker is at the end of the line and the lure tied to a short dropper, it will not interfere with the snap cast as much as a separate dropper and two lures of relatively equal weight. Some West Coast anglers use pencil lead, held in place with a short piece of surgical tubing, but this also is a little unwieldy. Nevertheless, tandem rigs are popular everywhere.

There's another reason, besides the additional weight or ability to cast with casting tackle, that some anglers like to use double lures. Two lures in the river are twice as effective as a single lure in presenting a lure to the shad. Tandem rigs also are good when first starting to fish for the day, since they allow you to use two different lures to explore the preferences of the shad. You can use darts of two different colors, sizes, or styles; spoons of two different finishes, types, or sizes; or a dart/spoon, dart/spinner, jig/spoon, spoon/spinner, jig/dart, or similar combination.

At the same time, there's also a chance of losing lures twice as fast, especially if you're fishing close to the bottom, where most of the best American shad fishing is found, or around snaggy structure or bottoms.

It's no wonder that in some areas, vendors travel the riverbanks selling shad darts and spoons to anglers whose losses have exceeded both their expectations and their stock of lures.

Multiple-lure rigs vary in different parts of the country. The most popular is a combination of two darts of different colors, or a dart with a small spoon on a short dropper 18 inches to 2 feet up the line. In Virginia, Huntington Drone spoons and Nungesser spoons are used with darts, while farther south in North Carolina, the size 1 Reflecto spoon is the choice to use with a dart. Often the spoons of small local companies, or companies that are locally popular, become favorites, even though shad seem to have no brand loyalty.

The Cather rig has been popular on the St. Johns River in Florida, where the late Joe Cather was known as one of the top shad anglers. His rig consists of a small dart with a spoon on a short, 6-inch dropper. When the rigs became commercially available some years ago, two different color choices were offered: a red-and-white dart teamed with a silver spoon, and a red-and-orange dart used with a gold spoon. A popular Susquehanna River rig consists of two darts—one on the end of the line and the other on a short dropper. In some other areas, rigging two spoons is a popular tandem rig.

SPECIAL RIGS

One unusual yet practical method of fishing for hickory shad was developed before the day of spinning tackle to allow the use of baitcasting outfits while fishing for shad at Chincoteague Inlet, Virginia, according to Claude Rogers, former director of the Virginia Sportfishing Tournament. To make this rig, start with 3 feet of stiff 20-pound-test monofilament. Tie two dropper loops, each about 3 inches long and about 7 or more inches apart from each other. Cut one end of each dropper loop close to the knot to make two separate single dropper lines of about 6 inches long. Tie shad darts to the end of each dropper. Since the line is stiff and heavy, the darts are kept away from the main line, preventing the rig from tangling. Tie a snap to the bottom of the rig, at least 7 inches below the bottom dropper knot, and add a Hopkins S-1 hammered spoon. The spoon adds weight for casting and also to lure the small bluefish that are found in the inlet during the same time period. Tie a loop at the other end for easy attachment to the fishing line. The entire rig weighs about ½ ounce, an easy weight for anglers using baitcasting outfits to get the darts out to the fish. It looks somewhat like a bait bottom rig.

This same outfit can be easily modified for spinning and fishing for American shad. Just remove the hammered spoon and substitute a lighter and smaller one or another small shad dart. Keep the same droppers with the two other shad darts. The rig becomes lighter and more manageable to cast with spinning gear and will still get down deep to the American shad. You'll have to use the slow position, pause, and cast method used with bait and described above for tandem rigs.

BAIT RIGS

Where not illegal, you can try fishing with a shad scale tipped onto a bare hook, or by chumming with shad scales scaled off into the current. Fish the shad scale just as you would a dart, spoon, or fly, using weight on the line to get the scale down to the shad. Other possible baits could include small minnows, especially for the hickory shad, which are more piscivorous than are the American shad.

SPINCASTING WITH FLIES

Another method with spinning tackle is to cast flies. To do this, tie the fly to the end of the line, and use a spinning bubble or sinker about 18 inches up the line to give the rig enough weight to cast. The spinning bubble is a small, clear plastic ball, fitted with a cork or closure and with eyes on opposite sides for line attachment. To use, fill the bubble with enough water to weight it for your casting. It's best to leave the bubble with a small air pocket so that it floats, while still holding enough water for casting weight. The bubble usually retains enough water for weight. Though this is not fly casting, it is fishing with a fly, but only by using enough additional weight to get the fly to the fishable water. The bubble will keep the fly suspended, just like a worm below a float, whereas using a sinker will get the fly deep, but with the added danger of snagging and losing the rig. Shorebound anglers on the American River in California have for years used spinning tackle successfully this way, floating a spinning bubble tied 2 to 3 feet above the shad fly.

A third alternative is to use the Statech Spinfly lines with spinning gear. These are essentially short (several feet), very thick fly lines that are used by feeding the line out from the rod tip and then making a slow, lobbing cast with spinning gear to throw the short, thick line and fly. In use, the short line is rigged with a short leader and fly tied to the end. To cast, pay out line past the tip of the rod, then make a long, sweeping cast, releasing the rig on the forward cast, just like fishing a bait rig or fly fishing with only one back-and-forth false cast. They are available in both floating and sinking models.

Some Washington and California shad anglers use a fly in place of shad lures with their spinning gear. To do this, they place split shot on the line about 1½ to 2 feet above the fly that is tied to the end of the line. Weight is kept to a minimum—just enough to permit a cast with the fly. Fly patterns for spinning anglers are the same as those used by fly anglers.

Spin fishermen usually use weighted darts or jigs, or a spoon with an in-line sinker, to get down. Fly fishermen don't have this luxury, although weighted flies help somewhat. There are also other methods of sinking a fly, as discussed in chapter 4. Sinking or sinking-tip lines are a must to get down in big rivers. With a sinking line or a spinning outfit, it is also possible to get even deeper by casting upstream, allowing some slack line and more time for the lure or fly to sink by the time the line starts to make an arc and swing in the current.

SHAD-FISHING QUESTIONS—AND SOME POSSIBLE ANSWERS

When the shad are thick in the streams and rivers, there are times when it seems that almost any lure, fished at any depth in any way, on any cast, and at any river position, will take fish. But there are other times when it seems that nothing will take shad, regardless of what is used, when, where, or how it is fished, or who fishes it, in any type of water or any part of the river.

One day on the Susquehanna River in Maryland, I was fishing with a then-new fishing partner who had never been shad fishing before. It was mid-April, early in the season. Dogwood blossomed along the banks, and the lush growth of the wildflowers and plants promised good fishing.

Donning waders and working slowly into the swollen waters of the river, we tied identical shad darts to the 4-pound-test line of the light spinning outfits we were using and began to cast slightly upstream, letting the lures swing down through the current on a snug line, waiting for a few minutes at the end of the swing before starting the retrieve and readying another cast.

Unfortunately, the fishing that day didn't materialize as it should have. Though I hooked and released some fish, my buddy wasn't having any luck. "Try that spot there," I suggested, pointing to a small eddy in the main current close to the bank.

It was a spot typical of those where shad hang out while resting from the efforts of fighting the main current in their trip to the spawning grounds. It was an easy cast and retrieve close to the shore, and any shad would be holding close, with the likelihood of a hit just as the lure started straight upstream.

I watched his first several casts, then resumed fishing. Soon I felt a jolt and saw the leap of a well-hooked shad.

"There's something wrong! How come you can catch fish and I can't?" my buddy yelled upriver. After releasing the protesting buck shad, I hooked the shad dart in the keeper ring of the rod, waded out of the water, and wandered the few dozen yards to his shoreline casting position.

"Let me try . . . " I cast the lure out into the current and watched the line swing in the current and come to rest straight downstream. It hung in the current for a few minutes until I began a slow, slightly jerky retrieve. The sudden hit of a shad on my line did little to bolster my buddy's ego. I handed him the rod with the jumping bucking shad and had the fun of watching him battle and land his first shad.

The sixth sense for hooking shad—or any fish—is hard to describe and harder for the beginner to realize, but it is there, and all experienced shad anglers have it. If I had not experienced it myself, I would not believe it, but most experienced anglers claim that they can almost sense the hit of a shad before it happens. I think that sometimes this is a result of the shad bumping the lure or fly before the fish finally takes it with a hard hit.

Fortunately, shad are often more predictable as to their preference for lures and their performance, and they don't always offer that much trouble for a beginner. But even some of the so-called well-established habits of shad are not always consistent on any river and sometimes vary widely from river to river.

LIGHT SENSITIVITY AND FISHING TIMES

One of the main characteristics of shad is their well-known and apparent sensitivity to light. Hickory shad seem to exhibit this characteristic even more than American shad, and thus, through most of their range, take lures and flies well at morning and evening and slack off in midday, from about 10 A.M. to 4 P.M. Some photos in my files show shad anglers at midday, sitting dejectedly on a rock in midstream, finally admitting defeat after often spectacular early-morning catches and nothing but casting practice the rest of the day. This pattern is so well known that most shad anglers will fish only from the inky black just before dawn to first light, when the shad stop hitting, or in the evening, staking out a fishing position in late afternoon to be in the right location when the shad turn on again in early evening.

The shad still run in midday, they just don't hit—or hit as well. This "fact" is well established on the Susquehanna River in Maryland, yet a few miles south, on the Rappahannock River at Fredericksburg, Virginia, some anglers think that the reverse is true. There, anglers often skip the morning fishing to fish throughout the day—often with excellent success—and then into the evening.

Landing a hickory shad on a fly rod.

The fact that American shad do not seem to exhibit the same light sensitivity may be due to the fact that they run deeper in rivers than hickory shad. Also, hickory shad seem to exhibit a sensitivity to light more in the small streams that are shallower and as a result have more light penetration. These same small streams are seldom frequented by American shad. American shad fishing stays better throughout the day than does hickory shad fishing.

Even so, morning and evening still rate as top times with experienced shad anglers. Most anglers on California streams and rivers rate the evening hours best, morning next, and the rest of the day third.

In North Carolina, many American shad anglers in the Tar River area fish only the morning hours, feeling that this is their best time, and use the rest of the day and evening for other fishing or chores.

LOCATING THE FISH

For the shorebound or wading angler, one of the most important factors in shad fishing is casting location; for the troller or anchored boat angler, it's the depth of retrieve or lure. Most fish are not found uniformly distributed in any water, and shad are no exception. Finding shad in the rivers often means looking for a certain type of water, necessitating reading the water, as does a trout angler. But the shad fisherman looks for different signs.

Even though shad run up the same streams each spring, they do not run all the time. If the temperature drops, they pause or even reverse themselves in estuaries and the mouths of rivers. They run seeking the channel of the river but often are near the bottom, where there is less current to fight, or near a seam of the main current, where they can follow the river flow but not have to fight its full force.

American shad usually run deep in the coastal rivers, requiring deep fishing. "If you aren't losing shad darts, you aren't fishing right," is how one shad angler once described the fishing to me. And he's right—for most shad in most waters. When necessary, shad do go over riffles in shallow water or between pools. These shallow riffles become more frequent as the fish move upstream into shallower and smaller waters and closer to the spawning areas.

One of the real advantages of hickory shad for East Coast anglers, aside from providing some fishing slightly before the main run of American shad, is that they can be taken in smaller streams and tributaries that are seldom, if ever, used by American shad. This opens up a lot more fishing water for light spinning and fly anglers. Hickories stick to about the same pattern as American shad, holding to river channels and channel edges, resting at the head and tails of pools, and fighting their way up through the riffles.

Deep fishing is also required in the deep pools of rivers, where shad congregate—presumably to rest—before pushing upstream. Often the best spots on such stretches are at the head of the pool, just before it goes into another riffle or rapids, or at the tail of a pool, just above a riffle or rapids. At both such spots, the shad move and mill around more, are more likely to see the lure, and are not as deep as they will be in the middle of the pool.

Fishing riffles is more difficult, only because it is more difficult to spot the specific area where the most shad might run upstream. On the Feather River near Oroville, California, there are some long, rifflelike flats, which are ideal for shad, but there is a lot of width to the river here from which to choose a fishing spot. On stretches like this in any river, it takes careful reading of the water to find a run where a shad lure or fly can swing through the current to a spot where the shad are resting or making their upstream push.

Shad also congregate around islands, large boulders, and rocks in rivers. Islands and boulders provide a cushion of quiet water along the tail, head, and both sides. This makes it easy for shad to rest for a while before venturing upstream again and fighting the main current. Such spots where shad are resting are prime locations for a cast, drifted or trolled lure, or fly.

One of the best places to find shad is below a dam blocking their progress. On the Columbia in Washington, Bonneville Dam blocks their progress so that the fish spread out close to the banks, giving the shore angler more of a chance than elsewhere on the river. On almost any river, the shad will congregate at these spots since they can't go any farther and will not reverse their run until they spawn. Even if there is a fish ladder, they are still found in large numbers, since the fish ladders can only take a small portion of the fish at a time. Conowingo Dam on the Susquehanna River in Maryland and Enfield Dam on the Connecticut are popular spots for the same reason. Fortunately, or unfortunately, most rivers have high hydroelectric dams (like the above), low mill dams that are a remnant of an earlier time, or dams built to create a water supply for a neighboring town or city. In many places, there are efforts to remove these dams, which ultimately will be good for shad and shad fishermen by providing more river area for both spawning and fishing.

WATER TEMPERATURES

Knowing the preferred water temperatures for shad is valuable information. A thermometer is just as important to the shad angler as is the depth finder to the bass fisherman and polarizing glasses to the trout fly fisherman (both of which have their use in shad fishing as well).

Research indicates that American shad begin their spawning between 60.8 and 66.2 degrees F (16 to 19 degrees C), while hickory shad prefer temperatures of 53.6 to 71.6 degrees F (12 to 22 degrees C). Since no river is the same as any other, and all fishing spots are at different distances from the mouth of the river, these temperature preferences probably vary slightly from spot to spot and river to river. Carry a thermometer, and use it to establish a pattern on your favorite shad waters.

SHAD MYSTERIES

Despite the many consistencies of shad fishing, there are still many mysteries. One of the most baffling is the tendency of a shad to hit a newly tried fly or lure color on the first few casts, and then completely ignore it after that, only to hit another color immediately when the fly or lure is changed. I've experienced this enough times, as have many other shad fishermen, to convince us that it really happens. We know that shad are milling around all the time, and that they are constantly moving upstream, yet it almost seems as if the shad are talking among themselves and telling everyone not to hit a certain color, since a buddy just got hooked on it!

The first time this happened, I thought I had the whole color problem solved—at least for that morning. I was fishing a small river for hickory shad, using a red-and-white fly that had previously been an excellent pattern. But the shad did not think so that morning. As the sky grew lighter, I changed the fly to a purple pattern. Throwing the fly across the stream as I had done dozens of times with the red-and-white pattern, I held the rod slightly high to allow the fly to swing in an arcing belly and straighten up downstream. Just as it straightened out, a hickory shad hit it and erupted with a spray of water. It was the first of several jumps before I was able to grab the leader and release the fish.

"Aha! I've got the pattern now!" I thought to myself while checking the fly before the next cast. But two dozen casts later, I had nothing to show for my efforts. Then I changed to another fly—yellow wing and green body this time—and immediately (well, the second cast) got a hit and a shad. After a few similar experiences like this, of hits on the first few casts of a fly and then nothing, a pattern began to develop—catch a shad and change the fly. I still have days like this, and while the change-a-fly system works, no one seems to understand it or why it works or why a color that works once will not work again.

Another strange aspect of shad is how they hook themselves—or are hooked, as the case may be. Most flies tied on standard ringed eyes, turned-up eyes, or turned-down eyes will rest point down in still water. But we don't fish in still water. In the roiling rivers and streams, flies drift and swim, turn and twist, tumble and fall, ending up in all sorts of positions when they are hit. Yet in a high percentage of cases, shad are hooked in the center of the lower jaw. This happens even though shad seem to swipe at the fly, when you think that they would be hooked in the side of the jaw, upper jaw, or randomly around the mouth.

The same thing happens with flies tied and fished on jig hooks, and with standard shad darts, which most of the time ride and drift with the point up. The question is, why? Does the shad turn on its side to take the fly or dart, or turn over, or turn the fly in its mouth? It's not an important question, since they are hooked, but it's one more mystery of shad and shad fishing.

CHAPTER 9

Shore- and Boat-Fishing Techniques

While basic fishing techniques allow ways to present flies or lures to shad and shad lies, some added special tactics are helpful to know for boat, shore, and wade fishing. These special tactics don't change or alter the basics, but merely provide different ways to get the fly or lure to the shad in the best possible way, the maximum number of times.

SHORE FISHING

Finding the right spot for shad is even more important for the shore or wading angler than for the boat angler. This is because the right spot from the shore or in a river is necessary for getting the right drift of the fly or lure to the shad as they fight through riffles or hold in pools. With boat fishing, you can lengthen or shorten the anchor rope to adjust upstream-downstream position, or even move sideways to change how the fly or lure drifts into a pool or over the shad. Much of the best shore fishing, both for American and hickory shad, is near the edge of a channel or chute or at the tail of a pool where shad are congregating and often more easily caught. In deep water, American shad will be deep, and such spots are less easily recognized. Most of the better spots are well known to old-time shad anglers, and it's often necessary to get to such spots early to stake a claim to a shoreline location or, if wading, to a spot in the river.

Fly Versus Spin Shore Fishing

Often shad fishermen can end up fishing shoulder-to-shoulder if spinning, perhaps only a few yards from each other if fly-fishing. Fly fishermen are often working a fly almost straight downstream or quartering downstream, whereas spin fishermen are often casting directly across current to allow their darts to drift with the current. Ultimately, their darts end up straight downstream the same as the fly anglers' flies.

Fly fishermen and spinning anglers seldom work well together under such tight conditions, since the spin fishermen is working a heavy lure using monofilament line that sinks, while fly fishermen may be using a sinking, sinking-tip, or floating line. Also, their casting angles and techniques are often different. If the lines are crossed, tangles are almost surely to result.

Below hydroelectric dams are especially popular spots, since the shad must stop there, either permanently or to position themselves for the fish ladder that will allow them to go farther upstream. Such places are often crowded, filled shoulder-to-shoulder with spin-fishing shad anglers. One solution for the fly fisherman, or for the spin fisherman who wants to get away from the crowd, is to get a topographical map of the area you wish to fish, and then spend a little time exploring roads, concentrating on those that cross rivers and streams that are tributaries of known shad rivers or that parallel known shad areas. Barring blockage by a dam, pollution, or insurmountable falls, shad should be in these smaller tributaries also, in addition to the well-known spots. And that goes for every area, East and West Coast alike.

Shore Fly-Fishing Problems

Shore fishing creates some problems for the fly rodder that the spin fisherman does not have to contend with. The backcast of the fly rod requires open space to prevent hanging up in trees or brush. Ideally, a small point of land, jetty, pier, or any man-made structure that extends out into the river will provide an open area in back of you to allow for a standard backcast.

Lacking that, there are some other solutions. One is the roll cast, in which you cast or flip as much line as possible in front of you, then slowly bring the rod slightly past a horizontal position, with the line hanging down in back of the rod. Flip the rod forward, almost like hammering a nail but at a slightly upward angle, to throw the line in the air, rolling out into the water. Done right and repeatedly, this will place the fly far enough out to catch shad without the necessity of the backcast.

Another alternative, if the brush in back of you is low, is to make a steeple cast, in which you throw the backcast high—almost like trying to throw it straight up in the air—then immediately coming through with the forward cast to get the fly out on the water. Timing is critical, but this cast does allow almost normal results, even if the casting style and technique are different. Distance will be less than that possible with a standard cast.

A change-of-direction cast is another possibility. Here you make forward casts and backcasts parallel to the shoreline to avoid tangles, then, at the last minute and on the last forward cast, change the direction of your rod to throw the final forward cast at a right angle to the bank and out over the water. It will not travel at a true right angle, but will get out far enough for a quartering downstream (or upstream) cast and fly presentation to the shad.

A final possibility, should you fish a bank with tall trees and no low backcasting hazards, or to throw under a bridge or tall pier, is to make a low, horizontal backcast under the tree limbs or bridge, then follow with a brisk forward cast to get the fly to the good water.

Shore Spinning Concerns

Spinning anglers seldom have these problems, although overhanging tree limbs, brush around you, and similar obstructions can catch a lure during an overhead cast or side cast. Also, since spinning is often done with anglers shoulder-to-shoulder, you *must* practice proper safety and use caution at all times to prevent hooking a fellow angler, or one changing position and walking in back of you. This usually means an overhead cast to prevent hitting someone to the side of you, and always checking in back of you, where other anglers may be moving into position or moving back and forth along the bank. Crowds are common in shad fishing, but safety must be paramount at all times.

Wading

Wading, whether you are spinning or fly-fishing, requires proper boots and safety techniques. In shallow water, hip boots are fine, but for deeper wading, wear chest-high waders. Since this is early-season fishing, when the streams are often fed with snowmelt from high elevations and the water is cold, use neoprene waders or insulate yourself. (See chapter 7 for details on wading gear.)

Wade sideways to the current, since this will present less of a profile to the water pressure. Be wary of taking a final fishing position on a sandy or gravel bottom. Current will erode the sand or gravel around your feet, placing you ever deeper. If standing in such a spot, move periodically to prevent ending up in a hole. Even while fishing, it helps to stand sideways to the current if possible, especially in a strong flow. Make sure that you have a solid base and are not on slippery or wobbly rocks.

Ed Russell with a hickory shad caught on a fly rod while wading a small stream.

Some rivers, such as the Rappahannock River near Fredericksburg, Virginia, can be very treacherous for wading fishermen. Fishing for shad from a mid-river rock, this angler can see the rough water and rapids.

Wading is often more effective than fishing from shore. Often, though not always, the farther you get out into the water, the better your chances of hooking fish. Wading also separates you from the competitive row of other shad anglers lined up along the bank. Just be careful as you get into increasingly deeper water.

While wading can be very effective and produce better sport, it can also get you into trouble. Chest-high waders can get you into twice as deep water—and at least twice as much trouble—as hip boots. This is true especially in areas below hydroelectric dams, where the fishing is often excellent. Most such areas have both visual and sound warnings when gates are to be opened or more water released. The danger is that some anglers too far downstream might not see or hear the warnings, and other anglers often ignore the warnings, wanting to get in just one or two more casts. *Don't do it!* Get out of the river immediately.

Years ago, fishing below Conowingo Dam on the Susquehanna River, I saw a shad angler wait until too late. The rocky island to which he had waded got smaller and smaller as the water was released from the upstream gates and the river rose higher and higher. He then had a cold swim back to shore, where several other anglers grabbed the exhausted and slightly hypothermic angler. He almost lost his rod and reel, did lose some of his other tackle, and could have lost his life. On any river, in any situation, under any circumstances, delays for one more fish or one more cast are not worth it. Get out as soon as you know water conditions are changing.

When wading, it's also important to make as little noise as possible. A recent study by the University of Maryland has shown that shad can hear high-frequency sounds. The theory is that by hearing these sounds, it may help them to escape their principle ocean predators, dolphins. Shad can hear sounds in the range detected by most fish, that of about 0.2 to 0.8 kHz, and they can also detect higher-frequency sounds in the range of 25 to 180 kHz. Humans hear sounds from the range of about 0.2 to 20 kHz. This suggests that wading anglers should be particularly careful to not make clicking sounds underwater by stumbling over rocks or hitting them, since this could make shad wary and less likely to take lures or even to stay in the area.

BOAT FISHING

The two anglers pulled the boat up to the dock and lifted the stringer from the water. It was as big as the grins on their faces. They said that they had never been shad fishing before but had wanted to try the fishing that attracts a lot of coastal anglers each spring.

Renting a boat and clamping their small outboard to it, they had headed out into the river, tying the newly purchased shad darts and spoons to the end of their lines. Trolling slowly upriver, they maneuvered among the rocks, channels, and islands that peppered the fast water. They were hooked on shad fishing when the first fish hit near the head of an island. Experienced in other facets of the sport, they reasoned rightly that if one shad hit near the island, others must be there also, and so maneuvered their boat back into trolling position. They didn't get a shad on the next troll past the island, but did the following time. Ultimately they learned that shad are found in spots that give the fish respite from battling the current of the swollen springtime rivers. The maneuverability of a boat allowed them to reach shad that would have been impossible if shore fishing or even wading. Boat fishing for shad works and will get you to spots impossible to reach any other way.

That is one of the pluses of boat-fishing for shad—both experienced anglers and beginners can get out on the water and aren't restricted to one spot that may not be a good location. Boats also allow fishing far beyond the length of a cast from the shore or waded position. Finally, by trolling or trying different spots, even boat anglers lacking knowledge of shad, specific spots, or river fishing can often find and catch shad.

Though boat fishing is an ideal method for catching shad, it has some disadvantages. First and foremost is the popularity of the sport in many areas, which places launch ramp use and rental boats at a premium. Often it is necessary to reach the boat livery before dawn to be sure of getting a boat for the day. This is particularly true in more northern areas, where the shad hit best during the early morning and late evening, and less so in southern waters, where fishing seems to be more consistent throughout the day. If possible, make reservations for a boat before planning a trip. You can avoid this problem if you own a boat, although the lineup at the boat ramp for trailered boats is sometimes almost as bad as the wait in line for a boat rental.

On upriver situations and smaller rivers where smaller boats are safe and suitable, cartopping is one happy solution, since these can be launched at any place along the river having parking and access. Check for permission on private land, and observe all regulations on local, county, state, and federal lands for launching cartop boats.

Boats and Accessories

Since shad fishing often involves early-spring river fishing, when currents can be strong and rivers sometimes high, the right boat for the river and your fishing is a must. This will vary with each river—in fact, with each part of a river. The large, 18-foot boat that might be needed for trolling lower reaches or the mouth of a river will be overkill on the upriver stretches, where a 14-foot V-bottom is ideal for anchoring in midstream and soaking shad darts. All boats should be open, with no clutter. Store nets out of the way but accessible so they will be instantly available to land shad. While johnboats are sometimes used, V-bottom boats are best for most rivers. Don't overload the boat with anglers, even though everyone wants to go spring shad fishing. Most small boats are best when fished by two, and some larger ones can be fished by three or maybe even four. Check the Coast Guard or BIA rating for the number of passengers and weight of total equipment. Make sure you have all proper safety equipment and boat equipment, even beyond what is required by the Coast Guard.

A handy item for boat fishing—especially when anchored with rods resting in rod holders—is a clamp-on seat for each fisherman. This allows you to rest comfortably while waiting for hits. Equally important, if the boat is lacking built-in gunwale or transom rod holders, are clamp-on rod holders to hold each rod being fished. Another must is a long-handled net to avoid having to stretch too far to land a fish. The soft upper jaw of shad and the possibility of losing one at the critical landing time make long-handled nets vital. A heavy anchor with a long enough rope is also very important to hold the boat in a strong river current. Most experts recommend an anchor rope seven to ten times as long as the river depth. And since boats can be pulled under if an anchor hangs up with too short a line, you should have a sharp knife, ready to use and next to the anchor rope, in order to sacrifice the anchor to save the boat, and perhaps lives. This is especially important when fishing below hydroelectric dams, where water is periodically released, increasing the current and depth almost instantly. Though wearing a PFD may not be required (carrying one for each occupant is), it's best if each angler wears a comfortable vest-style PFD. Check local regulations, since on some rivers at some times of the year, wearing a PFD is legally required.

Locating the Shad

Once on the water, you need to know how to locate the shad. Ask knowledgeable area river fishermen, check out rocks, pools, riffles, islands, and similar protected and seam areas near currents where shad are likely to hit. Seam areas occur where two currents meet, where a current runs adjacent to a quiet pool or eddy, or where a rock or obstruction creates a fast current next to a quiet backwater area.

Boat-Fishing Methods

There are several methods of boat-fishing for shad, as follows:

Trolling

Trolling involves running the boat at slow speed to position lures at the best possible spots for shad. Often this means running the boat through deep pools and watching the approximate lure position (length of line out) to place the lures at the tails of pools, in riffles, around rocks and islands, adjacent to cliffs and shelves, and through the depths of long pools and runs.

On big water, trolling can be nothing more than randomly running the boat around all the fishable spots until a shad hits. That's not always as easy as it sounds, since you have to avoid all the other boats with the same idea, and also avoid the trolled lines running from the stern.

I still remember my first such trip on the Susquehanna Flats in Maryland. My fishing partner and I rented a boat, clamped on my small outboards, and moved out into the quiet water of the flats, where shad mill around as they leave the head of the Chesapeake Bay and start their run up the Susquehanna River. The water here, while laced with channels, is relatively shallow. Shad are possible anywhere and everywhere.

Out on the water, small boats and some larger ones wandered in seemingly aimless circles, trying to avoid the lines of other anglers, and usually succeeding. Into this maze of boats we went, working into a fleet that from the air probably resembled a flock of disoriented water boatman insects. That we got shad on that trip—as did most other boats—was less a credit to our angling skill than to luck. Since that date many years ago, many springtime shad anglers have switched to the river for shad, leaving the flats for the increasingly popular early-season catch-and-release striper fishing.

Fortunately, most shad fishing is less crowded and more orderly, at least for the trolling angler. In a wide river, the best course is usually upriver, trolling against the current. This allows throttling the outboard back, which together with the river current, keeps the boat barely moving. The slow movement against the current keeps the lures in one general area long enough for shad to find them and, with luck, hit them. And because the channels of most rivers are relatively straight—at least for some distance—it is possible for a number of boats to run in a straight course upriver without navigation or right-of-way problems.

Anchoring and still-fishing

Anchoring and still-fishing requires more knowledge of the river, since it involves anchoring the boat in a location so that the lures, either plain or with in-line or drop sinkers, will be positioned where the shad are most likely to hit them. This positioning involves not only the right spot in the river, but also the right depth in the water column. Depth in the water column can be controlled by either the amount of weight on the line or the amount and type of line played out from the boat. Weight can be from the size of the dart or darts used, or a sinker combined with a dart or spoon. The line affects the vertical location of the lure in the water and is controlled by the length of line and the diameter. Generally, the more line out, the deeper the lure. Also, the thinner the diameter of the line, the less water resistance and the deeper the lure.

This type of fishing is popular, since local anglers often know and try to get favorite spots on the river. It requires getting an extremely early start to get your boat into the right location and drop the anchor with enough anchor rode (length of anchor line) to hold bottom, be safe, and position the boat where the lures can be fished effectively. Lures can be fished on short or long lines, but this will also vary the depth. Depth can be adjusted by adding or removing sinkers. You can only fish in a straight up- or downstream track, since moving to another side current entails moving the boat, and you also must make sure that you do not interfere with other boats or their fishing lines.

Downrigger fishing

Downrigger fishing is really the same as anchored-boat fishing, but using downriggers and depth finders to locate the shad and then to position small shad darts, spoons, or flutter spoons right in front of the shad at their depth. If you don't have a downrigger, you can use a substitute downrigger consisting of a short, stout boat rod, heavy line, heavy sinker, and downrigger clips to place the lure deep. The big advantage of this over standard boat anchoring is that you have exact knowledge of the depth of the lures, you can fight the fish without fighting the sinker at the same time, and you use far less of the river to position lines.

CHAPTER 10

Where to Find Shad

Although shad are confined to coastal streams, many of these streams extend far inland and provide good fishing each spring for millions of anglers. Major human population centers and areas of growth are located along both the Atlantic and Pacific coasts, and good shad fishing is usually available within a short drive of these large demographic areas.

Often certain rivers and streams in a locality are renowned for their shad fishing and attract all the attention. But consider exploring other nearby streams that have open access to the ocean—not blocked by slugs of pollution, dams, or impassable falls. Such areas often provide almost untouched virgin fishing. In the Chesapeake Bay area, for example, the Susquehanna River and its tributaries, such as Deer Creek and Octoraro Creek, along with the Potomac River near Washington D.C., get all the attention. However, other rivers running into the Chesapeake Bay have historically provided good shad runs. Today most of these rivers, such as the Patuxent, Sassafras, Chester, and Choptank, provide some shad fishing, and there is the potential for even better returns in the future.

The shad spots listed below, state by state and in the maritime provinces of Canada, have over the years provided good fishing. Without serious water pollution, new dams, or increased fishing pressure, they should continue to provide good shad fishing far into the future. Many are even getting better year by year, as old dams are being removed and new fishways and fish ladders built.

The information given here is as accurate as possible at the time of writing, but conditions of the rivers and shad runs can markedly change in the future. Fishing regulations are not included here, since they would quickly become outdated. Regulations vary widely and are likely to change frequently as more and more dams are removed and shad populations increase, leading to greater shad-fishing possibilities and access to sportfishing. Before you go, check for accurate, up-to-date information on the areas you wish to fish from one or more of the following sources:

- Call your local newspaper and ask to speak to the outdoor columnist. Outdoor writers or editors (different papers use different titles) are tuned in to the local seasons, fish species, and fishing conditions, and can be of immense help with the best times, places, techniques, flies and lures, and regulations and license requirements.
- Check with your state fish and game agency. The name varies among states, but it will appear on any information you get when you buy your fishing license. Additionally, all of these agencies are listed in the phone book. Call them or check their Internet website for information on fishing spots, restoration efforts, dam removal, or fishway construction. Also check for license requirements, seasons, and creel and size limits. Some states have no restrictions on the taking of shad, some have some regulations, and some allow only catch-and-release shad fishing. Find out before fishing.
- Check with local tackle shops in coastal or shad-fishing locations. All have information, tackle, and lures and flies for shad fishing. Stop in to get to know the clerks and shop owner and to learn about the best shad-fishing possibilities in the area.
- Check out local fishing clubs. It's good to belong to such clubs anywhere for the information and camaraderie they provide. You'll be able to get good information from many club members on shad-fishing conditions and hot spots. Some clubs are general fishing clubs, whereas others are geared only to fly fishing. To get a listing of such clubs, check with a tackle shop or the reference librarian at your local library.
- Ask any of the above about a shad-fishing hotline. Some are run by the state, some by tackle shops, and some by fishing clubs, such as the large Delaware River Shad Fishermen's Association. Some of these phone hotlines are toll-free; for others, you may have to pay long-distance charges. Most are operated seasonally and provide information on shad catches, river flows and conditions, top lures, and hot spots.

ATLANTIC COAST

Nova Scotia

Plenty of shad are found in the Bay of Fundy, where they are primarily taken by commercial fishermen. There seems to be little sportfishing here, even though the shad spend a lot of time here from midsummer through midfall before heading south in the open ocean. The popularity of sportfishing for shad has been growing over the years, however, with most of the fishing now on the Annapolis River near Middleton. The run peaks in the last week in May and lasts about three weeks.

Quebec

Shad enter the Gulf of St. Lawrence in May and then continue their migration up the St. Lawrence River. Between May 12 and 20, they appear south of Green Island (Isle Verte), where they are found in the greatest concentrations. Some shad get as far upstream as Montreal, and some enter the Ottawa River. They are also occasionally reported in the Saguenay, but this river is too deep and large to be fished effectively for shad.

New Brunswick

The St. John River does have a shad run, but most of the catches are incidental to the catching of other species. Salmon fly anglers occasionally hook shad. Shad runs can be found in the St. Lawrence, Miramichi, St. Mary, Mersey, Tusket, Annapolis, Shubenacadie, Petticodiac, and the seas adjacent to the mouths of these rivers.

Maine

A number of dams block some of the potentially best shad rivers in Maine, although this is improving as a result of dam removal on some rivers. The best fishing in the state is on the Narragaugus River, where about 150 to 200 shad are taken by sportfishermen each year. A 1968 through 1971 study showed a total run at there of only about 500 fish annually.

Other rivers with American shad (the only shad species currently found in Maine) include the East Machias and the Dennys. Of less importance for the sport angler are the runs in the Kennebec, Sheepscott, Nonesuch, Kennebunk, Cathance, and Eastern Rivers, and the tributaries of the St. Croix estuary.

The best fishing is from early May through mid-June, with the peak usually around Memorial Day.

New Hampshire

When my first book on shad fishing was published in 1974, there was no shad fishing to speak of in New Hampshire, although there were plans for anadromous fish passages. Fish lifts and fish ladders have since been added to dams at Lawrence and Lowell, Massachusetts, and at Manchester, New Hampshire. Power agreements currently being negotiated may allow additional fish passages at other upstream dams at Bow, Franklin, and Bristol, New Hampshire.

Rivers in coastal New Hampshire also produce shad, with the Squamscott and Exeter River offering the best opportunities. (The Squamscott and Exeter are the same river, with the Squamscott the tidal portion, the Exeter the freshwater portion.) The fish can move up the fish ladder at the Exeter dam and continue several miles upriver, where they are stopped at the Pickpocket Dam. The Salmon Falls River, bordering New Hampshire and Maine, also offers shad fishing to the dams at Rollinsford, New Hampshire, and South Berwick, Maine.

Connecticut

Enfield Dam on the Connecticut River is still nationally known for its shad fishing. But according to Steve Gephard, supervising fisheries biologist for the state, the dam has deteriorated markedly over the years. Boat fishing is best here today, although in past years shore angling was more popular. Anglers new to the area should note that this water sometimes has constant waves as a result of the water flow through the dam and can be dangerous. Stable large boats with high sides are recommended for this river. Most of the fish are taken right at the dam. Some trolling is done, but the best fishing is casting darts from an anchored boat. In heavy flows, add sinkers to the rigs to get the darts down.

The area along the shore from the Enfield Dam downstream to the Windsor Locks Bridge and immediately below the railroad bridge above Windsor Locks is also good. The now out-of-print booklet *Shad Angling on the Connecticut,* published by the Windsor Rod and Gun Club of Windsor, lists the following areas in the state, ranked in order of past angling success:

1. Enfield Dam controlled area (west side more productive than east side).
2. King's Island launching site, below Enfield Dam.
3. Windsor Locks boat rental area.
4. Windsor Locks bridge.
5. Enfield Dam.
6. Farmington River and similar tributaries of the Connecticut River. (Trolling produces well on the Farmington, although casting results in good catches from the banks below the dam at Pequonnock on the Farmington or at the river's mouth. The Farmington can be reached by boat from the Connecticut River also.) The best access here is from Route 159 or from Bart's, a general store that locals can direct you to. The flow is less here than on the Connecticut, so willowleaf flutter spoons are more commonly fished than darts.

Albin J. Sonski, Kensington Fish Hatchery supervisor, says that the shad population in the Connecticut has dropped off in recent years, down to several hundred thousand shad from a high of 1.5 million in 1992. He notes that the best fly fishing is at the mouth of the Farmington River, with a shooting lead taper fly line from an anchored boat. He likes fishing at the Dexter Coffin bridge on the Connecticut and about a mile or two up from the mouth of the Farmington at the Loomis-Craffee School, fishing from shore or trolling from a boat.

Two other good areas are the Shetucket River near Norwich and the Housatonic River near Shelton. Fish the Shetucket in the Greeneville area, where a fish elevator on the hydroelectric dam there is restoring the shad to the upper reaches of this river. The best access is from the southeast side of the river with public access and public parking for fishermen at the corner of Roosevelt and 8th.

The Housatonic—another tidal-border river—with the Derby Dam is also good. A shad restoration plan is in place, but there is no fish lift or ladder at this writing. These spots do bode well for the future, however.

Another good area is the Hammonasset River north of Clinton and Madison, although this is a smaller river and is best for fly fishing rather than spinning.

The best fishing for shad in Connecticut waters is from late March and into June, with the peak fishing in mid to late May at Enfield Dam and other shad hot spots.

Massachusetts

In Massachusetts, shad fishing is done primarily on the Connecticut and Merrimack Rivers, according to Massachusetts anadromous fish project leader Caleb Slater. Most are American shad, with very few hickory shad mixed in. The shad pass over five dams: Lawrence and Lowell Dams, on the Merrimack; Holyoke Dam, the first dam on the main stem of the Connecticut River from the ocean; Turners Falls Dam and the DSI dam on the Westfield River, a major Connecticut River tributary.

The DSI fishway was built about 1995 and has opened 14 miles of habitat to anadromous fish. The most intense fishing is at and right below Holyoke Dam, where an annual shad derby contributes to spring interest in these fish.

Another good fishing area is at the mouth of the Chicopee River, a Connecticut River tributary that enters the river several miles below Holyoke. Slater says that the lower Westfield River in West Springfield and the Agawam below the DSI dam also have good shad fishing.

The Connecticut River rus through Massachusetts, Connecticut, and Vermont and produces the best shad fishing in all three states. In Massachusetts, the best fishing on the river is at the South Hadley Falls Dam and the Williamansett Bridge, farther downstream. Excellent fishing extends above the falls at Hadley and into Vermont. The dam at Holyoke has a fish trap and elevator for transporting the shad farther upstream. There are also migrations of shad up the Palmer River near Rehoboth and the North River near Plymouth. These shad streams are often less crowded than others of the area. More dams are being removed, with one project under way to remove the remains of an already breached dam on the Concord, a tributary of the Merrimack, to allow the passage of river herring, which will allow for the passage of shad also. There are also plans to construct a fishway at the first dam on the Manhan River in Northampton.

The best fishing is from late April through early June, with the run usually peaking from about May 20 to May 25.

Vermont

Shad fishing on the Connecticut River extends into Vermont, with good fishing along most of its length up to Bellows Falls, which is impassable to shad. The best fishing is from late May through mid-June.

Rhode Island

The best and only really serious fishing for American shad is in the Pawcatuck–Wood River system, according to Rhode Island fisheries biologist Phillip Edwards. The Wood runs into the Pawcatuck, forming this two-river system. There is fishway passage past the first two dams, at Potter Hill and Bradford. Shad are stopped at the upstream dams at Alton on the Wood River and at Shannock on the Pawcatuck River. Most of the American shad fishing is done with darts.

Hickory shad can be caught on the Narrow River in the summer and along the coast through the summer and fall. Most of the fishing is blind casting with darts or flies to find the fish, or following the stripers, which are presumably feeding on the shad that summer in the estuary areas throughout New England. Sometimes jumping hickory shad signal their presence in an area, and once they are located, repeat catches are common until the school moves or is lost.

New York

Most shad fishing in New York is in the Delaware River (see sidebar). The cleanup of the Hudson River has also resulted in a revival of shad fishing there over the past twenty-five years, with shad festivals reintroduced beginning in 1974. In the late 1800s and early 1900s, almost every town along the river had such festivals, when the shad ascended 160 miles upriver. Fishing is for American shad, since there are no appreciable numbers of hickory shad found in the river. American shad are presently able to get past Albany and up to the Troy Dam, about 10 to 12 miles above Albany. There is a lock at the dam that shad can get through, but few do, making shad fishing above the dam marginal at best. The tailway of the Troy Dam is one of the hot spots on the river, which is tidal up to this point. Shad fishing is somewhat spotty downstream; here it's best around the mouths of tributaries to the Hudson. Good fishing can be found around the towns of Hudson and Cheviot. Fishing on the slack tides is best in these tidal waters. Some shad fishing can also be had on the lower reaches of the Neversink, a tributary of the Hudson. Most of the fishing is around Port Jervis. Farther upstream the Neversink is fine trout water. The best New York shad fishing is from mid-May through June.

A new fall fishery for hickory shad has begun, with the shad showing up in Long Island Sound in the early to mid-1990s. Before that, locals say hickory shad were not found in the estuaries in the summer and fall, as they are now. They are often caught in Niantic Bay (really, Connecticut waters). Fishing is mostly catch-and-release, although some anglers keep the hickories to use as bait for blues and striped bass. The best of this late-season hickory shad fishing continues from early summer through late fall.

For valuable background information on shad in the Hudson, consult Robert H. Boyle's excellent book *The Hudson River.*

New Jersey

Shad are occasionally found in the small rivers along the coast, but there is no targeted fishery for them at this time. In the 1980s some American shad were stocked in the Raritan River, and a fish passage there shows about three hundred shad passing up the river annually at the time of this writing. Shad have always spawned in the lower reaches of the Raritan, as they have in other coastal tidal streams, but the fishery has been getting better since the transplantation of Delaware River shad in the early 1980s. The Rancocas, a tributary of the Delaware, is now showing a sizable worthwhile shad fishery. Most of the serious shad fishing takes place in the section of the Delaware River (see sidebar) that is shared with Pennsylvania. The small streams all along the New Jersey coast hold shad, but in such minimal numbers that they are not worth targeting.

The Delaware River

The Delaware River hit its shad-fishing peak around 1900. At one time, it had the most extensive shad population and fishery above tidewater of any river in the United States, with the fishery concentrated at Scudders Falls area (today the Route 95 bridge), but many years of pollution led to nearly half a century of almost nonesixtent shad fishing. In 1972 the Federal Clean Water Act resulted in the cleanup of the river and elimination of much of the pollution factors, and today shad in the Delaware have the longest run in the country—almost 300 miles. Bordered by the states of New York, Pennsylvania, New Jersey, and Delaware, the Delaware River run extends from Delaware Bay, where the shad enter from the ocean, up to Cannonsville, New York. The runs are good, with the 2000 survey of 382,000 shad almost matching previous years' records, after an admittedly suspect low count of 24,700 shad in 1999. Previous records of shad migrations in the Delaware River were 327,800 (1992), 289,900 (1995), 524,300 (1996), and 392,700 (1998).

Early-season shad fishing on the Delaware usually begins during the third or fourth week of March at the Trenton Falls area, just below Trenton, New Jersey. Shad fishing on the Delaware is especially good in the Yardley, Pennsylvania, Scudders Falls area; Lambertville, New Jersey; Lumberville Dam, Pennsylvania; Bulls Island State Park, New Jersey, at the wing dam; Byram, New Jersey; Phillipsburg, New Jersey; Easton, Pennsylvania; and within the Delaware Water Gap National Recreation Area.

Above Easton, shad fishing is popular at the Martins Creek Pool

Pennsylvania

Shad fishing is primarily done in the Delaware River (see sidebar) and in Pennsylvania west-bank tributaries of the Delaware, such as the Lehigh River, which has had a shad festival and planking for years. The Lehigh is a success story so far, with fishways added to three of the five dams on the river as of 1999. Fishways are located at the Easton Dam at river mile 0.0, the Chain Dam at 3.0 miles, and the Hamilton Street Dam at 17.0 miles. Other upriver dams (though lacking fishways) are the Cementon and Francis E. Walter Dams, at river miles 24.0 and 76.5. Returns of shad and Sandts Eddy, Pennsylvania. Foul Rift, near Portland, Pennsylvania, is also a good place to fish for shad. Sandy Beach and Pardee Beach, in the same area, are also excellent, with Pardee Beach perhaps the top hot spot.

The Belvidere, New Jersey, area is also good for shad. The river from the Delaware Water Gap all the way up through Flatbrookville; Dingmans Ferry, Pennsylvania; Montague; and Milford, Pennsylvania; to Port Jarvis, New York, also provides continual good shad fishing from mid-May through mid-June.

The famous Lackawaxen area and the Zane Grey pool (so named for the writer, who lived here in his youth) are especially good and deservedly popular. In the New York section of the Delaware River, shad ascend the main river and the East and West Branches, although the fishing is more marginal in the West Branch. Shad fishing is good at Barryville, Narrowsburg, Skinners Falls, Long Eddy, the Junction Pool, and as far north as Cannonsville. The best times to fish these upper stretches of the river are from mid-May through June, and sometimes as late as early July.

Access to the river is plentiful, with twenty-four public and commercial beach and ramp access points for boat anglers in Pennsylvania and New Jersey. In some areas, boat rentals are available. A listing of current boating access areas is available from the fisheries departments of the states that border the river.

Because of the long shad run in the Delaware River, the best times to fish depend on the section of the river. The run begins in mid-March below Trenton and extends to early July in the headwaters of the spawning areas in New York State.

through the Easton fishway have increased from 87 in 1994 to 3,293 in 1998, promising good future shad fishing for this river.

Delaware

The only four shad-fishing streams in Delaware are the Delaware River (see Delaware River sidebar); the Nanticoke River, which runs through Maryland and empties into the Chesapeake Bay; Broad Creek, west of the junction of routes 3 and 24; and the Brandywine. (The Brandywine runs close to the DuPont research labs and is where a researcher first tried nylon monofilament as a possibility for fishing line.) The best fishing is from mid-April through early May.

Maryland

The two hot shad rivers in the state, producing both hickory and American shad, are the Susquehanna River, up to the Conowingo Dam near the Pennsylvania border, and the Potomac River (wholly owned by Maryland, but along the border with Virginia). The Potomac River is best in the Washington, D.C., area, with a lot of fishing around Fletcher's Boathouse and just below Great Falls, which is at the fall line of the river. The river is deeper here than the Susquehanna, and deep-water techniques, heavier darts, and sinking fly lines are often required.

In addition, there are a number of smaller streams with only hickory shad. (It is thought that the deeper-swimming American shad do not frequent these streams because they are shallow. These include Deer Creek and Octoraro Creek, Susquehanna River tributaries popular with fly fishermen.)

Other, lesser-known rivers are also good for shad fishing, even if less publicized. On the western shore of the Chesapeake Bay are the Bush, Gunpowder, Severn, and Patuxent Rivers. On the eastern shore of the bay, consider the Northeast, Bohemia, Chester, Choptank, and Nanticoke Rivers and their tributaries, along with the C & D Canal, at the head of the bay.

The best fishing is from mid-April through early May for hickory shady, and from late April through late May for American shad.

Virginia

As in Maryland, both hickory and American shad are taken in most of the rivers. And also as in Maryland, the American shad prefer the deeper waters, wheras the hickory shad run up into shallow streams that the American shad avoid.

Popular and well-publicized shad fishing occurs in the James River at Hopewell; in the Chickahominy (tributary of the James) below Lexana, at Walkers Dam on the Chickahominy, the Mattaponi (tributary of the York River) below Aylett; in the Rappahannock River at Fredericksburg and below Port Royal; and in the Piscattoway near Tappahannock. Other good shad rivers include the James, York, Pamunkey (a York tributary), Occoquan River (below the reservoir), Swift Creek, Four Mile Creek, Cat Point Creek, Appomattox River, and Nottoway River. Some Virginia fishermen fish from shore in the Potomac, although the river belongs to Maryland.

The best fishing is in late March and early April for the hickory shad, and a little later (early April through late April) for the American shad. Spring weather is extremely variable in the Mid-Atlantic area, causing fluctuations of shad fishing seasons from year to year.

North Carolina

American shad seem to favor the Cape Fear River and the Tar River; hickory shad are more prevalent in the Neuse and are also found in the Roanoke and Tar Rivers. Catches of shad in the Cape Fear River run about 99 percent American to 1 percent hickory. The Cape Fear River locks 1 and 12 are the best places for casting anglers, with most of the fish taken between 7 A.M. and 12 noon. Trolling has proven less effective than casting.

Other good fishing for both species is had in the Chowan, Trent, Black, Pamlico, Whiteoak, and New Rivers. Around Grifton, a shad festival is held each year for hickory shad, with most of the fishing done in Contentnea Creek and nearby Pitchkettle Creek.

The Black River, a tributary of the Cape Fear, is good in the area between the Route 53 bridge and Route 41 near Tomahawk. Another Cape Fear tributary, the North East Cape Fear River, has good shad fishing between Route 53 and Tin City. American shad fishing is good within the city limits of Rocky Mount and in the Tar River from the railway bridge upstream to the Textile Mill Dam, a distance of about a mile. The fishing is not as good downstream from there to Tarboro, although it is still fishable. The junction of Pitchkettle Creek and the Neuse River, east of Kinston near Fort Barnwell, is another shad hot spot.

The best fishing is from late February and early March through mid-March for hickory shad, and early March through late March for American shad.

South Carolina

Though the shad fishery in South Carolina is not as large as that found in Florida or Georgia, both hickory and American shad do ascend most tidal streams and rivers. The best shad fishing for both species is on the Edisto River from Penny Creek upriver to Givan's Ferry. In this area, the best fishing is at the West Bank Landing at Jacksonboro. Most of the fishing involves trolling the river channels, fishing near the bottom with small bucktails or shad darts, often tandem rigged.

Other favorite shad streams and rivers for American shad are the Combahee, Salkehatchie, Black, Santee, Waccamaw, Pee Dee, and the Little Pee Dee. Hickory shad can be caught on the Cooper River, including the tailrace area of the canal at Lake Moultrie. Some American shad are found here also, but most of the shad catches are incidental to the spring striped bass fishing.

The best fishing is from the first of January, when the hickory shad begin to arrive, through March. The American shad run occurs from late February and continues into March and early April.

Georgia

One popular hot spot is on the Ogeechee River, in the area between the U.S. Route 80 bridge at Blichton and U.S. Route 17 bridge at Richmond Hill. There is some commercial fishing for shad on the Altamaha River, but no sportfishing to speak of.

Good shad runs for sportfishing can be found on the Woodbine, Satilla, Altamaha, and Savannah Rivers. The Savannah produces the best shad fishing in the northeast part of the state. One of the best spots for this is at the New Savannah Bluff Lock and Dam, just southeast of Augusta. This is a clear-water area below the dam that provides shore access and boat fishing. This is far up the river—about 175 miles from the ocean—so fishing here can extend into May. For most of the rest of the state, the shad arrive in late January through early February, with the fishing continuing through late March and early April.

Florida

The St. Johns River is without exception the best-known shad-fishing river in the state, and it is widely known throughout the country. Both American and hickory shad are caught there. There are about 75 miles of good fishing here, beginning at Crows Bluff west of Deland and extending south of Lake Poinsett. This latter portion of the St. Johns coils as it flows along, taking on the appearance of a snake. It has good shad fishing in areas such as Mullet Lake, Lemon Bluff, Puzzle Lake, Lake Cane, Hatbill, and Possum Bluff.

The heaviest spawning, according to fisheries biologists, is around the Lemon Bluff area near Sanford. South of Route 250, the shad fishing is not quite as good, although some shad are caught as far south as Lake Sawgrass, west of Melbourne. Less than a half mile below Route 250, shad are considered scarce. The best fishing on the St. Johns is from late November through February, when the waters are cool enough for the shad to feel comfortable to enter and spawn.

The little-known Alabama shad is found along the Florida Panhandle area. This area offers virgin fishing for anglers interested in exploring the rivers there for an unexploited species. A study done some years ago indicated that Alabama shad were caught on hook and line at a rate of one for every twenty-nine minutes of fishing, considerably better than the angling opportunities some areas offer for American or hickory shad. The best areas for the Alabama shad include the Apalachicola and Chipola Rivers. The Apalachicola River is formed by the junction of the Chattahoochee and Flint Rivers at the Jim Woodruff Dam. The Chipola River joins the Apalachicola River farther downstream. The shad enter the rivers starting about early January and can be caught through early March.

GULF COAST

Alabama

There is no real shad fishery in Alabama for any of the shad species, not even the Alabama shad. Alabama shad are only caught incidentally when fishing for other species, although they can be caught on the Chattahoochee River below Lake Eufaula.

Louisiana

For all practical purposes, there is no shad fishing here, even though Alabama shad are found in some rivers. In a 1971 research study, only one specimen of the Alabama shad was caught here, with no catches of American or hickory shad.

WEST COAST

Washington

American shad are caught primarily in the Columbia and Chehalis Rivers. Most of the fishing on the Columbia is done from shore, as the river is often too swift for boat fishing. The best fishing is within a mile or two below Bonneville Dam, with good access from the Washington side along Route 14. Small boats can be launched at the Oak Park bridge. Trolling in Camas Slough at the mouth of the Washougal River is productive near the city limits of Camas.

Two productive shad-fishing spots are the mouth of the Washougal River between the towns of Camas and Washougal, and in the tailrace section below Bonneville Dam on the Columbia. The shad school below the dam and can be taken by casting from the shoreline.

Anglers can determine the relative numbers of shad in the river by checking the daily tallies of the numbers of shad going over the dam. Monthly totals of shad going over the dams reveal that the best fishing is during June and July.

Fishing on the Chehalis River is best just below the Skookunchuk, which enters the Chehalis close to Centralia. Fishing on both rivers is good from early June through mid-July. The Willapa River is also a good shad hot spot.

Oregon

Fisheries biologists state that shad are probably found in every major river along the Oregon coastline. They have definitely been documented in the Yaquina, Alsea, Siuslaw, Columbia (forming the border between Oregon and Washington), Willamette (a tributary of the Columbia), Smith, Sandy, Umpqua, Millicoma, Coos, Coquille, and Rogue Rivers.

Adult shad are found in the rivers as early as March, but the actual spawning run is from April through June. The peak of the migration—and of shad fishing—is from late May through early June. Shad start arriving in April on the Umpqua, and a little later than this on the Rogue River. The best fishing on the Umpqua can be found between the towns of Elkton and Scottsburg, and along the North and South Umpqua near Roseburg.

Columbia River anglers familiar with shad watch the daily fish ladder counts in the May newspapers to determine the time to start fishing. As a general rule, counts of about 30,000 per day are considered good, although counts often go higher (to over 140,000 at the peak of the run). Most of the shad fishing (about 80 percent, according to Department of Fish and Wildlife estimates) occurs in the 3 miles below the Bonneville Dam. Over 70 percent of this fishing is done by bank or shore fishermen. The peak fishing on the Columbia was in about 1990, with 4 million fish passing upstream, and is now down to just below 2 million fish as of 1999. There is some fishing upstream of Bonneville Dam to just below the John Day and McNary Dams, but this is not well monitored.

The best fishing usually starts about late April and continues through June or early July. I-84, on the Oregon side of the Columbia River, provides good access to the fishing there.

There are also good runs on the Snake River (a tributary of the Columbia) and the Willamette, which drains into the Columbia at river mile 102. Shad do not seem to use the fish ladder at Willamette Falls, but they do seem to travel through the lock there to get upstream.

California

The Feather, Yuba, Russian, American, Trinity, Klamath, San Joaquin, and Sacramento Rivers have the best shad runs in the state, with shad running in them from the first of April through the end of July, depending on the area, length of the run, and latitude. The Yuba and Feather are considered the two best shad rivers.

The Feather River, a tributary of the Sacramento River, is best between Oroville Dam and the Sacramento, with the best fishing between Marysville and the dam. It is a large river with fast-flowing water, often necessitating sinking fly lines and weighted flies or heavy darts.

The best shad fishing along the Yuba River, a tributary of the Feather, is the 20-mile section from the town of Marysville northeast and paralleling Route 20 upriver to the Daggero Point Dam. This is as far as migrating shad can travel. Productive pools exist all along the river.

The Klamath is a very large river and thus not the best for fishing shad, since it is really too big and deep, with a high volume of water, to be fished for shad effectively and efficiently. Any fishing here requires heavy lead-core lines and weighted flies if fly-fishing, or heavy darts, often rigged tandem, if spin-fishing.

Located in the northern part of the state, the Trinity River is the main tributary of the larger Klamath. The best fishing is in the area of the Hoopa Valley Indian Reservation, early in the morning or late in the evening.

The Sacramento River, where lead-core lines are also necessary, is larger even than the Klamath. Shad fishing is sometimes good at the mouth of Butte Creek, a tributary of the Sacramento.

The American River has a short section of fishable shad water extending from the Nimbus Dam (the farthest that shad can travel upstream) to where it joins the Sacramento River, a distance of about 16 miles. The water just below the Nimbus Dam and the junction pool where the American joins the Sacramento are two of the hot spots on this river. The season extends from April through August.

The San Joaquin River is large and has the additional disadvantage of being used for irrigation of nearby ranches and farms, making the water supply for shad and shad fishing unreliable. Also, recirculation of the water often keeps it roiled and muddy. The Surgeons Bend area, near Tracy, reportedly has the best fishing. Because of the roiled water, fluorescent, or even phosphorescent (glow-in-the-dark), flies are best. Fishing can be good from late May through early June.

The Russian River has good shad fishing from Jenner, where the shad enter the stream, to Healdsburg.

EUROPE

Interest in fishing for shad is increasing in Europe as well. In France, the allis shad is the species targeted by anglers. England has both the allis shad *(Alosa alosa)* and the twaite shad *(Alosa fallax).* Both species are currently protected, but the United Kingdom Environmental Agency is conducting efforts to define coastal shad areas and identify shad spawning areas. The allis shad, the rarer of the two, is found around the British Isles but has no breeding sites there; the nearest recognized population is in Loire, France. The twaite shad are known to spawn in the Severn, Usk, Wye, and Tywi Rivers.

CHAPTER 11

Shad Recipes

Even before the shad became a sport fish, it was a popular food fish. In the early colonial days, meals of shad were a necessity in the hard life on the frontier. Later they became a popular and staple food fish each spring. Today shad and shad roe are properly considered a gourmet's delicacy. Recipes for shad have been developed over the years, with the first method perhaps that of planking shad—pegging the shad to a plank to be cooked while facing an open fire. Note this one from the 1884 book *Fishes of the East Atlantic Coast,* by Louis O. Van Doren.

> A large fish is taken and split along the belly from head to tail, and is then fastened with the meat side outward to a smooth oak plank and slowly roasted before an open coal fire. It is then, when nicely cooked (and right here lies the delicacy and success of the operation), served up with lemon on a hot dish, having been previously buttered and seasoned.

Before cooking shad, it is necessary to bone it for most recipes. Boning is a method of filleting the fish, removing even the small bones that lace through the shad's muscular body. An alternative to this is to use one of the various slow-baking methods that will dissolve the small bones.

There are several methods of boning a shad. In most cases, boning is done only on the larger American shad, since the smaller hickory shad take just as much time for less meat. Only American shad are considered for the commercial seafood markets, although where legal, anglers can keep and bone the smaller hickory shad.

One simple method of boning involves scaling both sides of the shad, starting with the tail and working up to the pectoral fin. Cut off the head, starting the blade at the back of the gill plate, and then, with a rocker

Adrian Bonaventure, of Gibby's Seafood in Timonium, Maryland, is an expert shad boner.

The first step in boning a shad is to scale it.

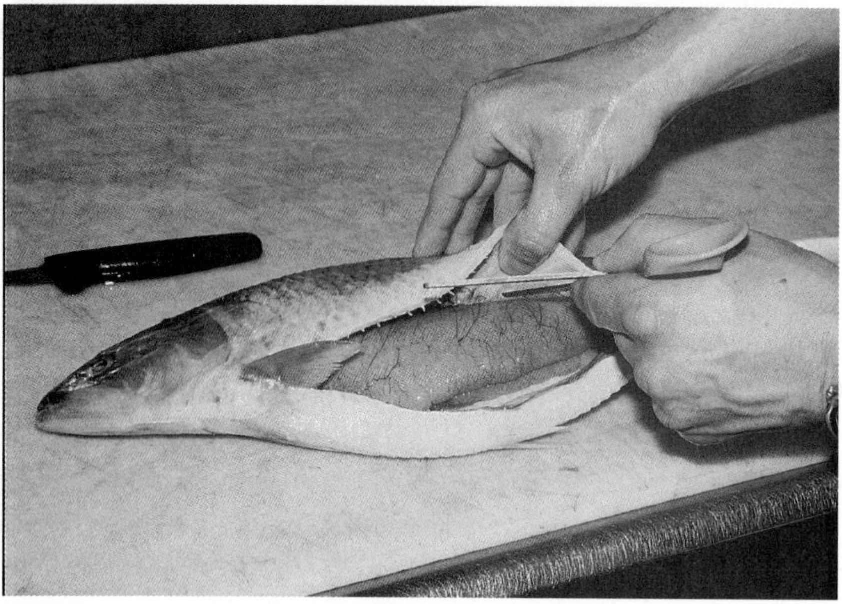

Step two is to cup open the body cavity to remove the entrails and the shad roe.

motion, working down to the belly and back toward the backbone. Cut along the belly of the fish, but be careful to not hurt the roe sac if it is a female. Remove the roe from the fish, and place it aside for cooking or other preparation. Cut the fish, removing all the entrails, including the blood line (actually the kidneys) that runs along the backbone. Wash the fish under cold, running water, and clean the filleting board.

At this point, a good filleting knife is necessary, along with a sharpening steel. A sharp knife is extremely important for boning. Slice with the knife along the back, right next to and parallel to the backbone, splitting the fish completely in half. At the same time, remove the other fillet from the backbone to leave three pieces—the central backbone and tail (which is discarded) and the two fillets, still with the bone in them. Taking one side at a time, remove the ribs, which run next to the body cavity and were cut through in splitting the fish. Run the knife along the edge of the bones, being careful to not remove the meat that is there.

The boning process will remove the two main sets of bones that run parallel along the length of the shad and give the shad a reputation as a bony fish. Probing carefully with the blade without removing the meat of the shad, cut along the length of the fish under where the ribs were.

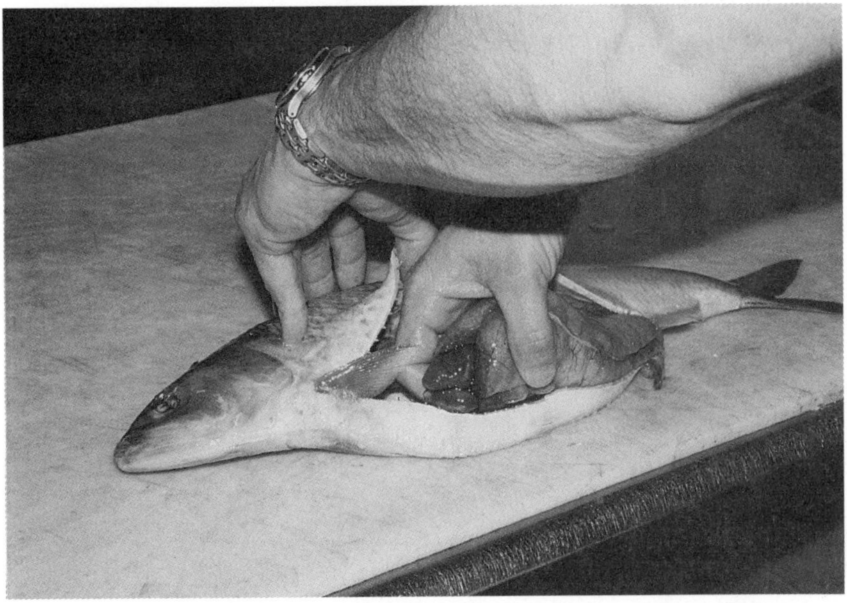

The shad roe is removed.

The "set" of shad roe alongside the shad.

Next, the head of the fish is removed.

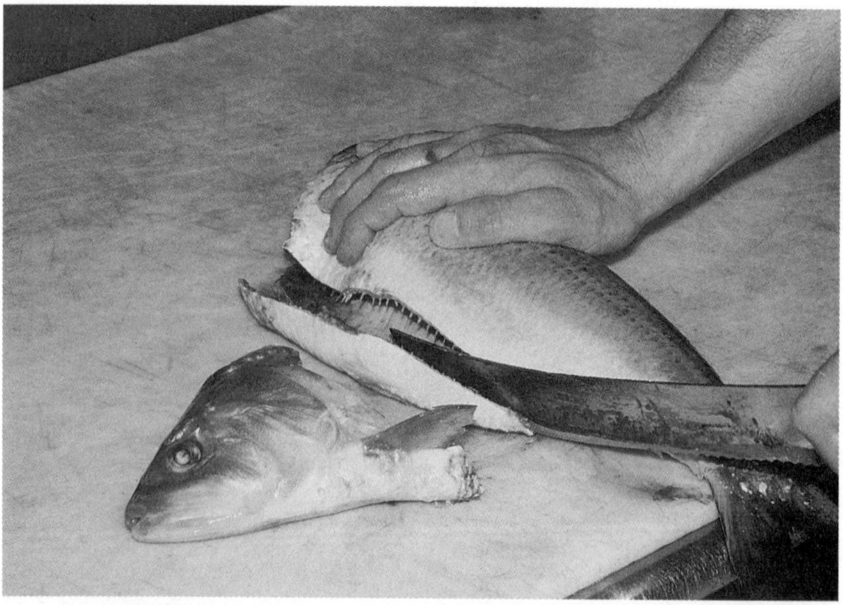

Once the head is removed, the belly is cut off, exposing the ribs.

With the body cavity open, a knife is used to remove the "blood line" (actually the kidneys of the fish) from along the spine.

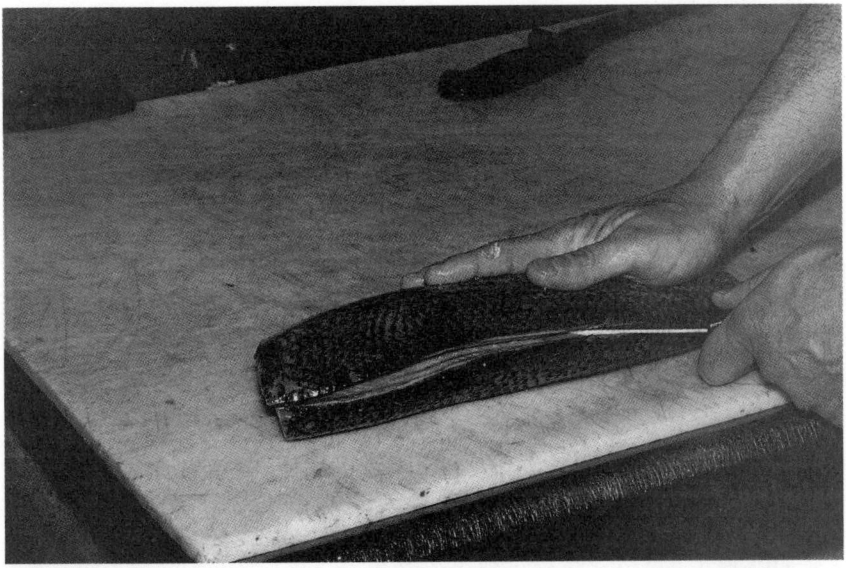

After the fish is cleaned, a sharp knife is used to cut the first fillet from the body. This cut is made along the backbone.

Here, the first fillet is next to the remainder of the fish.

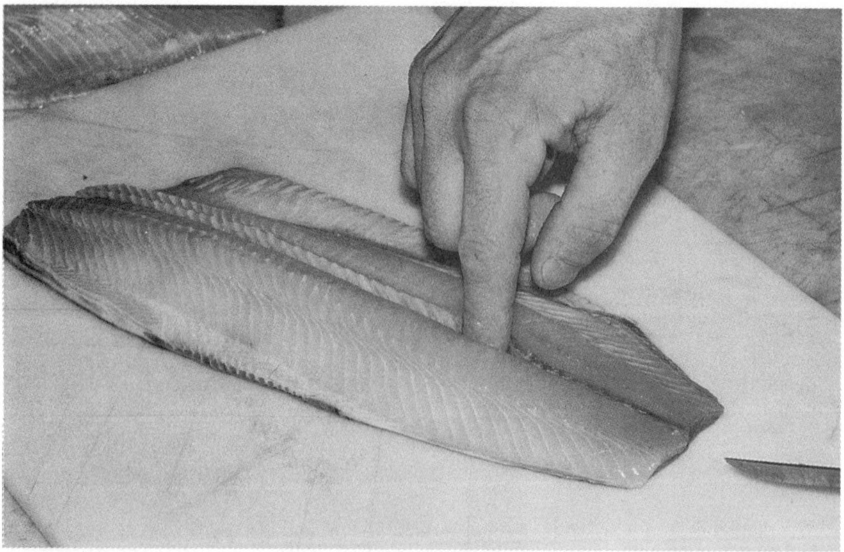

Use a finger to feel the extra bones that are along the ribs and make a cut along these bones, using the finger as a guide. This is the single most important part of boning a shad, and the part that differentiates boning from filleting.

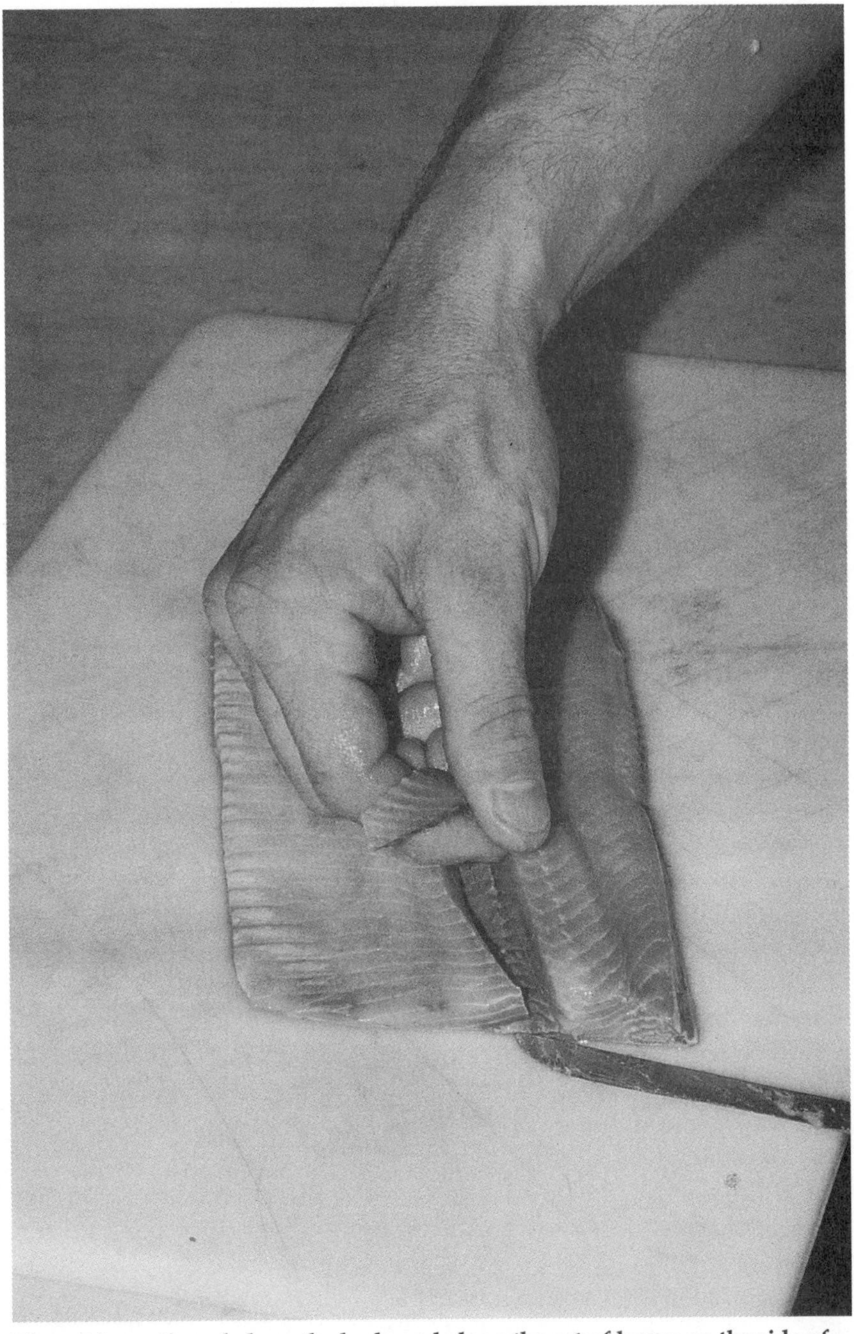

The cut is continued along the body and along the set of bones on the side of the shad.

The strips of bones are removed from the rest of the fillet.

After making this cut, make a second parallel cut along the other side of the bones to cut a groove for removal of the strip of bones. Throw away the bones. On the first few shad, it may be necessary to feel in the slit for other bones to be removed if the first cut did not do a complete job.

A second main row of bones also exists in the shad, parallel to the first, and like the first, they can be felt with the fingers. Repeat the same operation with this row of bones, making first one cut, then a second to isolate the strip of bones for removal. This process will remove about 90 percent of the bones. It's also an easy process since the hand can run along behind the cutting blade to feel any bones that are left for later removal. There is no danger of cutting yourself.

An alternate, more complex method of boning a shad, as described in the California Department of Fish and Game booklet *How to Catch, Bone and Cook a Shad,* is as follows:

1. Clip off all the fins except the tail fin, using shears for this. Bone shears, kitchen shears, or poultry shears are good for this operation.
2. Scale the shad, working from the tail up to the head.
3. Cut the shad between and under the gill covers, using a very long, thin knife.

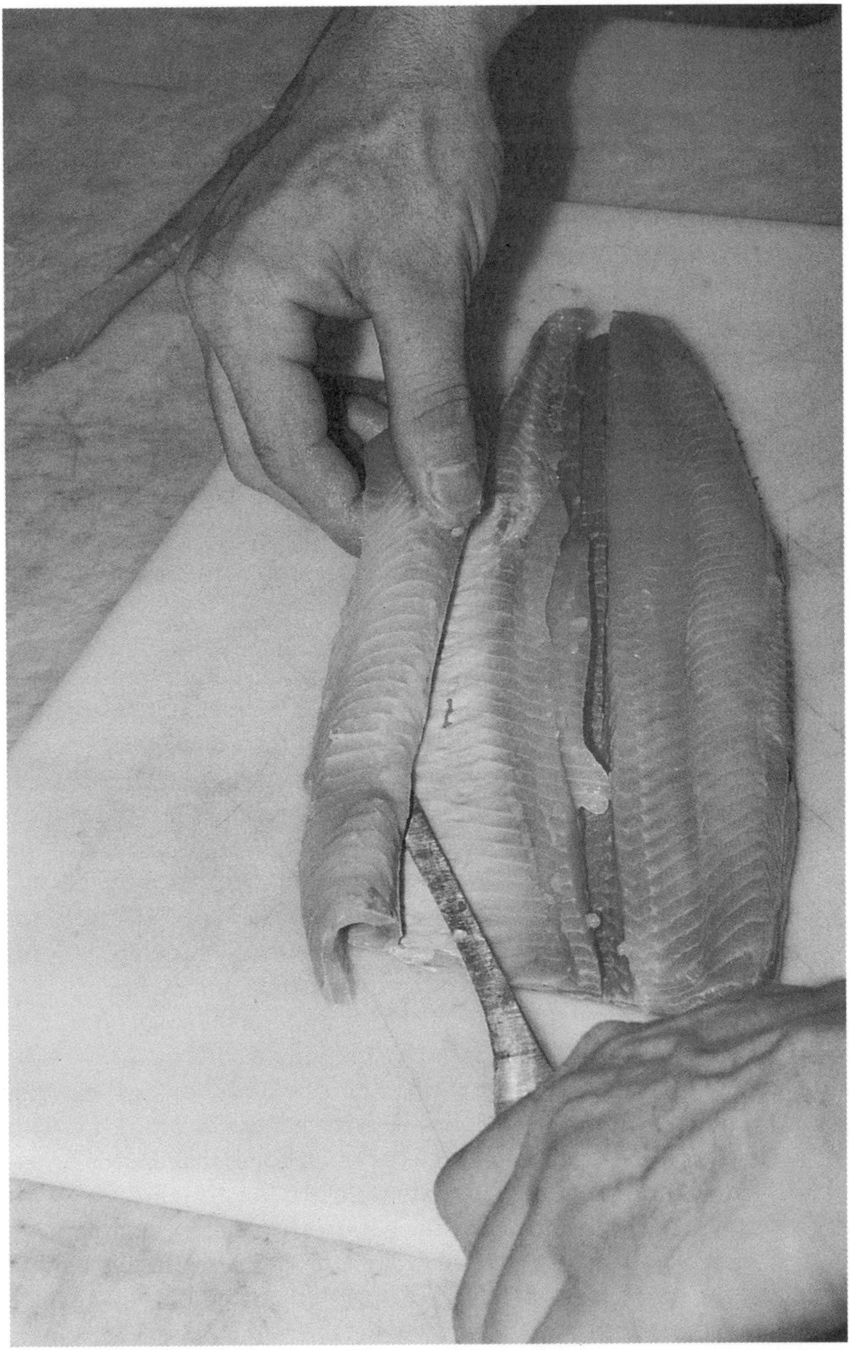

The ribs of the shad are removed.

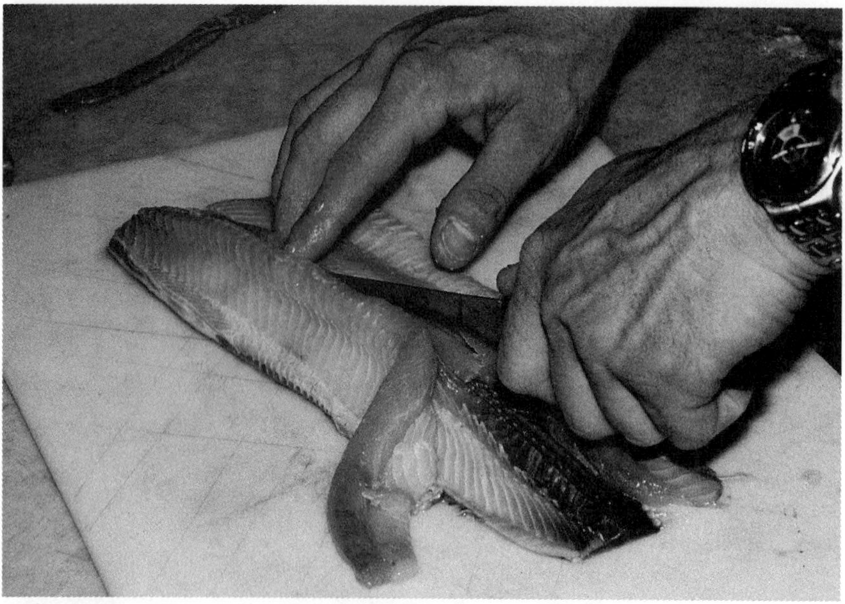

A second set of bones along the body must also be removed, using a finger to find the tips of the bones and guiding the knife to cut on both sides of this row of bones. Once this is complete, the fillet is ready for cooking.

4. Insert the filleting knife into the body cavity and cut the shad open, being careful to cut between the roe and the body wall. If the fish is a male, the operation will be the same, except that the roe will not be present.
5. Lift up the body wall to expose the roe and entrails.
6. Lift the roe out and wash before preparing it for cooking.
7. Cut off the head close behind the base of the pectoral fins.
8. Cut off the belly ridge (keel), cutting through the small bones that extend from the belly ridge up to the body wall.
9. Cut along the left side of the backbone and base of the dorsal fin. This cut is made closely parallel to the bones that are in line with the vertebrae, cutting through the small bones that are connected and which extend into the body wall.
10. Continue cutting alongside the backbone (vertebrae), through the small bones but not cutting through the rib cage. Cut the flesh off of the rib cage as closely as possible so that the fillet will be thick and there will be little lost meat.
11. Pass the knife over the rib cage to remove the fillet. Toward the tail, cut alongside but not through the backbone.

12. Repeat the above steps (9 through 11) to remove the fillet from the other side.
13. Use a shad boning board of soft wood, slightly larger than the shad. Recommended is a shad board about one inch longer and wider than the fillet. Thus, if different fish are being worked on, different size shad boards will be required. The advantage of this shad-deboning board is that the shad fillet can be placed on the board and left there for the remainder of the process, allowing the shad to be positioned by moving the board as required.
14. Start with the right fillet, with the flesh (inside) exposed. Blot the fillet dry with paper towels or with a cloth and place it on a boning board. At this time, check the fillet to find the rows of small bones that run parallel to the length of the shad. The ends of these bones have been cut through in the filleting process and can be felt and seen. They extend from this position into the flesh of the fish, curving around into the muscle tissue.
15. Start by cutting along the belly (ventral) side of the fillet making a cut parallel to the length of the fish and continue the cut along the row of bones. Make a second cut parallel to the first on the other side (dorsal) of the same row of bones. Cut almost to the skin, being careful not to cut through it. The two cuts make a wedge of bone and little meat.
16. If the cuts have been made properly, the wedge of bone can be lifted out and discarded. In some spots, it may be necessary to loosen this wedge from the fillet with the knife.
17. Now feel the bones that poke out of the fillet along the back of the shad. They will begin at the head end close to the wedge that was just removed, and separate from it going toward the tail.
18. Cut down to the skin, but not through it, along one side of the row of bones (cut along the side closest to the center), cutting down to about halfway to the tail where some other bones will be felt. Do not cut through these bones.
19. Approximately halfway down the length of the shad the bones start curving. At this point, let the knife ride over the bones by turning the edge of the knife into the direction of the bones. Continue cutting in this fashion to the tail.
20. Begin the next cut at the head of the fillet just above (dorsal to) the row of bones on which you were working. Cut down deep to the skin (but not through it) to the center of the fillet where the bones begin to curve into the muscle of the shad.
21. Turn the knife blade outward to continue the cut and let it follow,

or ride over, the bones. Continue this cut to the tail of the shad fillet.

22. Turn the boning board so that the head is close to you. Lay back the fleshy part of the fillet and carefully cut it away from the bones. Let the knife ride over the bones, being careful not to cut through them.
23. Separate the bony wedge of bones from the rest of the fillet. Start to remove them by lifting the wedge and freeing any uncut portions with a knife. Do not cut through the skin.
24. Continue to separate the bones from the meat of the fillet, working toward the tail. Discard this bony strip.
25. Turn the fillet so that the tail portion is facing you. Find one more row of bones that project out of the fillet, about one-fourth the distance of the fillet from the head end and next to the first wedge of bones that was removed. This row of bones curves outward from the center of the fillet and curves toward the tail and central side (belly). Begin the cut dorsal (along the back) to the ridge of bones and follow the bones with a knife.
26. At the end of this strip of bones, you will note that the bones end in fibers that must be cut through.
27. Begin the next cut near the head of the fillet on the ventral side of the row of bones just cut. Cut toward the tail, riding the knife blade over the bones. About halfway down the fillet, turn the edge of the blade outward to allow it to ride over the bones.
28. Continue to cut the fleshy section from the bones but leave it attached to the skin at the outer edge of the fillet. Separate the bony and fleshy strips.
29. Turning the boning board for convenience, start at the head end and carefully separate the bones from the skin.
30. Continue to cut the bones from the skin, allowing the knife blade to run along this strip, until the tail is reached.
31. Once the last strip of bones is removed, the fleshy strips of the fillet can be folded back into the fish. The three strips of bone are discarded if this has not yet been done.
32. The fillet can be stored in a cold dry place, wrapped in a meat paper. Do not allow the fillet to come into contact with water or ice (a good practice with any fish), since this will discolor it and cause it to deteriorate more rapidly. After some practice with this California method, a shad can be turned into two completely boneless fillets in about 15 to 20 minutes.

Various methods for cooking shad range from planking to baking, broiling, and frying. For those interested only in the basics, these methods are described in the North Carolina Department of Natural and Economic Resources booklet *Spring Gourmet with Shad,* as follows:

BAKING—Place fillets or whole fish in a greased baking dish. Brush with seasoned butter and bake in a preheated oven at approximately 350° F or at the same temperature suggested in any recipe. Stuff whole fish with a herb and bread stuffing, or marinate fish before baking.

BROILING—Arrange fillets or whole fish on a preheated well-greased broiler rack. Brush with melted fat or basting sauce. For fillets, place rack two inches from heat; for whole fish or split fish, place rack three to six inches from heat. Serve immediately.

PAN-FRYING—Bread the fish by dipping, first into milk, then into corn flakes, cracker or bread crumbs. Use melted shortening or vegetable oil to cover the bottom of the pan ⅛ inch deep. Fry fish until light brown, turn and brown other size. Serve on a hot platter.

PLANKED—Whole fish or fillets may be used in planking. Oil plank or board carefully and heat slowly in oven. Arrange cooked vegetables around fish, piping hot mashed potatoes around the edge, and return to the oven for final baking. Serve on a plank.

While most recipes have been developed for the commercially available American shad, they will work equally well for the smaller hickory shad. Times and temperatures might have to be adjusted, since the hickory shad are smaller, and thus fillets and whole fish are thinner and will cook faster than the larger American shad.

TYPICAL SHAD RECIPES

STUFFED SHAD ON A PLANK

Recipe origin: Maryland

3-pound shad, pan dressed
lemon and pepper seasoning
1 pound crabmeat (preferably backfin)
¼ to ½ cup canned cream of mushroom soup or canned Newburg sauce
4 strips bacon
seasoned hot cooked rice or mashed potatoes
seasoned hot cooked vegetables (such as corn on the cob and asparagus)
cold, ripe cherry tomatoes

Wash and dry fish thoroughly. Sprinkle inside of shad with lemon and pepper seasoning. Remove all cartilage from crabmeat. Mix with mushroom soup or Newburg sauce. Put 2 strips of bacon on a preheated oiled wooden plank or greased bake-and-serve platter. Place fish on top. Stuff with crabmeat mixture, and secure edges loosely with foil. Put remaining bacon on top of fish.

Bake at 350° F for 45 to 60 minutes, or until fish flakes easily when tested with a fork. Arrange rice or potatoes and vegetables around fish. Serves six.

PLANKED SHAD

Recipe origin: Virginia

3- to 4-pound shad
vegetable oil
salt and pepper
4 tablespoons melted butter
juice of 1 lemon

Clean and split the fish down the back. Heat a wooden plank very hot. Lay fish on it, skin side down. Brush fish with oil, and sprinkle with salt and pepper. Bake 35 minutes in a very hot oven. When cooked, pour melted butter and lemon juice over the shad. Serves six.

BAKED SHAD, MAINE STYLE

Recipe origin: Maine

1 average-size shad
stuffing of 1 cup breadcrumbs
    1 tablespoon melted butter
    1 tablespoon minced parsley
    1 tablespoon minced onion
    ½ teaspoon salt
    ⅛ teaspoon pepper
salt and pepper
melted butter
flour
lemon butter sauce (½ cup butter and 2 tablespoons
    lemon juice)

Scale fish and wash thoroughly; wipe dry. Stuff with the dressing mix as above. Place stuffed fish on baking rack, sprinkle with salt and pepper, brush with melted butter, and dredge with flour. Place over dripping pan with bottom covered with boiling water and dots of butter. Bake 15 minutes for every pound of fish in 400° F oven. Baste occasionally with gravy from the dripping pan. Serve with lemon butter sauce.

SPICY BROILED SHAD

Recipe origin: Maryland

2 pounds shad fillets or steaks, boned
¼ cup (½ stick) margarine or butter
½ teaspoon prepared mustard
½ teaspoon salt
¼ teaspoon lemon and pepper seasoning
¼ teaspoon seafood seasoning
⅛ teaspoon tarragon
⅛ teaspoon rosemary
½ cup dry white wine (or water)

Wash and dry fish thoroughly. Place in single layer, skin side down, on foil-lined shallow baking pan or cookie sheet. Melt margarine; add rest of ingredients, and heat over low heat until warm. Brush fish generously with sauce. Put in preheated broiler about 4 inches from flame for 5 minutes. Pour remaining sauce over fish. Broil 5 minutes more, or until fish flakes easily when tested with a fork. Serve immediately. Serves six or eight.

OVEN-FRIED SHAD FILLETS

Recipe origin: North Carolina

2 pounds shad fillets
1 tablespoon salt
1 cup milk
1 cup browned dry bread crumbs
¼ cup melted fat or oil

Cut fillets into serving-size portions. Add salt to milk. Dip fish in milk, and roll in crumbs. Place fish, skin side down, in a single layer in a well-greased baking pan. Pour fat over fish. Bake in an extremely hot oven, 500° F, for 10 to 15 minutes, or until fish flakes easily when tested with a fork. Serves six.

BROILED SHAD ROE

Recipe origin: North Carolina

1 shad roe sac
salt and pepper
3 strips bacon

Sprinkle salt and pepper on shad roe sac (American or hickory). Wrap with bacon strips. Place on shallow rack in heavy frying pan or broiling rack. Broil about 20 minutes.

SHAD WITHOUT BONES

Recipe origin: New England

1 shad
1 tablespoon finely chopped onion
1 tablespoon finely chopped celery
1 bay leaf

Place shad on rack in baking pan, filling the pan below with water. An upturned tin of any kind will do if you do not have a rack. Place 2 or 3 cups of water in the pan. Then, with the cover on, bake the shad for 5 hours—not 4 or 3, but the whole 5 hours. Baste frequently, and renew water if necessary. A tablespoon of finely chopped onion, chopped celery, and bay leaf added to the water gives the shad a delicious flavor. A few minutes before serving, remove the cover and let the shad brown. Bake at 300° F.

In addition to the above recipes, shad roe is often combined with other foods, such as roe with eggs, bacon, and mushrooms, or roe on toast. Shad fillets can be combined in a seafood salad, barbecued, made into a tomato casserole, stewed, or combined with various condiments.

Future Possibilities

On May 20–23, 2001, *Shad 2001: A Conference on the Status and Conservation of Shads Worldwide,* was held at the National Aquarium in Baltimore. The conference was sponsored by the Hudson River Foundation for Science and Environmental Research, Inc., the National Aquarium in Baltimore, Exelon Generation, the Center for Marine Biotechnology, and seven other governmental, scientific, and conservation groups. The conference focused on the importance of the 30-plus species of shad found throughout the world. Specific goals were to examine the current status of shad and shad fisheries and to consider conservation and restoration methods available for shad.

The conference, which involved scientists from as far away as New Zealand, included three days of specific presentations and a half-day field trip to Conowingo Dam, courtesy of the owner of Exelon Generation. This allowed for both formal and informal exchanges of ideas by scientists, as well as viewing sport shad fishing and shad fishing techniques on-site.

The presentations concluded that shad are an important species of fish for commercial, recreational, economic, biological, and social reasons. That we have lost shad from historical highs is without question. Historically, there were 130 streams/rivers along the East Coast holding major runs of shad. Today, there are only 68.

The conference covered a full range of shad history, with keynote speaker Tom Horton pointing out that in Crisfield, Maryland, in 1922, 150 railroad carloads of shad were shipped to other parts of the country. Today, there is no effective shad fishing in the area and all shad fishing, both commercial and recreational, is banned in Maryland. (Maryland anglers are allowed to catch hickory and American shad under a catch-and-release program, but may not keep shad.)

Presentations on African shad, the American shad, the hickory shad, shad fisheries monitoring, oriental Hilsa shad, American shad restoration on the Susquehanna River, the allis and twaite shad of Europe, and restocking of shad, proved the high degree of optimism in the future of shad fisheries.

Some information on shad is still lacking, however. For example, although hickory shad fishery in sounds and estuaries is becoming increasingly popular in summer and fall, because hickory shad have little commercial importance, they are less studied. Anecdotal information on hickory shad fishery over the last ten years has increased, but there have been no coastwide studies or other research done on a possible change of habits or habitat of these smaller cousins of the American shad.

Still there is room for more optimism than ever before. The conference confirmed that intercept fishery, or commercially taking shad at the mouths of major river systems, will be phased out completely by 2004/2005. In addition, hundreds of miles of rivers are now being opened up to shad and river herring. For example, Conowingo Dam once stopped all upstream migration of shad about 8 miles above the head of the Chesapeake Bay. Today, an elevator lift there and additional fish ladders past upstream dams will make shad able to ascend throughout their original range through Pennsylvania and all the way to Cooperstown, New York.

In addition to fish ladders and lifts, restocking and placing shad above dams are helping to restore shad. Returning shad and fall juveniles are able to traverse the large turbines in these hydroelectric dams with minimal mortality. Studies on the Susquehanna River, with its four dams, indicate that there is a 95 percent survival rate of fish through large blade turbines, with populations going through turbines of all four dams (Conowingo, Safe Harbor, Holtwood, and York Haven) still maintaining a survival rate of about 73 percent.

Even if shad numbers may never reach their abundance of 150 years ago, the future for shad looks good. The reduction and ultimate stoppage of the river mouth intercept fishery, the dam reduction and passage to allow increased upstream access to shad, and refined tackle and techniques mean that for now at least, there is a bright future for shad and for shad fishing on both coasts for millions of anglers.

Glossary

Anadromous Said of fish that live their adult lives in the ocean but return to fresh water to spawn, such as shad and salmon.

Anchor rode The amount of line (rope) necessary to hold bottom when anchoring. Usually expressed as a ratio, which a standard of 7:1, meaning 7 feet of line (rope) is necessary for each foot of depth. Often extended to 10:1 in fast rivers.

Bass bug taper One type of weight-forward fly line.

Boning The process of removing the several rows of small bones from a shad. These bones are in addition to the backbone and rib cage found in all species of fish. They must be removed for normal cooking of fillets, although some slow methods of baking will dissolve these bones.

Boning knife A short, stiff-bladed knife used to cut out the many rows of bones in the process of boning a shad fillet.

Buck The male of a fish species. Male shad are also called cocks.

Bug taper See *weight-forward line.*

Casting bubble A small, generally transparent bubble that can be partially or completely filled with water for casting weight to allow the use of spinning or casting tackle to fish very light lures or flies for shad.

Cather spoon A small, slim spoon used primarily along the South Atlantic coast for shad fishing. This spoon was designed with shad fishing in mind.

Doll fly A form of commercial bucktail that in small sizes is ideal for shad fishing.

Downrigger A trolling tool that, when fitted to the gunwale or transom of a boat, allows fishing deep. The device controls a heavy ball or weight on a strong downrigger line. Downrigger clips fastened to the downrigger line hold the fishing line and allow a lure to be fished at a predetermined depth. When a fish hits, the line springs free of the clip to allow fighting the fish without any weight.

Filleting knife A knife with a long, thin, flexible blade necessary for removing fillets from a shad during the boning process.

Fish ladder A series of steplike pools connected together that ascend from the water level below a dam or falls to the water level at the top of the dam or falls. Artificially constructed to allow for the passage of anadromous species such as shad and salmon to points above the obstruction. Usually built along the side of the dam or falls, with gates to allow for controlled water flow. Several types are made, depending on the prevalent view of fisheries biologists, current technology and knowledge at the time they were built, and the species for which they are principally designed. Also sometimes called a *fishway.*

Fish lift An elevatorlike device designed for lifting shad from the water level at the base of the dam, up and over the dam, to the water level at the top of the dam, so that the shad can continue their upstream journey. Also called a *fish elevator.*

Fishway See *fish ladder.*

Flutter spoon A small, thin spoon used for both casting and downrigger shad fishing. Originally made by soldering a long-shank gold Aberdeen hook to the concave side of a willow leaf blade, then painting the blade bright flourescent colors. Also available commercially.

Fuse wire A thin lead wire used by electricians for fuses. Fly tiers wrap this wire around the hook shank before tying a fly to add weight. Similar lead and nontoxic nonlead wires are now sold in fly shops and catalogs specifically for this purpose.

Hen A female or roe shad.

Lead-core line A line that consists of a lead core inside a braided nylon sleeve. It is normally used for deep trolling. Sections of this line are used by shad fishermen to make their own fast-sinking shooting-taper fly lines for casting long distances and for getting a shad fly deep.

Milt The sperm of a fish, a milklike fluid.

Mylar A modern material of very thin plastic, generally with a bright silver or gold coating. It comes in sheet, ribbon, and braided forms and is widely used in fly tying. For shad flies, it is used sparingly to avoid too much flash, which might scare the fish.

Pequea Quilby Minnow A commercially made lure manufactured in Strasburg, Pennsylvania. Though no longer made, it was the most popular lure for shad for a long time, and the basic colors of yellow tail, silvery body, and red head are the basis for many of the shad flies and shad fly colors used today.

Roe The egg sacs of a mature spawning fish. Shad roe is a delicacy that shows up in the food and fish markets each spring. The term roe shad is used to describe a female shad.

Saltwater taper See *weight-forward line.*

Shad dart A small, specialized type of lead lure or jig, patterned after the original Pequea Quilby Minnow of years ago, but with a painted lead body. Typical darts have straight tapered sides and a slanting head, and come in a variety of colors. Sizes range from 1/64 ounce to as large as several ounces, with the larger sizes used for striped bass and other saltwater game fish. Most shad darts are less than 1/4 ounce.

Shad fly Any of dozens of flies tied specifically for American or hickory shad. Most are tied in bright or fluorescent colors and in sizes 1 through 10. Most popular sizes are 6, 8, and 10.

Shooting taper A short (generally 30-foot-long) length of fly line that is connected to a running line or shooting line of monofilament and used for casting long distances. These originally came in sinking versions only, but today floating shooting tapers are also available. Also called a Shooting Head or shooting line.

Sinking fly line A fly line that sinks. Various sink rates are available for slow, medium, or fast sinking of the line.

Sinking-tip fly line A fly line that has a floating running belly and a tip section that sinks. Most manufacturers make them, and several different designs are available. The sinking-tip end can vary from 5 to 30 feet. Sink rates of the sinking section also vary.

Tandem rigging A rigging in which a second fly is used in addition to the main fly tied to the end of the leader.

Weighted fly Any fly that has weight added during the tying process. Methods include wrapping the body with lead or similar nonlead wire; using dumbbell eyes, metallic beads, or metallic cones; or tying on a tiny jig head, which has a molded leadhead on a jig hook.

Weight-forward line A fly line with a heavy belly, placed in the front of the forward section of the line and designed for distance casting. These lines are generally the choice of shad fishermen and vary in line length, type of taper, and length of belly. Check line manufacturer catalogs to find the best line for your purpose. A long-belly, weight-forward line is best for most shad fishing, although a short-belly line or shooting taper will give the maximum casting distance. Saltwater tapers and bug tapers are examples of these.

For More Information

Shad Museum, Higganum, Connecticut. Dr. Joseph Zaientz, P.O. Box 336, Higganum, CT 06441, telephone (860) 267-0388. To the best of my knowledge, this is the only shad museum in existence.

Shad Journal, published on-line at http://www.cqs.washington.edu/~hinrich/foundation.html. The *Shad Journal* was started some years ago by Richard Hinrichsen for the dissemination of information on shad. While of prime interest to shad and fisheries biologists, it does contain good up-to-date information on shad and shad fisheries worldwide.

Atlantic State Marine Fisheries Commission home page, www.asmfc.org. Click on programs, then Interstate Fisheries Management Plans, and look for shad.

American Rivers, 1025 Vermont Ave. NW, Suite 720, Washington, DC 20005, telephone (202) 347-7550. A nonprofit national conservation group working to conserve rivers. Video "Taking a Second Look: Communities and Dam Removal" and two books, *Paying for Dam Removal* and *Dam Removal: A Citizen's Guide to Restoring Rivers.* Website is www.americanrivers.org.

Delaware River Shad Fisherman Association, 4110 Shannon Ave., Bethlehem, PA 18020, telephone (610) 797-1957, (610) 867-7010, or (610) 691-6383. Contact names include Mike Misiura, George Magaro, and Rick Reichard. Shad hotline numbers for river conditions, shad-fishing locations, and possibilities are (610) 954-0577 and (610) 954-0578. The shad hotline on the Internet is www.geocities.com/shadhotline.

Other shad-fishing information from the Delaware River Shad Fishermen's Association is available from www.geocities.com/shad_fishermen. This major shad-fishing association is dedicated to the preservation of the American shad and the Delaware River environment. It has fought to get fish ladders on the two lower Lehigh River dams for upriver shad movements, and conducted logbook surveys while cooperating with government agencies in data collection on shad fishing in the Delaware River system. It is an ideal source of inforamtion on fishing and shad in this area. Information on membership can be obtained by calling one of the above numbers or sending e-mail to drsfa@hotmail.com.

Chesapeake Bay Foundation, 162 Prince George St., Annapolis, MD 21401, telephone (410) 268-8816, (410) 269-0481 (from Baltimore), or (301) 261-2350 (from Washington, D.C.), e-mail chesapeake@savethebay.cbf.org, website www.savethebay.cbf.org. The Chesapeake Bay Foundation is involved with all things concerning saving the bay and its wildlife, including shad fisheries. Its mission statement is "to restore the Bay's ecosystem by substantially improving the water quality and productivity of the watershed and to maintain a high quality of life for the people of the Chesapeake Bay region."

The Hudson River Foundation, 40 West 20th Street, 9th Floor, New York, NY 10011, telephone (212) 924-8290, (212) 924-8325-fax, e-mail: info@hudsonriver.org, website www.hudsonriver.org. The Hudson River Foundation supports scientific and public policy research, education and projects to enhance access to the Hudson River. It was established in 1981 under agreement with environmental groups, government agencies, and utility companies to effectively resolve controversies concerning environmental impact of power plants on the Hudson River.

Bibliography

Many of the following books and references are out of print, but they are available in libraries or from used bookstores or sporting collectible book catalogs. Some are current and provide additional information on local shad fishing, changing shad populations and access to shad, productive fishing, lures, tackle, and flies. For state publications, write to the state agency involved. Also check the Internet for resources of a given state or area for more information about American and hickory shad.

Bates, Joseph D., Jr. *Spinning for American Game Fish.* Boston, MA: Little Brown and Co., 1948.

———. *Spinning for Salt Water Game Fish.* Boston, MA: Little Brown and Co., 1957.

———. *Streamer Fly Tying and Fishing.* Mechanicsburg, PA: Stackpole Co., 1966. An excellently researched book on the subject, with information on shad fishing and fly tying.

Beatty, Christopher. *The Susquehanna River Guide.* Corvallis, OR: Ecopress, 1998. A thorough guide of the Susquehanna River, with detailed maps.

Boyle, Robert H. *The Hudson River.* New York: W. W. Norton, 1969. A thorough book covering the history and ecology of the Hudson, an important shad river.

Brooks, Joe. *Salt Water Fly Fishing.* New York: G. P. Putnam's Sons, 1950. One of the first books to mention shad fly fishing in detail, with emphasis on the sport in the Mid-Atlantic area.

Budworth, Geoffrey. *The Complete Book of Fishing Knots.* New York: The Lyons Press, 1999.

Delaware River Shad Fishing. Pennsylvania Fish Commission. A collection of shad-fishing articles from *Pennsylvania Angler* magazine.

Dick, Lenox. *Experience the World of Shad Fishing.* Portland, OR: Frank Amato Publications, 1996. Basic information on shad fishing, with emphasis on the West Coast.

Gerlach, Rex. *Creative Fly Tying and Fly Fishing.* New York: Winchester Press, 1974. Some shad flies are listed in this volume, which covers many other fly-tying patterns and techniques.

Gerstell, Richard. *American Shad in the Susquehanna River Basin.* University Park, PA: Pennsylvania State University Press, 1998. A history of commercial shad fishing—and some recreational shad fishing—and the importance of shad in the Pennsylvania–New Jersey area.

Grucela, Buddy. *Guide to Better Shad Fishing on the Delaware River.* Self-published. An excellent book of shad-fishing tips and hot spots along the entire range of the Delaware River.

Hart, J. L. *Pacific Fishes of Canada.* Ottawa, ONT. Fisheries Research Board of Canada, 1973. A good basic book on the shad of Canada's Pacific coast.

Haw, Frank. *Angling for Salmon, Shad and Sturgeon in Fresh Waters of Washington State.* Olympia, WA: Washington Department of Fisheries, Department of Fish and Game, 1971. A good book with detailed information on fishing for the three species mentioned, up to the date of publication.

Haw, Frank, and Raymond M. Buckley. *Salt Water Fishing in Canada.* Stanley Jones, Publisher, 1971.

Hellekson, Terry. *Fish Flies.* Portland, OR: Frank Amato Publications, 1995.

Jones, Stan. *Washington State Fishing Guide.* Stanley Jones, Publisher, 1970. A basic book on fishing in Washington State, with information on top spots for shad.

Jorgensen, Poul. *Dressing Flies for Fresh and Salt Water.* New York: Freshet Press, 1973. An excellent fly-tying book by one of the world's foremost fly tiers. Includes a chapter on shad flies.

Kreh, Lefty. *Fly Fishing in Salt Water.* 3d ed. New York: Lyons Press, 1997. An excellent book on the subject that includes information about shad fishing.

———. *Longer Fly Casting.* New York: Lyons Press, 1991. For fishing big rivers for shad, you will want this book.

———. *Solving Fly-Casting Problems.* New York: Lyons Press, 2000. An excellent book on the subject of longer, more accurate casts.

Ovington, Ray. *Spinning in America.* Mechanicsburg, PA: Stackpole Co., 1954.

Owen, Peter. *The Field & Stream Fishing Knots Handbook.* New York: Lyons Press, 1999.

Pennsylvania Fish and Boat Commission. *Guide to Public Fishing Waters and Boating Access.* Harrisburg, PA: Pennsylvania Fish and Boat Commission, 1997. A guide to all Pennsylvania waters, including the shad rivers of the Susquehanna and Delaware.

Pfeiffer, C. Boyd. *The Complete Book of Tackle Making.* New York: Lyons Press, 1999. A thorough coverage of the construction of all types of tackle, including rods for shad, along with shad darts, jigs, and spoons.

———. *Fly Fishing Saltwater Basics.* Mechanicsburg, PA: Stackpole Books, 1999. Complete coverage of saltwater fly fishing, with a little information on shad fishing, along with basic fly-fishing techniques.

———. *Shad Fishing.* New York: Crown Publishers, 1975. The only book to completely cover all types of shad fishing, up to the date published.

Punola, John A. *Fishing Delaware River.* Madison, NJ: Outdoors, USA, 1993. A general guide to fishing the Delaware River, with information on shad fishing, techniques, and hot spots.

Radovich, John. *How to Catch, Bone and Cook a Shad.* California Department of Fish and Game. A fine booklet that covers the subject well, with catching emphasis on California waters.

Scott, W. B., and E. J. Crossman. *Freshwater Fishes of Canada.* Ottawa, ONT. Fisheries Research Board of Canada, 1973. An excellent book that includes shad and the range, biology, and habitat of shad in Canada.

Shewey, John. *Northwest Fly Fishing: Trout and Beyond.* Portland, OR: Frank Amato Publications, 1992.

Sosin, Mark, and Lefty Kreh. *Practical Fishing Knots.* New York: Lyon Press, 1991.

Stranahan, Susan Q. *Susquehanna, River of Dreams.* Baltimore: Johns Hopkins University Press, 1993. A book on the history of the Susquehanna River, but with information on shad and a chapter on shad restoration.

Walburg, Charles H., and Paul R. Nicols. *Biology and Management of the American Shad and Status of the Fisheries, Atlantic Coast of the United States, 1960.* U.S. Fish and Wildlife Service, 1967. Basically a research paper, highly detailed and somewhat technical, with emphasis on commercial fishing. A good basic volume on the history of shad fishing and its status up to 1960.

Warren, Joe J. *Tying Glass Bead Flies.* Portland, OR: Frank Amato Publications, 1997.

Washington Department of Fisheries. *What's So Great About . . . Shad?* Olympia, WA, 1991. A small booklet of shad recipes.

Waterman, Charles. *Modern Fresh and Salt Water Fly Fishing.* New York: Winchester Press, 1972. A good book, with some information on shad fishing, particularly in Florida waters.

Wilson, Geoff. *Geoff Wilson's Complete Book of Fishing Knots & Rigs.* Portland, OR: Frank Amato Publications (dist.), 1997.

Index